FRESH CATCH OF THE DAY
...from the
FISHWIFE

by Shirley Rizzuto

Art Direction and Design	Chuck Johnston
Illustrations	Leslie Hata
Editing	Monica King
Composition and Layout	Brad Deffenbaugh and Gordon Price
Project Coordination	Ellen Johnston

First Edition

Published by
HAWAII FISHING NEWS
HONOLULU, HAWAI'I

Introduction

In 1986, "Fish Dishes of the Pacific. . . from the FISHWIFE" made its debut on bookstore shelves and it was instantly embraced by fish lovers. Thanks to you, the book has sold over 40,000 copies worldwide.

Now, 10 years later, you're reading "Fresh Catch of the Day. . . from the FISHWIFE." It will seem familiar to you in many ways—same size and format, another spectacular cover and appealing illustrations by Les Hata, art direction and design by Chuck Johnston, careful editing by Monica King, composition and layout by Brad Deffenbaugh and Gordon Price, Fishwife's Tips and inspiring creations from many of Hawai'i's celebrated chefs.

I've responded to your request for "healthful" ways to prepare the fish you are most likely to find at your local fish counters–tuna, billfish, dolphin fish, wahoo, snapper and salmon–and to your cry for moonfish, shrimp and squid recipes. Cooking lean, the culinary focus of the '90s, was my mission as I researched and developed recipes that kept fat to a minimum without sacrificing flavor or ease of preparation. However, for the occasional indulgences we all crave and deserve, you'll find a few "guilty pleasures" to satisfy your momentary weaknesses!

Acknowledgements

I'll say it again: I owe boundless gratitude to friends and family who shared their time, energy and talent with me throughout this project.

My resident fisherman went above and beyond to buoy me up when necessary and reel me in when I was frantic. For his loving support and for cleaning pounds of squid and octopus, my thanks.

HAWAII FISHING NEWS Editor Monica King and my daughter Rahna, during a visit from her home in New York, took my mass (and mess) of material, organized and categorized it, scrutinized the recipes with their keen eyes and gourmet cooking backgrounds and then hypnotized me into believing this project would be easy.

Thanks also to these wonderful recipe testers and hand-holders: Mary and Paul Barthelemy; Mebane and Alan Boyd; Sheila and Gary Cadwallader; Mike Dahlager; Margie and Chris Dunlap; Judy Furtado; Lillie Garrido; Terri and Andy Gedo; Judy and Will Hancock; Everold Hosein; Kerry Kakazu; Art Kamisugi; Roberta Kasperowicz; Mary Kleschen; Mark Lee; Marjorie Lincoln; Suzanne McNaughton; Helen Miller; Josephine Munos; Kendra Nash; Alison Pape; Phyllis Richards; Ticia Rizzuto; Tony Rizzuto; Neljane and Steve Rizzuto; Becky Rude-Ozaki; Dan Saracino; Mike Schultz; Cheryl Shrum; Sharon Shutes; Al Sullivan; James Takemoto; Craig Tooman; and Juan Waroquiers.

For exceptional recipes (and patience with the Fishwife's questions, calls and correspondence), my thanks to Hawai'i's creative and generous chefs who are true ambassadors of the *aloha* spirit.

Thanks to the staff of the Ocean Services Branch of the Department of Business, Economic Development and Tourism for inviting me to numerous seafood promotion functions and for the contributions to this book.

Finally, my appreciation to Chuck and Ellen Johnston for their patience and support of this project.

Table of Contents

BILLFISH

MAHIMAHI (DOLPHIN FISH)

ONO (WAHOO)

OPAH (MOONFISH)

SNAPPER

SALMON

SHRIMP

SHRIMP continued...

SQUID AND OCTOPUS

SEAFOOD PASTA DINNERS

SOUPS, STEWS & COMBOS

SAUCES, MARINADES & RELISHES

Sauces

Marinades

Tuna

'Ahi: Bigeye tuna, Yellowfin tuna, Albacore tuna, Skipjack tuna

Tuna has earned a worldwide reputation as a premier fish for all palates. The growing appeal of Asian food and sushi bars and the recognition of fish as a healthy food source have increased the popularity of 'ahi and other tuna.

Tuna's fat content makes it particularly flavorful and also determines its price. Fish wholesalers test the fish's fat content by rubbing a small piece between their fingers. The more buttery it feels, the higher the quality of the meat and the higher the price the 'ahi will bring, particularly during holiday celebrations, when island residents honor their guests by serving decorative sushi platters of claret-colored tuna.

Yellowfin and bigeye are widely used in raw dishes; albacore is used less often because it does not have the deep red color of the other tuna and its soft flesh is difficult to cut as thin as is preferred for sashimi. Albacore's light pink flesh makes it a popular choice for those who prefer mild fish. Tuna is best prepared smoked, grilled, sautéed and, of course, raw. It can also be baked and adds a special richness to soups and stews.

Tuna is available in markets year-round: yellowfin is most plentiful from May through September, bigeye from October through April, and albacore from April through mid-October.

NOTE: 'Ahi is used to identify all of the varieties of tuna. ATLANTIC SUBSTITUTIONS: Blackfin and Bluefin Tuna.

Blackened Tuna With Coconut-Wasabi Sauce
courtesy of Paul and Mary Barthelemy

2 pounds fresh tuna

SPICE MIXTURE
2 tablespoons Szechwan peppercorns
1 tablespoon ground black pepper
¼ teaspoon cayenne pepper
2 tablespoons paprika

COCONUT-WASABI SAUCE
1 cup chicken stock (preferably homemade)
1 can unsweetened coconut milk
  Lime juice (to taste)
1 to 2 tablespoons wasabi (to taste)
1 tablespoon cornstarch, mixed with
  2 tablespoons cold water (optional)

GARNISH
  Watercress
  Wasabi
  Pickled Ginger

PREPARATION

Cut the fish into steaks, fillets or loins. (You will sear it on all sides and then slice it thinly for the presentation.)

Grind the spice mixture until fine. (Paul uses a mortar and pestle, but other methods are acceptable.) The mixture may need to be passed through a sieve or strainer to remove the husks of the peppercorns. Rub this mixture into the fish pieces. Set aside.

Heat the chicken stock, coconut milk, lime juice and wasabi in a saucepan. Stir to combine well. Cook this sauce down until reduced somewhat. To thicken, add the cornstarch mixed with the cold water at the end.

Heat a cast-iron skillet or large wok over very high heat until a bit of the spice mixture smokes when placed on it. Quickly sear the steaks on each side so that the spice mixture is blackened somewhat but the fish is still raw or rare on the inside. Do not overcook. Slice the fish thinly.

Place the sauce in a soup plate. Lay strips of the seared fish on the sauce. Garnish with watercress, a dab of wasabi and pickled ginger.   SERVES 6

FISHWIFE'S TIPS

1. Skin fish before cooking. All tuna have a dark strip running along each side of the backbone. This section is stronger in flavor and can be cut away, if you prefer, especially when serving fish raw.

2. Watch for a condition known as "burnt tuna." Tuna are among the few fish that can regulate their own body temperature. When under exertion, a tuna can change its body temperature as much as 18°. It does this to increase muscle efficiency during a fight. As the fish's temperature rises, acidity builds up in the flesh, causing chemical changes and deterioration. This, coupled with improper refrigeration once the fish is on board, results in reduced quality.

Burnt tuna is characterized by whitish spots and mushy, soft flesh, which makes the fish unpalatable for raw consumption.

It also means less money at the market for fishermen, so they try to bring the fish up fast to cut down on the struggle. Then they ice the catch immediately, always bleeding the fish first.

The only way to tell if a tuna is burnt is by looking for whitening of the flesh, usually near the spine, and for watery, soft flesh. Fortunately, most tuna is sold at market quartered, chunked or steaked, so the flesh can be examined before buying. If you find yourself with burnt tuna, cook it in a strong-flavored sauce, like misoyaki or any of the tomato-based sauce recipes in this book.

3. Eat tuna fresh. Freezing affects the flavor of the meat, changing a once firm fish to a mushy one and giving the fish a slimy, iridescent-green cast.

Tuna Carpaccio With Black Bean Aioli, Ginger Vinaigrette and Roasted Red Peppers

courtesy of Douglas Lum, Sunset Grill at Restaurant Row, Honolulu

1   pound #1 grade fresh tuna
2   tablespoons Black Bean Aioli
¾   cup Ginger Vinaigrette
½   large red pepper, roasted, peeled, seeded and diced
1   bunch Chinese parsley (cilantro)

BLACK BEAN AIOLI

1   egg yolk
    Salt and white pepper
1   tablespoon white wine vinegar, or
    ½ tablespoon lemon juice
¾   cup oil
2   tablespoons garlic and black bean paste

GINGER VINAIGRETTE

1½ cups shoyu
½   cup rice wine vinegar
¾   cup sugar
5   ounces ginger
¼   cup olive oil

PREPARATION

To prepare the Black Bean Aioli, beat the egg yolk with a pinch of salt and pepper and half of the vinegar until thick. Add the oil, drop by drop; whisk constantly. When 2 tablespoons of oil have been added, the rest of the oil can be added more quickly. When all of the oil has been mixed in, adjust the seasoning with more vinegar, or lemon juice, and more pepper, if desired. Mix with black bean paste, and chill until needed.

To prepare Ginger Vinaigrette, combine all vinaigrette ingredients in a bowl or jar with tight-sealing lid. Blend (or shake) well until sugar is dissolved.

Slice fish, and arrange on a plate in a manner that is appealing to the eye. Place red pepper pieces atop the slices of fish followed by small dollops of the Black Bean Aioli placed next to the pepper. Drizzle with Ginger Vinaigrette, and garnish with Chinese parsley.
SERVES 5

Douglas Lum

Executive Chef Douglas Lum oversees the San Francisco inspired, exhibition-style kitchen at Sunset Grill in Restaurant Row in Honolulu. Chef Lum's culinary creativity has helped Sunset Grill garner Honolulu Magazine's prestigious 4-star Hale Aina Award in 1991, 1992 and 1993 and recognition as Best Brasserie in the Hawaiian Islands by the international guidebook "Best of the Best." He works closely with California and European vineyards to complement the restaurant's offerings at its monthly Winemaker Dinner Series. Chef Lum completed an extensive apprenticeship with Sheraton Hotels after high school and served in various kitchen positions, including saucier and banquet chef at the Sheraton Palace Hotel in San Francisco. He was also the assistant food and beverage manager for Hornblower Dining Yachts Inc. in San Francisco and San Diego, with duties that included managing the staff of on-board cooks aboard the luxury dining yachts.

Tuna Won Ton

½ **pound fresh raw tuna, ground or minced, or 1
1 cup cooked and flaked tuna (see Fishwife's Tip)**
1 **tablespoon peanut oil**
1 **large garlic clove, minced**
2 **teaspoons minced ginger root**
2 **tablespoons minced green onion**
¼ **cup shredded carrot**
¼ **cup chopped water chestnuts or
bamboo shoots**
1 **tablespoon shoyu (or oyster sauce)**
1 **tablespoon sake or white wine**
1 **egg white, beaten
(or 2 teaspoons cornstarch)
Freshly ground black pepper to taste**
½ **package won ton wrappers (24)**

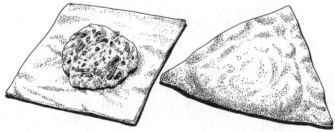

FOLDING TRADITIONAL WON TONS

FOLDING STAR WON TONS

PREPARATION

Heat the oil in a non-stick skillet large enough to hold all ingredients. Sauté the garlic and ginger briefly. Add the fish, and sauté until it turns white, just a minute or two. Remove the skillet from the heat immediately. Stir in the green onion, carrot, water chestnuts, shoyu, sake and egg white.

To prepare the won tons, place 1 rounded teaspoon of the fish filling in the center of a won ton wrapper. Shape the won ton in the traditional Chinese manner, or as you would an egg roll (folded in half), or bring all 4 points together on top (reminiscent of a star fruit). Regardless of the shape you choose, wet the edges that will be joined with water. Pinch together to seal.

To deep-fry won tons, heat oil to 375° and fry the won tons until they are golden brown, about 2 minutes. Remove from oil; drain on paper towels or paper bags.

To oven-fry won tons, preheat the oven to 375°. Lightly brush won tons with peanut oil, and bake for 8 to 10 minutes, or until golden brown.

To boil, drop won tons into boiling water (use a large pot, and don't boil too many at once) until they cook, 5 or 6 minutes.

If you are not going to cook the won tons right away, place them on a cookie sheet, cover, and refrigerate for 2 or 3 hours. You may also freeze them.

MAKES 24 WON TONS

FISHWIFE'S TIP

If you use cooked, flaked fish, you do not need to sauté it. After the ginger and garlic are sautéed, add the cooked fish to the skillet with the other ingredients and proceed.

Wok-Charred Tuna Appetizers

courtesy of Peter Merriman,
Merriman's Restaurant

2   pieces 8-ounce fresh tuna loins, scored on top
    for cutting
½   cup clarified butter
2   teaspoons grated fresh ginger
2   teaspoons chopped shallots
2   teaspoons crushed chilies
1   teaspoon dried thyme
2   teaspoons crushed garlic
1   teaspoon dried marjoram
½   teaspoon cayenne pepper
1   teaspoon salt
    Juice from ½ lemon

PREPARATION

Mix together clarified butter, ginger, shallots, chilies, thyme, garlic, marjoram, cayenne pepper, salt and lemon juice. Heat wok until metal begins turning white. Dredge tuna loins in butter mixture, and then sear in wok 20 seconds on each side. Slice, and serve.

Peter Merriman's note: The sauce we use is 4 parts shoyu (soy sauce), 1 part mirin, 1 part lime juice and wasabi to taste. The sashimi dip is ¼ cup wasabi to 2 cups shoyu; wasabi must be made into a thick paste with water before it is mixed with shoyu. Fresh tropical fruit makes an excellent accompaniment.   SERVES 6

Peter Merriman

Credited as the "galvanizing force" behind the non-profit organization Hawaii Regional Cuisine Inc., Peter Merriman was recognized as a crusader for fresh Hawai'i products early in his culinary career at the Mauna Lani Bay Hotel. When he opened Merriman's in 1988, continental cuisine was still the norm at most hotels, with ingredients brought in from the mainland. Chef Merriman went right to the local farmers, fish markets and ranchers for his ingredients, as did other Hawai'i's chefs, which changed Hawai'i's local products from being underutilized assets to key ingredients in a cuisine unique to Hawai'i. Chef Merriman points out that the mission of Hawaii Regional Cuisine Inc. is to promote the cuisine and to promote producers and growers. "Our goal is for Hawai'i Regional Cuisine to develop as a cuisine of truly good food, not a gimmick. Chef Merriman recently opened the Hula Grill on Maui.

Chinese Pan-Fried Tuna

1   pound fresh tuna fillets (¾ inch thick)
2   cloves garlic, minced
1   tablespoon shoyu
½   tablespoon minced ginger root
2   teaspoons hoi sin sauce
1   tablespoon vegetable or peanut oil
½   cup minced green onions (garnish)

PREPARATION

Combine the garlic, shoyu, ginger and hoi sin sauce in a bowl. Mix well, and set aside.

Heat oil in a wok or large skillet. Add fillets, and fry on both sides until half-cooked. Lower heat, and add the sauce mixture. Cover wok, and simmer fish for 3 minutes, or until done. Place tuna on a platter, garnish with the green onions, and serve.   SERVES 4

Alison's Grilled Fish 'n Fruit Special

courtesy of Alison Pape

1½   pounds fresh tuna fillets
½   cup olive oil
     Juice of ½ lemon
     Juice of ½ small lime
     Salt and pepper to taste

SALSA
1   cup diced pineapple
1   pear, diced
1   apple, diced
1   mango, peeled and diced
1   small papaya, peeled and diced
½   small red onion, diced
2   jalapeno peppers, seeded and diced
     Squeeze of fresh lemon
     Squeeze of fresh lime
     Chopped cilantro

PREPARATION

Marinate the fillets in the olive oil, lemon and lime juice and salt and pepper in a non-reactive pan for 15 to 30 minutes. Turn fillets once.

Combine all salsa ingredients. Chill to serve.

Grill the fish. Turn fillets once. Remove when fish turns opaque. Serve with salsa.   SERVES 4

Mebane's Blackened Tuna

1½   pounds fresh tuna steaks, ½-inch thick
4   tablespoons butter or margarine, melted

SPICE MIXTURE
1   teaspoon onion powder
½   teaspoon garlic salt
¾   teaspoon cayenne pepper
¾   teaspoon black pepper
¾   teaspoon dried thyme leaves
¼   teaspoon ground sage (optional)

PREPARATION

Prepare your barbecue to hold a large cast-iron skillet directly on the hot coals.

Combine all spice mixture ingredients in a small bowl. Set aside.

When the fire is hot, place your unoiled skillet directly on the coals. Let it heat until it is very hot–at least 5 minutes. (Watch for the bottom to turn an ash-gray color, or test it by sprinkling a bit of water on the pan; it should sizzle.) Brush the fish with the melted butter (or dip fish into the butter, if you prefer), and coat both sides of the fish with the spice mixture. Use it all, and pat it gently on the the fish to keep the fish from sticking to the pan.

When the pan is hot enough, cook fish for about 2 minutes per side. You may drizzle more melted butter on the fish while it is still in the pan or after you have transferred it to the serving dish. The tuna should be pink inside.   SERVES 4

FISHWIFE'S TIPS
To prepare blackened fish indoors, preheat your skillet over medium-high heat for 5 minutes or until drops of water dance on the skillet's surface. The skillet should not be white-hot.

Blackened Tuna on Green Papaya Salad With Soba Noodles and Oriental Vinaigrette

courtesy of Eberhard Kintscher, Executive Sous Chef, Prince Court Restaurant, Hawaii Prince Hotel

4   tuna steaks, 6 ounces each
4   tablespoons Blackening Spice
1   pound soba noodles, cooked

PAPAYA SALAD

2   cups green papaya, julienned
1   teaspoon anchovy paste, or 4 anchovy fillets, chopped fine
1   clove garlic
1   tomato, cut in strips
   Juice of 1 lemon

BLACKENING SPICE

10 tablespoons paprika
1   tablespoon ground white pepper
1   tablespoon ground black pepper
2   tablespoons cayenne pepper
2   tablespoons garlic salt
2   tablespoons onion salt
1   tablespoon oregano powder
1   tablespoon marjoram powder
1   tablespoon coriander powder
1   tablespoon chili powder
1   tablespoon salt

ORIENTAL VINAIGRETTE

2   ounces (¼ cup) shoyu
4   ounces (½ cup) mirin
1   ounce (2 tablespoons) apple juice
2   ounces (4 tablespoons) orange juice
1   tablespoon fish sauce
1   teaspoon chili paste
1   tablespoon chopped ogo
   Juice of 1 lime
1   tablespoon sesame seeds, toasted
2   tablespoons chopped green onion
1   tablespoon chopped cilantro
4   tablespoons diced red and green bell peppers

PREPARATION

Combine Papaya Salad ingredients and let sit for at least 1 hour.

Mix together all blackening ingredients. Set aside.

Prepare Oriental Vinaigrette: Combine the shoyu, mirin, fruit juices, fish sauce, chili paste, ogo and lime juice in a saucepan. Bring to a boil and thicken with ½ teaspoon of cornstarch mixed with 1 ounce (2 tablespoons) apple juice. Let vinaigrette cool then add the sesame seeds, green onion, cilantro and bell peppers.

Heat an iron skillet or non-stick pan until very hot. Dust fish with blackening spice and cook for 20 to 30 seconds on each side.

Arrange soba noodles on plate and place fish on top. Garnish with the papaya salad and generously spoon sauce onto plate. SERVES 4.

Eberhard Kintscher

Hawaii Prince Hotel Executive Sous Chef Eberhard Kintscher served his apprenticeship at the Black Forest Hotel in Germany and worked in Holland and Switzerland before he came to the U.S. After 5 years in Beverly Hills, including the responsibility as sous chef in the fine dining restaurant of the Regent Beverly Wilshire Hotel, Chef Kintscher moved to Hawai'i.

CHEF KINTSCHER'S HEALTHY TIPS

1. Take any recipe from your favorite cookbook, and cut the portion by half. Substitute unhealthy fats, such as butter, with light olive oil. Substitute egg whites in recipes that ask for eggs.

2. Herbs and spices can substitute for salt. Parsley, cilantro and basil can be added to almost any fish. Tarragon, thyme and lemongrass are best for fish (or chicken).

3. Add a piece of fruit as garnish. The fruit acid will help to digest the food more easily.

Tuna With Mac Nut, Melon and Pear Salsa

1⅓ pounds fresh tuna, cut into 4 steaks or loins
¼   cup coarsely chopped dry-roasted, unsalted macadamia nuts
1   cup cubed honeydew melon, diced
1   cup cubed cantaloupe, diced
2   pears, diced
½   cup chopped parsley
1   large clove garlic, peeled and sliced lengthwise
2   tablespoons olive oil
    Freshly ground black pepper

SAUCE
3   cloves garlic, minced
1   tablespoon brown sugar
¼   cup Thai fish sauce
2   tablespoons lime zest
¼   cup lime juice
1   small, fresh jalapeno pepper, minced
⅓   cup minced cilantro

PREPARATION

To prepare the salsa, toast macadamias until golden brown. Cool, and set aside. Combine sauce ingredients in a large, non-reactive bowl. Mix well. Add the fruit, parsley and toasted nuts. Mix gently until well-blended. Cover salsa, and refrigerate for at least an hour. (This salsa will keep in the refrigerator for 2 days.)

Rub the fish on all sides with the cut garlic clove. Brush the fish on all sides with the olive oil, and season with black pepper. Let stand for 10 or 15 minutes. Grill close to the fire so you can sear the sides of the steaks. Remove fish from grill before the fish is cooked; you want it pink inside. Serve with salsa.

SERVES 4

BBQ Tuna With Geoff's Marinade

2   pounds fresh tuna, sliced into pieces ¼ to ¾-inch thick

GEOFF'S MARINADE
¾   cup virgin olive oil
½   teaspoon crushed peppercorns
1½ teaspoons chopped garlic
1½ teaspoons chopped chives
1   teaspoon chopped fresh thyme (or ½ teaspoon dried)
¾   teaspoon chopped fresh dill (or ¼ teaspoon dried)
1½ teaspoons chopped fresh rosemary (or ½ teaspoon dried)
    Juice of ½ medium lime

PREPARATION

Mix all marinade ingredients together, and marinate the fish slices for 1 hour. Turn fish occasionally. Broil fish over the coals until done, 6 to 8 minutes.

SERVES 6

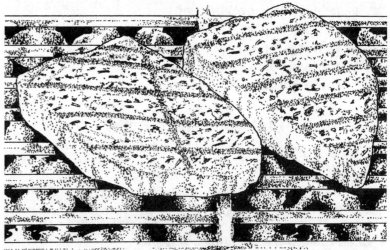

Tuna in Fresh Tomato Sauce

2 pounds fresh tuna
(small skipjack can be used)
3 cloves garlic, pressed or minced
¼ cup olive oil
Juice of one lemon
2 tablespoons olive oil
1 onion, diced
½ cup dry white or red wine
2 cups chopped tomatoes (peeled, if you wish)
½ teaspoon thyme
½ teaspoon oregano
Salt and pepper to taste

PREPARATION

Slice the fish into serving-sized pieces ¾ to 1 inch thick, and place in a non-reactive dish. Mix the garlic, ¼ cup oil and lemon juice together. Pour mixture over fish, and let it marinate for 1 to 2 hours. Turn fish occasionally. When ready to cook, drain the marinade into a skillet, heat it, and quickly sear the fish on both sides. Then remove fish to a plate.

In an oven-proof skillet, heat the 2 tablespoons of olive oil, and sauté the onion pieces until they are tender. Add the wine, tomatoes, thyme, oregano, fish and salt and pepper. Cover the skillet, and bake at 425° until fish is done, about 8 minutes.

SERVES 6

FISHWIFE'S TIP

1. You can cook the entire recipe on the stove. After you add the fish, cover the skillet, lower the heat to a simmer, and cook until the fish is done.
2. If you want the tomatoes to break down more, do not add the fish until the tomatoes are the consistency you want.

Tuna Broil With Citrus Mustard Marinade

2 pounds tuna steaks of even thicknesses
¼ cup shoyu
1½ teaspoons grated lime peel
3 tablespoons fresh lime juice
2 cloves garlic, minced
1 tablespoon minced ginger root
2 teaspoons prepared mustard (Dijon is best)
3 tablespoons peanut oil
3 to 4 stalks green onion, chopped
Pepper to taste

PREPARATION

Place the tuna steaks in a non-reactive baking pan. Combine all remaining ingredients, and pour mixture over the fish. Cover, and refrigerate for at least an hour. Turn once during every hour you marinate the steaks.

Before broiling or barbecuing, let the marinade drip off the fish, then place on a broiler pan or on a barbecue rack. If you broil, place pan 4 to 6 inches from heat source and turn steaks once during cooking.

SERVES 4 TO 6

Tuna Tempura

¾ **pound tuna steak or loin**

TRADITIONAL DIPPING SAUCE
1 **cup dashi (fish stock)**
3 **tablespoons shoyu**
1 **tablespoon mirin**
3 **teaspoons sugar**
¼ **cup grated, peeled daikon (Japanese radish), (optional)**
3 **teaspoons grated ginger root (optional)**
   Oil for deep-frying, about 6 cups

TEMPURA BATTER
1 **egg (optional)**
1½ **cups ice water**
1½ **cups flour**
¼ **teaspoon salt**
2 **teaspoons baking powder (optional)**

FISHWIFE'S TIPS
1. A batter of flour and water is lighter in color and weight and produces a lacy tempura texture. The addition of an egg (or an egg yolk) creates a heavier, more golden brown batter. Baking powder makes a puffier batter.
2. Stir the batter occasionally to keep it from separating.
3. Dashi can be made from scratch (see Sauce chapter) or you may buy powdered, instant dashi (soup stock) in the Oriental foods section of your supermarket.
4. Maintain an even oil temperature during cooking.

PREPARATION

Cut fish into 2- by 1-inch pieces. Pat pieces dry with a paper towel.

To prepare the dipping sauce, combine the dashi, shoyu, mirin and sugar in a small pan. Heat to boiling over medium heat; remove from heat. Divide the grated daikon and ginger root into 4 small bowls. Set aside.

Heat the oil in a large pan over medium-high heat. The amount of oil you use will depend on the size of the pan. You want the oil at least 1½ inches deep.

Prepare tempura batter while the oil is heating: If you use an egg (see Fishwife's Tips), beat it in a bowl. Add the ice water. Beat lightly to mix well. Add the flour and salt (combined with the baking powder if you are using it) all at once. Stir to combine well, but do not overmix. Batter will be lumpy. Set aside.

When the temperature of the oil reaches 360°, test your batter. The temperature is right if the batter sinks to the bottom then rises to the surface immediately, puffing up and turning golden brown.

Dust your fish pieces lightly with flour. Shake off excess. Dip each piece in batter, then slide it into the oil. Don't crowd the pan. Fry 3 or 4 pieces at a time. Cook until golden brown, about 3 minutes, turning pieces once during cooking. Remove fish from oil, and drain on paper towels or brown paper bags.

When serving, pour about ¼ cup of warm sauce into each of the small bowls you set aside.

SERVES 4

Broiled Tuna With Parsley and Ginger Vinaigrette

courtesy of Executive Chef Richard DeWitt Jr.,
Royal Waikoloan

8 6-ounce fresh tuna steaks, at least
1 inch thick
Salt and white pepper to taste

VINAIGRETTE

½ cup rice wine vinegar
1 tablespoon finely minced green onion, white part only
3 tablespoons fresh lime juice
2 tablespoons shoyu
1 cup peanut oil, smoked (see Chef's Note)
½ cup finely chopped ginger
Salt and white pepper to taste

GARNISH

½ cup finely chopped fresh parsley
1 tablespoon finely diced red bell pepper

PREPARATION

Combine vinaigrette ingredients, and set aside.

Season the fish steaks with salt and pepper. Oil the grill to prevent sticking. Broil the steaks over a medium to hot fire until medium, or medium-rare, if you prefer. Never overcook your fish, or it will be too dry.

Place tuna steaks on a serving plate. Mix the vinaigrette well, and spoon over the steaks. Sprinkle a generous amount of the chopped fresh parsley over them, and then sprinkle a little of the diced red pepper on top for color contrast.

SERVES 8

Richard DeWitt Jr.

Executive Sous Chef Richard DeWitt Jr., known as JR at the Royal Waikoloan, became interested in cooking as a youngster. When he'd present his own "catch of the day" to his mother, she'd cook his newly caught fish every way but fried, mostly in the Japanese style. He remembers her suggestion that he think about becoming a chef, but, "I kind of shrugged it off and said I was going to be a bus driver." JR is an active participant in culinary events throughout the state, from chili cook-offs to cooking classes in the Tiare Room kitchen. His advice to all cooks: "It's not recipes or ingredients; it's timing and balance."

Chef's Note: Smoke your oil (this is a Chinese technique). Bring the oil to the smoking point, and then let it cool down. This will give the oil a cooked taste or a roasted flavor. Be very careful; always watch for the oil to start smoking, then turn off the heat immediately. The oil can catch fire at this point if you're not careful. (If you have an electric stove, remove the pan from the heat immediately.) Also any liquid spilled or added at this point will splatter explosively, so, again, be very careful.

Zesty Tarragon Tuna

1½ **pounds fresh tuna fillets or steaks**
½ **cup white wine**
½ **cup white vinegar**
1 **teaspoon dried tarragon, rubbed or crushed**
2 **teaspoons Worcestershire sauce**
  (or to taste)
½ **cup flour**
  Salt and pepper to taste
2 **tablespoons olive or peanut oil**
2 **tablespoons butter or margarine**
1 **clove garlic, minced**

FISHWIFE'S TIP

If you prefer to broil the 'ahi over coals, which is delicious, too, leave out the flour, butter and margarine. Add the salt and pepper, oil and garlic to the marinade.

PREPARATION

Marinate the fish (use a non-reactive container) in a combination of the wine, vinegar, tarragon and Worcestershire sauce 15 to 20 minutes per side if the fish is thick, or 30 minutes without turning if fish is not. Remove fish from the marinade, and let it "drip dry" before patting dry. Season the flour with the salt (not much because the Worcestershire sauce is salty) and pepper, and dust each piece of fish with the flour mixture.

Heat the oil and butter or margarine in a heavy skillet over medium heat. When oil begins to sizzle, add the fish and garlic. Cook fish on both sides until golden brown (no more than a total of 10 minutes per inch of thickness of the fish). Serve immediately.

SERVES 4

Wok-Fried Tuna in Nori and Cornmeal Crust With Coconut Tomato Sauce

courtesy of Mauna Kea Beach Hotel
Garden Restaurant

10 3-ounce pieces of fresh tuna fillet
1 cup teriyaki sauce
2 tablespoons wasabi paste
10 nori sheets
Japanese mirin (amount varies)
Egg wash
¼ cup yellow cornmeal (or more if needed)
¼ cup flour (or more if needed)
Peanut oil for frying

COCONUT TOMATO SAUCE
1 tablespoon sweet butter
4 fresh tomatoes, peeled, seeded and chopped
1 sweet onion, diced
1 teaspoon diced garlic cloves
1 tablespoon curry powder
½ cup sherry wine
½ cup fish stock
½ cup coconut milk
½ cup whipping cream
1 tablespoon chopped fresh cilantro
Salt and pepper to taste

FISHWIFE'S TIP
Expect the tuna to be medium-rare. The nori will burn before the tuna cooks through. If you want your tuna well done, cut the pieces smaller.

PREPARATION

Combine teriyaki and wasabi paste. Marinate fish pieces in the mixture for 10 minutes. Wrap each piece of fish in a nori sheet that has been moistened with mirin. (You can fold the nori over the fish envelope-style or bring edges up and tie off with a leek leaf or spinach stem.) Lightly dip the wrapped fish in the egg wash, and then dredge it in a mixture of the cornmeal and flour.

To prepare the sauce, melt butter in a saucepan over medium heat. Add tomatoes, onion, garlic and curry powder, and cook for 2 to 3 minutes. Add sherry and fish stock, and reduce to half. Add coconut milk and cream, and cook until desired consistency is reached. Add the cilantro, salt and pepper to taste, and remove the pan from the heat. Keep sauce warm.

Fry the tuna packets in hot peanut oil until the nori is golden. Serve immediately with the sauce.

MAKES 10 PACKETS

Tuna Appetizer, New York-Style

1½ pounds fresh tuna loins
1 tablespoon green peppercorns, crushed
1 tablespoon sesame seeds, crushed
(I use black, but white seeds are fine)
Salt and pepper to taste
2 tablespoons fresh lemon or lime juice
Lemon or lime wedges (garnish)

PREPARATION

Combine the crushed peppercorns and sesame seeds in a small dish. Sprinkle 'ahi loins on all sides with salt, pepper and lemon or lime juice. Dust the loins with the peppercorn-sesame combination (press the mixture against the fish so it will stick). The peppercorn-sesame mixture won't cover every inch of the loins, which is fine because green peppercorns are hot. Let stand for 10 minutes or so before slicing fish very thin. Serve with lemon or lime wedges.

SERVES 10

VARIATIONS:

1. Combine the peppercorns and sesame seeds with salt and pepper and enough of the lemon or lime juice to make a paste. Roll the loins in the paste. Let stand on a cake rack to dry before slicing.

2. Slice the fish very thin and overlap the slices on a platter. Sprinkle the salt, pepper and lemon juice over the top. Combine the peppercorns and sesame seeds in a small dish, and add ½ to 1 teaspoon water, just enough to make a paste. Smear this mixture over the top of the fish, and serve.

FISHWIFE'S TIP
Crush the peppercorns and sesame seeds in a small grinder to the consistency you prefer (chunky to fine), or put the whole peppercorns and sesame seeds in wax paper and pound them with a mallet or rolling pin to crush.

Cold Tuna Salad With Kidney Beans

1½ pounds fresh tuna
½ pound red kidney beans (dried)
1 tablespoon dried oregano
2 teaspoons rock salt
1 teaspoon rock salt
1 red onion, sliced thinly
3 cloves garlic, minced
2 tablespoons chopped fresh oregano
3 tablespoons chopped fresh parsley
4 tablespoons red wine vinegar
2 tablespoons lemon juice
2 tablespoons olive oil
¼ cup water
1 teaspoon balsamic vinegar
1 teaspoon shoyu
2 tablespoons capers, drained and chopped
1 teaspoon Dijon mustard
Fresh ground pepper

PREPARATION

If you are using dried kidney beans, soak them overnight, cook (adding 2 teaspoons of salt toward end of cooking) according to package instructions, drain, and cool.

Poach fish in water with the dried oregano and teaspoon of rock salt. Drain, and let cool. Break tuna into chunks. Combine the fish with the drained beans, onion slices, garlic, fresh oregano and parsley. Toss gently but well. Combine the vinegar, lemon juice, olive oil, water, balsamic vinegar, shoyu, capers, mustard and fresh ground pepper in a jar. Cover, and shake well to blend. Taste and correct seasonings before adding to the salad. Combine well.

Transfer salad to a non-reactive container, cover, and refrigerate for at least 1 hour. Serve cold, or bring to room temperature.

SERVES 6

Tuna Carpaccio Salad With Avocado and Soy Wasabi Aioli

courtesy of Chef Paul Heerlein,
The Gallery Restaurant

1 8-ounce fresh tuna loin well-chilled
4 cups mixed organic greens
   (such as frissee, Lola Rossa, arugula)
1 teaspoon kosher salt
1 teaspoon cracked pepper
¾ tablespoon olive oil (Sita extra-virgin)
¼ cup julienned red onion
¾ cup peeled and julienned tomato
   (approximately 1 medium tomato)
2 tablespoons lemon juice

SOY WASABI AIOLI

1 egg yolk
¼ teaspoon finely chopped garlic
½ cup Bertolli olive oil
3 teaspoons Yamasa soy sauce
¼ teaspoon wasabi
¼ teaspoon mirin

GARNISH

½ cup finely julienned nori seaweed
½ medium avocado, peeled and diced
   Avocado and 2 ounces enoki mushrooms

Paul Heerlein

Chef Paul Heerlein joined The Gallery Restaurant staff in 1992 and has since created an entirely new menu concept for the restaurant, which reflects a Northern Italian cuisine with Asian influences. He uses the freshest of ingredients and relies on vinegars, wines, olive oil, basil and tomato reductions to create flavorful dishes that are low in fat. His favorite dishes are those prepared with very fresh shellfish and fish. Chef Heerlein has been in the restaurant business since he was 14. Inspired by his mother, a private chef for East Coast estates, he climbed the culinary ladder by working in restaurants across the country, including The Post House in Southampton, New York, The Pier House in Key West, Florida, and the Four Seasons, Newport Beach in California.

PREPARATION

To prepare Soy Wasabi Aioli, combine egg yolk and garlic in a small bowl. Slowly drizzle in oil, little by little, while whisking constantly. Combine soy sauce, wasabi and mirin in a separate bowl. Mix together. Drizzle this mixture into egg mixture, whisking constantly, until a thin mayonnaise consistency is reached. Strain.

Slice chilled fish paper thin. Combine mixed greens, salt and pepper, Sita olive oil, red onion, tomato and lemon juice. Toss well. Serve fish on greens with a drizzle of Soy Wasabi Aioli. Garnish with nori, avocado and enoki mushrooms.

SERVES 4

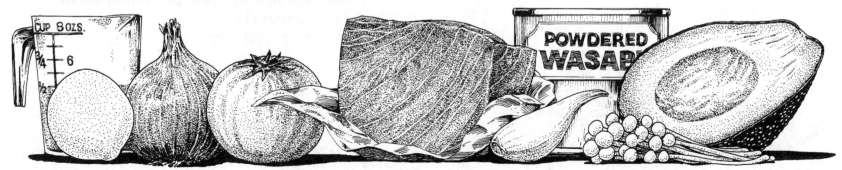

Seared Sashimi
courtesy of Mark Ellman,
Avalon Restaurant & Bar

1   2-ounce piece of fresh yellowfin tuna–
    top fillet only
1   tablespoon macadamia nut oil

HERBS (chopped and mixed):
1   tablespoon basil
1   tablespoon mint
1   tablespoon cilantro

SAUCE
4   ounces Chardonnay wine
1   ounce shiitake mushrooms, sliced
¼   ounce ginger, chopped
¼   ounce garlic, chopped
¼   ounce sweet onion, chopped
1   tablespoon butter
1   tablespoon Marumasa soy sauce
1   tablespoon green onion

PREPARATION

Coat fish in macadamia nut oil, and roll fish in herbs. Sear fish for 5 seconds on each side in a very hot pan. Remove, and slice ⅛-inch slices on the bias.

Reduce the first 7 sauce ingredients over high heat until halved in volume. Add green onions. Nap plate (lightly coat the center of the plate with sauce), and fan sashimi over sauce.   SERVES 1

Mark Ellman

Mark Ellman is a self-taught chef who dazzles critics with his unique approach and blend of Pacific and Asian cuisines. He and his wife, Judy, fulfilled their dream of owning a restaurant on Maui when they opened Avalon Restaurant and Bar in 1989, but the road to Avalon began many years before. As a teen, Mark flipped hamburgers and pizza crusts before working under French Chef Tony LeBlanc and others. In 1977, the Ellmans opened a catering company, "Can't Rock and Roll, But Sure Can Cook," and later a small restaurant called "Cuisine, Cuisine." Avalon opened in January 1988. Mark, along with his sister Gerry, his assistant chef, creates innovative dishes influenced by the cuisine of California, Indonesia, Vietnam, Thailand, China and Japan. Mark was recently a featured chef on NBC's "Today Show," where he cooked his whole 'opakapaka on the beach at Kapalua for Katie Couric. The Ellmans hope to bring the restaurant into the year 2000 with world-class status. With the recognition and accolades Mark has already earned, that should be easy.

Tuna Poke Temaki (Hand Roll)
courtesy of Roy Kaneko, Hilo, Hawai'i
First Place, Local-Style Poke
Sam Choy Poke Contest

½   pound fresh tuna, cubed
2   tablespoons finely chopped green onion
1   tablespoon finely chopped round onion
3   tablespoons shoyu
1½ teaspoons chili pepper oil

PREPARATION

Combine all ingredients in a large bowl. Mix until fish is evenly coated. Chill.   SERVES 2

This poke makes an excellent filling for hand rolls using your favorite sushi recipe and green yakinori (roasted seaweed).

Tuna Carpaccio

1 **pound fresh tuna loins, thinly sliced (as for sashimi)**
¼ **cup soft tofu**
2 **tablespoons rice vinegar**
1 **teaspoon mirin (or ½ teaspoon sugar)**
2 **tablespoons water**
2 **teaspoons wasabi powder (or to taste)**
¼ **teaspoon ground ginger**
2 **tablespoons shoyu**
1 **tablespoon sesame oil**
3 **tablespoons minced green onion**
2 **tablespoons sesame seeds**

PREPARATION

Arrange the fish slices on a serving platter. Cover platter, and refrigerate.

Combine the tofu, rice vinegar, mirin, water, wasabi powder, ground ginger and shoyu in a food processor. Blend until smooth. Slowly process in the sesame oil. Drizzle mixture over the fish, sprinkle with green onion and sesame seeds, and serve.

SERVES 8

FISHWIFE'S TIP
If you cannot slice your fish very thin, lay your slices on a sheet of wax paper, leaving room between slices. Cover with another sheet of wax paper. With the smooth side of a meat mallet or any smooth object, gently tap the fish slices until they flatten out and are as thin as possible. Remove them carefully (or they will tear) and place them (overlapping one another) on your platter.

NOTE: Whenever you make any of the recipes in which fish is served uncooked, it's best to use fresh fish. If frozen fish is used, the texture will not be firm and the fish, although edible, will tend to get slimy fast.

Seaweed Poke
courtesy of Jane Yamashiroya

1 **pound fresh fish (aku, 'ahi, marlin), cubed**
1 **tablespoon sea salt or rock salt**
½ **pound seaweed (Japanese *ogo*, scientific name: *Gracilaria coronopifolia*)**
2 **stalks green onion, chopped**
1 **small round onion, chopped**
Chili pepper flakes, optional

PREPARATION

Cube fish to desired size. Combine with salt, and let stand in refrigerator for at least 1 hour.

Wash seaweed, drain well, and chop to desired lengths (½ inch to 1 inch size is good). Combine seaweed, onions, pepper flakes (if desired) and fish.
Serve cold as an appetizer.

SERVES 8

Shoyu Poke

½ **pound fresh fish (aku, 'ahi, marlin, etc.)**
1 **teaspoon finely chopped ginger**
½ **cup shoyu**
1 **round onion, quartered and sliced**
1 **to 2 stalks green onion**
Chopped chili pepper flakes, optional

PREPARATION

Cube fish to desired size. Combine with ginger and shoyu. Let stand in refrigerator for at least 1 hour.

Combine with onions and pepper flakes (if desired). Serve cold as an appetizer.

SERVES 4

Jane Yamashiroya
Jane Yamashiroya, an educator of Home Economics for more than 20 years, experiments with local seafood dishes. Above, she offers two of her favorites.

Chinese-Style Poisson Cru Poke

courtesy of Judy Furtado, Kula, Maui
Second Place, Local-Style Poke
Sam Choy Poke Contest

5 pounds tuna, cut into ½-inch cubes
4 fresh limes
½ cup rock salt
2 cups green onion
2 large carrots, diced
1 medium sweet onion, diced
4 large cucumbers, peeled, seeded and diced
3 large tomatoes, seeded and diced
Salad oil for frying
5 packages mai fun noodles

VINAIGRETTE
¼ cup oil
1 tablespoon lime juice
½ tablespoon grated ginger
1½ teaspoons sugar

PREPARATION

Squeeze limes, and mix juice with rock salt. Add fish to mixture, and marinate 15 minutes. Rinse fish cubes gently in a colander. Combine fish with diced vegetables, toss, cover, and refrigerate.

Pour salad oil into a wok or deep pan, and cook mai fun noodles until puffy. Arrange noodles on a large platter.

Shake vinaigrette ingredients well in a jar with a lid, and pour vinaigrette over fish and vegetables. Toss, and arrange mixture on top of mai fun noodles.

SERVES 20

Mainland-Style Poke

1 pound fresh tuna, cut into ½-inch cubes
½ cup diced, seeded cucumber
¼ cup sliced green onions
3 cloves garlic, minced
½ teaspoon dried hot pepper flakes
3 tablespoons sesame oil
3 tablespoons shoyu
4 medium radishes, thinly sliced
3 cups spinach leaves, rinsed, dried and cut into thin ribbons
1 tablespoon roasted sesame seeds

PREPARATION

Put the fish in a large bowl. Add the cucumber and onions, and mix well. Sprinkle fish mixture with the garlic and hot pepper flakes, and mix again. Add the sesame oil and shoyu. Mix thoroughly, cover, and refrigerate until very cold, at least 2 hours.

Before serving, mix in the radishes. Serve fish mixture on top of the spinach. Sprinkle with sesame seeds.

SERVES 8

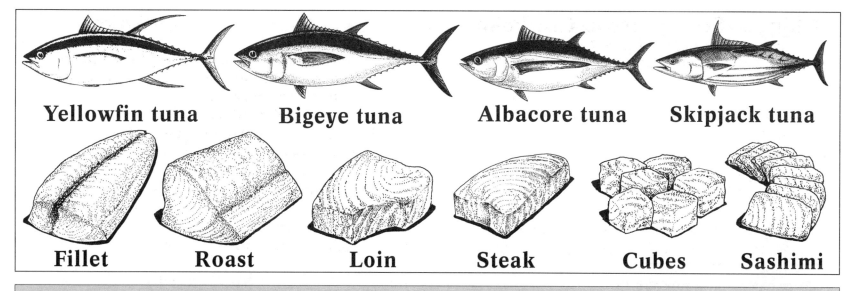

Yellowfin tuna **Bigeye tuna** **Albacore tuna** **Skipjack tuna**

Fillet **Roast** **Loin** **Steak** **Cubes** **Sashimi**

FISHWIFE'S TIP

Be careful of scombroid poisoning, a type of allergic reaction to fish that hasn't been properly refrigerated after capture. Tuna and other red-meat fish deteriorate rapidly and must be properly iced immediately upon capture.

HOW FRESH IS YOUR CATCH?

Fish is known to be one of the most tasty, healthy and nutritious forms of food available. However, there are certain precautions you should take and knowledge you should have as a consumer to avoid certain health hazards.

CONSUMING RAW FISH

Many of you are from island and coastal areas and are from fishing families or are fortunate enough to have friends, neighbors or family members who share their catch with you. If this is the case, you can be reasonably sure of both the freshness and care of the fish (which should be iced immediately after capture for maximum freshness). Such is not always the case for store-bought "fresh" fish.

Included in the chapters of this book are numerous recipes that call for the use of raw fish for *sashimi*, *poke*, *ceviche* and seared preparations (which leave the center of the meat very rare). We've included these recipes because they offer exciting, flavorful dining experiences, which explains their extreme popularity in Central Pacific island fine restaurants and at family gatherings.

If you are fortunate enough to know the source of the catch and can be certain that the fish is fresh and has been properly handled, these recipes can be prepared and served with the confidence that there will be no ill effects. However, we offer the following warnings and cautions you should be aware of and heed before choosing a raw fish recipe for consumption.

According to the "University of California at Berkeley Wellness Letter" (vol. 11, issue 9), "Fish and shellfish marinated in lime juice–known as ceviche, a Latin American specialty–are still raw fish. Like sashimi, ceviche could make you sick.

"Marinating infected seafood might kill cholera bacteria on the surface, but the interior is another matter. And *E. coli*, which can cause severe food poisoning, is hardly fazed by lime juice. Parasites could be a problem, too." Blanching before marinating is not sufficient, either.

"The FDA says that if the raw fish used in ceviche is commercially frozen first and then thawed, it might be safe. . . . But even frozen shrimp should be cooked for three to four minutes in boiling water to kill any microbes and other stowaways. This doesn't mean that ceviche is certain to make you sick. But, as with [sashimi] and poke, you're taking a risk.

"You could try cooking shrimp or other fish first and then adding the lime juice marinade for a cold dish. It's really not that different, except that it's reliably safe to eat."

In conclusion, if you do not have certain knowledge of who caught the fish, when the fish was captured and how it was cared for, it should be properly cooked and never eaten raw.

For fishermen new to the sport, we have included proper care and handling techniques for your catches.

Notes

Billfish

Broadbill swordfish, or shutome, are the main target of the commercial longline fleet. Shutome is a high-profile fish on the auction block, popular with chefs and home cooks. It is mild yet tastes rich, and chefs appreciate its adaptability to various cooking methods. The firm flesh takes well to grilling or broiling, sautéing and stir-frying but it can also be braised and poached successfully. Shutome is a migratory fish available year-round but most common from April through July.

Sport fishermen practice catch and release of marlin and spearfish as an important conservation measure. However, not all billfish can be released successfully. What do you do with a marlin that can't be released? Prepared correctly, marlin are excellent table fare.

Shortbill spearfish, or hebi, is considered by some as the best buy at the fish counters because it has not yet been "discovered" for its mild but flavorful flesh. Its texture is softer than that of other billfish, but it holds its shape well when broiled, sautéed and used in soups and stews. In Hawai'i, hebi is most common during the spring months.

Striped marlin, or a'u, is the most tender of the species and, as such, considered the best eating.

Pacific blue marlin, or kajiki, is popular broiled, stir-fry or barbecued. A winter fish, it is most abundant when sea temperatures drop a few degrees.

Billfish are moderately fatty, not as rich as tuna and not as lean as mahimahi or snapper. They take well to grilling, broiling, baking, sautéing and poaching and are often used as sashimi or poke.

> **FISHWIFE'S TIP**
>
> Watch for improper care of the fish. Because of their unwieldy size (Pacific blue marlin average 300 to 400 lbs, and striped marlin between 80 and 200 lbs), proper storage is difficult. Few marlin will fit into cold storage facilities on boats. Many times, all a fisherman can do is cover the fish with a blanket and keep it wet by sloshing it with ocean water. Evaporation helps draw off some of the heat and protects the meat from spoiling as quickly. If you are fortunate enough to receive some marlin meat, check it for freshness (see page 194).

SUBSTITUTIONS: Mako and Thresher Shark.

Broiled Hawaiian Shutome Crisp Stir-Fried Vegetables With Ginger Emulsified Butter With Oyster Sauce

courtesy of Dominique Jamain, Executive Chef, Kahala Hilton

10 2½-ounce shutome medallions
 1 ounce sesame oil (2 tablespoons)
    Salt and pepper to taste

VEGETABLES

 1 ounce red bell pepper strips
    (about ¼ medium pepper)
 1 ounce yellow bell pepper strips
 2 ounces bean sprouts
 1 ounce red onion strips
    (about ¼ medium onion)
 1 ounce green onion strips (about 1 stalk)
 1 ounce shiitake mushroom strips
 1 ounce snow pea strips (10 to 12 snow peas)
 1 ounce celery, peeled and cut into small strips
    (about 7 1-inch by 1-inch pieces, cut into strips)
 ½ teaspoon grated ginger root
 2 ounces (¼ cup) sesame oil
    Salt and pepper to taste

SAUCE

 3 cups fish stock
 ½ cup finely cut shallots
 ½ cup white wine
 2 sprigs fresh thyme
 1 ounce oyster sauce
    Juice from ½ lemon
 2 ounces butter, at room temperature
    Salt and pepper to taste

GARNISH

 1 ounce tomatoes, diced
    Black sesame seeds
    Cilantro sprigs

Kahala Hilton's Executive Chef Dominique Jamain, with his distinct style and regional flair, oversaw a crew of culinary artisans who captivated guests in 3 of the hotel's restaurants with unique dishes and elegant presentations. Under his supervision, the Maile Restaurant received the American Automobile Association's prestigious Five Diamond rating for 3 consecutive years and had been hailed statewide as the number 1 restaurant in Hawai'i. Chef Jamain had embraced the Pacific and Asian influences of island cooking in his creations, blending native fish, fruits and nuts with imported products new to O'ahu. Chef Jamain is the recipient of numerous international culinary awards dating back to 1982. He was honored in 1992 by The James Beard Foundation as one of the Great Hotel Chefs of America, and his guest appearances on Cunard's flagship QE2 have been among the most popular of the ship's World Cruise Guest Chef program.

PREPARATION

To prepare sauce, combine fish stock, shallots, white wine and thyme in a saucepan over medium heat; bring to boil, and reduce to 1 cup. Remove from heat. Add oyster sauce and lemon juice to the reduced stock; blend at high speed. Continue blending while adding the softened butter. Strain through a fine sieve, add salt and pepper, and set aside.

Season, oil and broil the shutome. *Do not overcook.*

Stir-fry vegetables separately. Toss together, and adjust seasoning.

Place broiled fish medallions over a bed of vegetables. Top with a little sauce. Garnish with diced tomatoes, black sesame seeds and cilantro sprigs.

SERVES 5

Swordfish Steaks Baked With Cheese

1½ pounds swordfish steaks, cut into pieces
  1 inch thick
  1 egg white
  2 tablespoons skim milk
  ½ cup bread crumbs
  ½ teaspoon dried basil, or oregano, crushed
  1 tablespoon freshly grated Parmesan cheese
  1 tablespoon freshly grated Romano cheese
  1 teaspoon dry mustard
  Salt and pepper to taste

PREPARATION

Preheat oven to 450°.

Whisk the egg white in a bowl large enough to dip fish steaks. Add milk, and blend well.

Blend the remaining ingredients in an equally large dish or bowl.

Dip each steak into the egg white-milk mixture. Remove, and dredge in the seasoned bread crumbs. Then place steak on a non-stick baking sheet (or use a baking sheet prepared with a vegetable cooking spray).

Bake until lightly browned, 8 to 10 minutes. Time the cooking carefully; fish can dry out fast.   SERVES 4

Barbecued Swordfish Burgers

1 pound swordfish, cubed
1 small onion, chopped
2 slices white bread, torn into 1-inch pieces
2 tablespoons butter
2 tablespoons plain, non-fat yogurt
2 teaspoons Dijon mustard
¼ teaspoon cayenne pepper, or hot paprika
  Salt and pepper to taste

PREPARATION

Combine the onion, bread, butter, yogurt, mustard, cayenne, salt and pepper in a food processor bowl. Process until smooth. Add the fish, and purée (using on/off turns).

Shape mixture into 4 or 5 patties, about ¾ inch thick. (Dust hands lightly with flour, if necessary.)

Lightly oil your barbecue rack. Grill patties (or broil in the oven) until cooked through, turning once, about 4 minutes per side. Offer with your favorite tomato relish.   SERVES 4

FISHWIFE'S TIP

1. Patties can be prepared a day ahead if kept in the refrigerator.
2. If you wish, purée only the fish and mix it with all remaining ingredients, as you would for a meat loaf or meatballs. Be sure to tear the bread into smaller pieces.

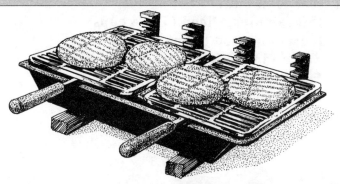

Swordfish á la Compleat Kitchen

1½ **pounds swordfish steaks, or fillets**
¼ **cup flour**
2 **tablespoons olive oil**
1½ **cups chopped plum (Italian) tomatoes**
¾ **cup pitted black olive halves**
3 **cloves garlic, pressed**
3 **tablespoons chopped fresh parsley**
1 **tablespoon lemon juice**
¼ **cup grated Parmesan cheese**
Fresh ground pepper to taste

PREPARATION

Cut fish into cubes about 1 inch square. Dust lightly with flour. Heat olive oil in a skillet over medium heat. Add the fish, and sauté for 4 minutes. Add the tomatoes and olives, and cook together for 2 more minutes. Add the remaining ingredients. Stir together for a minute, and then remove from the heat. Cover the pan, and let stand for another minute.   SERVES 6

FISHWIFE'S TIPS

1. Cooking time will vary depending on the size of your fish cubes. The rule here would be to cook the fish for no more than half of its necessary cooking time before adding the tomatoes and olives, and then proceed with the recipe above.

2. For additional flavor, substitute green olives with pimentos for some of the black olives.

Grilled Billfish, Greek-Style

1½ **pounds fish, cut into 1-inch thick steaks**
12 **large Kalamata olives, pitted**
3 **tablespoons olive oil**
1 **teaspoon dried thyme**
Freshly ground pepper
1 **medium tomato, chopped and seeded**

PREPARATION

Mince olives, and combine them with olive oil, thyme and pepper. Blend well. Marinate the fish in this mixture for 30 minutes. Turn steaks once. Grill fish, basting frequently with the olive marinade, for no more than 8 minutes. Turn once. Top with tomato.   SERVES 4

Oven-Baked Swordfish With Onions

2 **pounds swordfish steaks, cut into pieces**
1½ inches thick
1 **tablespoon olive oil**
1 **teaspoon butter**
3 **large onions, sliced (3 to 4 cups)**
1 **teaspoon dried thyme, or oregano**
Salt and freshly ground pepper to taste
Flour for dredging
⅓ **cup fresh bread crumbs**
1 **tablespoon minced fresh parsley**
⅔ **cup white wine**

PREPARATION

Preheat oven to 350°. Heat oil and butter in a large, non-stick skillet over medium-low heat. Sauté onions until tender. Add dried herb, stir well, and remove onions to a dish or bowl.

Season fish steaks with salt and pepper, dredge lightly in flour, and brown over medium-high heat in the same skillet for 1 minute per side. Remove fish, and place it in a baking dish. Cover fish with the onions. Combine the bread crumbs and parsley, and scatter on top.

Pour the wine around the fish, and bake, basting occasionally, for 20 minutes, until the top has browned slightly.   SERVES 6

Bloody Mary Barbecue

2 pounds swordfish, cut into serving-sized
  pieces ¾ to 1 inch thick
SAUCE
¼ cup chopped onion
2 tablespoons chopped celery
1 clove garlic, minced
¼ cup V-8 juice
⅓ cup white wine
2 tablespoons lemon juice
1 tablespoon Worcestershire sauce
¼ teaspoon salt
¼ teaspoon freshly ground pepper
4 to 8 drops hot pepper sauce (optional)

PREPARATION

Sauté the onion, celery and garlic in a large saucepan over medium-high heat until tender. Add the remaining sauce ingredients. Simmer for 5 minutes, remove from heat, and let cool.

Place the fish in a non-reactive baking dish in a single layer. Pour the cooled sauce over the fish, and let stand for 30 minutes, turning once.

Remove the fish, and place it on a well-oiled grill. Cook for no more than 8 minutes per inch of thickness. Turn fish once during cooking, and baste frequently with the sauce.
SERVES 6

Steamed Swordfish Steaks Oriental

1½ pounds swordfish steaks, cut into 4 pieces
  1 inch thick
  Freshly ground pepper to taste
1 teaspoon sesame oil
1 cup sliced fresh mushrooms
1 stalk green onions, cut into 1-inch lengths
1 large clove garlic, minced
1 teaspoon minced ginger root
¼ cup oyster sauce
¼ cup shoyu (low-salt works best)
¼ cup white wine, vermouth, sake, or water
1 tablespoon black sesame seeds

PREPARATION

Season steaks with pepper. Put 2 inches of water in a pan large enough to steam the fish. Place steaks on a steamer rack; cover, and bring the water to a boil over high heat. Steam fish until it is tender, about 5 minutes (it will not be completely cooked). Remove from heat.

Heat sesame oil in a large non-stick skillet. Add the mushrooms, onions, garlic and ginger, and sauté until the mushrooms are limp, 3 or 4 minutes. Add the oyster sauce, shoyu and wine; blend well. Add the fish to the skillet, and cook for 1 minute per side, turning once. When fish is done, remove to a serving dish. Top with sauce, sprinkle with sesame seeds.
SERVES 4

Swordfish Diane
courtesy of Margie Dunlap

1 **pound swordfish fillets**
¼ **cup flour**
    Salt and freshly ground pepper to taste
2 **tablespoons olive oil**
1 **tablespoon butter**
3 **tablespoons chopped green onions**
2 **teaspoons capers, drained**
1 **tablespoon chopped parsley**
1 **teaspoon Dijon mustard**
    Dash Worcestershire sauce
½ **cup chicken broth**
⅓ **cup white wine**

PREPARATION

Slice fish into 4 serving-sized pieces. Combine flour, salt and pepper. Roll fish in flour mixture; dust off excess. Heat oil in a non-stick skillet over medium-high heat. Sauté fish for 2 or 3 minutes per side, decreasing heat, if necessary, to keep from overcooking. (The fish should not be completely cooked at this point.) Remove fish from skillet, and pour off any oil that remains.

Melt the butter in the same skillet. Add the green onions and capers; stir for 30 seconds, or so. Add the parsley, mustard, Worcestershire sauce, chicken broth and wine. Cook for 2 minutes

Lower the heat to medium, and return the fish to the skillet. Cook for 2 minutes per side, or until fish is just done. Remove it to a serving platter. Pour sauce over fish, and serve.

SERVES 4

Swordfish
With Mint-Garlic Basting Sauce
courtesy of Suzanne McNaughton

1 **1½-pound swordfish fillet,**
    2 to 2½ inches thick

BASTING SAUCE
1 **tablespoon minced garlic**
2 **tablespoons chopped fresh mint**
1 **tablespoon raspberry vinegar**
    (or other mild red vinegar)
½ **teaspoon salt**
½ **teaspoon freshly ground pepper**
½ **cup non-fat plain yogurt**
    (or substitute non-fat mayonnaise)
    Mint sprigs

PREPARATION

Preheat oven to 450°. Combine basting sauce ingredients in a small bowl or dish. Coat fish with basting sauce; place skin side down in a baking dish or tray. Bake for 15 to 18 minutes, depending on thickness. Baste fish frequently (3 or 4 times) to keep it moist. Remove from heat. Top with mint sprigs.   SERVES 4

FISHWIFE'S TIP
To speed cooking and prevent fish from drying out when baking a large fillet, make a deep, lengthwise cut down the center of the fillet (or cut through completely, if you wish). This creates additional surfaces for the heat (and the basting sauce, too!) to penetrate.

Grilled Cilantro Swordfish With Lime Marinade

1½ **pounds fish, cut into 1-inch thick steaks**
2 **tablespoons fresh lime juice**
  Salt and pepper to taste
¼ **cup olive oil, as needed**
2 **small cloves garlic, minced**
¾ **cup minced cilantro**
¼ **teaspoon dried red pepper flakes**

PREPARATION

Place fish in a single layer in a non-reactive pan or dish. Pour lime juice over the fish. Season with salt and pepper, and marinate for 15 to 20 minutes. Turn steaks once.

Meanwhile, heat half the olive oil in a small pan over medium-low heat. Add the garlic, and cook briefly (about 30 seconds) before adding the cilantro and pepper flakes. Add more oil, if necessary. Cook for a minute or so, and remove pan from the heat.

Grill or broil the fish until it is almost done. Time it at approximately 5 minutes on the first side. Turn fish once, and watch it carefully so you don't overcook it. Brush it frequently with the cilantro mixture during cooking.   SERVES 4

Grilled Shutome With Nectarine-Plum Salsa

2 **pounds swordfish steaks, cut ¾ inch thick**
MARINADE
⅓ **cup oil**
2 **tablespoons balsamic vinegar**
1 **teaspoon dried basil**
SALSA
2 **firm, ripe nectarines, diced**
2 **firm, ripe plums, diced**
¼ **cup firmly packed basil leaves, minced**
¼ **cup chopped sweet onion**
1 **tablespoon minced fresh ginger root**
1½ **tablespoons balsamic vinegar**
1 **tablespoon honey**

PREPARATION

Combine the marinade ingredients in a non-reactive pan or dish large enough to hold the fish in one layer. Marinate the fish for 30 minutes. Turn steaks once.

To prepare salsa, combine all ingredients in a bowl. (You may serve it immediately, or let it stand for 20 to 30 minutes to blend flavors.)

Grill the fish, basting often with marinade. Remove steaks from the heat after 6 minutes. Serve with salsa.
                              SERVES 6

Swordfish and Vegetable Sauté

1 pound swordfish, cut into bite-sized pieces
   Juice from ½ lemon, or lime
2 tablespoons shoyu
¼ cup dry white wine
2 cloves garlic, chopped
1 tablespoon chopped or minced ginger root
¼ cup oil
3 green onions, chopped
1 cup each of 3 thinly sliced vegetables
   Salt and pepper to taste

PREPARATION

Combine the lemon or lime juice, shoyu, wine, garlic and ginger in a non-reactive container. Marinate the fish in the mixture for at least ½ hour.

Pour half of the oil into a hot wok or pan, and sauté the vegetables until just tender, about 3 minutes. Remove vegetables to a warm platter. Add remaining oil to pan, if necessary. Add fish and marinade. Stir-fry for 2 minutes. Return the vegetables to the pan, and mix well with fish. Season with salt and pepper.

Remove the mixture to a warm platter.

SERVES 4

FISHWIFE'S TIP
Increase the amount of shoyu if you prefer a stronger flavor, or add a splash of Worcestershire or ½ teaspoon of chili sauce.

Swordfish With Orange-Mustard Raisin Sauce

1½ pounds swordfish fillet or steaks
    Salt and pepper to taste
¼   cup flour
2   tablespoons olive oil
SAUCE
2   tablespoons butter
¼   cup minced onions
2   tablespoons orange juice
¼   cup raisins
1   teaspoon Dijon mustard
1   tablespoon balsamic vinegar
3   tablespoons chopped almonds
3   tablespoons rum
¼   teaspoon ground ginger
    Salt and freshly ground pepper to taste

PREPARATION

To prepare sauce, melt the butter in a saucepan over medium-high heat. Sauté onions briefly. Add the remaining ingredients, and boil until the mixture is reduced, 3 or 4 minutes. Remove pan from heat, cover, and set aside.

Salt and pepper the fish. Coat with flour; shake off excess. Heat oil in a non-stick skillet over medium-high heat. Sauté the fillet until done, turning once during cooking. Serve topped with sauce.

SERVES 4

Sautéed Swordfish With Cumin Seed and Black Bean-Corn Salsa

1½ pounds swordfish steaks, ¾ inch thick
 1 tablespoon olive oil
    Salt and pepper to taste
 1 teaspoon cumin seeds

SALSA
 1 cup canned black beans, drained and rinsed
 ¾ cup corn kernels, drained if canned
 ¼ cup chopped onion
 4 cloves garlic, minced
 ¼ teaspoon dried oregano
 ½ teaspoon ground cumin
 2 tablespoons chopped cilantro
 2 teaspoons lime juice

PREPARATION

To prepare salsa, mix black beans, corn and onion pieces together in a large bowl. Add the remaining salsa ingredients, and mix well. Let the salsa stand for an hour (at least) before serving. The salsa will keep in the refrigerator, covered, for 2 days.

Heat olive oil in a non-stick skillet over medium-high heat. Sprinkle swordfish steaks with cumin seeds, salt and pepper. Sauté the steaks quickly, 3 to 4 minutes per side. Remove from heat. Serve with the salsa.

SERVES 4

Swordfish Broil With Spicy Ginger Glaze

1½ pounds swordfish steaks, sliced 1 inch thick
 2 tablespoons fresh lime juice
 1 teaspoon grated lime peel
1½ tablespoons shoyu
 2 cloves garlic, crushed
 1 tablespoon minced fresh ginger root
 ½ teaspoon sesame oil
 1 teaspoon black sesame seeds
 1 teaspoon minced fresh jalapeno,
    or ¼ teaspoon dried red pepper flakes
 ½ teaspoon sugar

PREPARATION

Place steaks in a non-reactive baking dish. Whisk all remaining ingredients, and pour over the fish. Turn steaks to coat both sides. Cover tightly, and marinate for an hour in the refrigerator. Turn steaks at least once.

Preheat broiler. Place steaks on a broiler pan rack, and spoon some marinade over them. Broil 4 inches from the heat for about 2½ minutes, basting at least once before turning them. Spoon remaining marinade over the fish, and broil just until cooked through, about 2 more minutes. Baste again. Remove fish from heat, and spoon pan juices over steaks.

SERVES 4

Cured Kajiki Salad With Cucumbers, Tomatoes, Red Onions and Ogo Vinaigrette

courtesy of Chef Kirby Wong, Ilikai Hotel Nikko

6 ounces kajiki block
1 tablespoon sugar
1 tablespoon salt
⅛ teaspoon cracked black pepper
⅛ teaspoon Jamaican Jerk Blend (The Spice Hunter)
1 tomato, thinly sliced
1 Japanese cucumber, thinly sliced
1 red onion, cut into eighths and separated to form "petals"
2 tablespoons Ogo Vinaigrette (recipe follows)

PREPARATION

Mix together sugar, salt, pepper and Jamaican Jerk Blend. Season kajiki on both sides with mixture. Place fish in a container, and top with a heavy object to press out liquid. Refrigerate for 3 days. Discard excess liquid. Thinly slice fish, and arrange it on a platter with cucumbers, tomatoes and onions. Top with Ogo Vinaigrette.

SERVES 2

Chef Kirby Wong of the Ilikai Yacht Club has been instrumental in maintaining the high standards for which the Nikko Hotels are known. His nightly creations combine the seasonal island foods with a mix of Asian, Hawaiian and European influences. As a die-hard fisherman, Chef Wong takes special care with his seafood creations, using the freshest fish with mouth-watering combinations of flavors for patrons.

Ogo Vinaigrette

½ cup fresh ogo, chopped
½ cup rice vinegar
½ cup water
½ cup minced round onion
¼ cup sugar
1 clove garlic
½ teaspoon minced fresh ginger
½ teaspoon chili pepper water (Park's brand)
½ tablespoon minced green onions
¼ cup shoyu

PREPARATION

Simmer all ingredients except ogo in a saucepan over medium heat for 5 minutes. Add ogo. Remove from heat, and cool.

MAKES 2½ cups

Types of Billfish

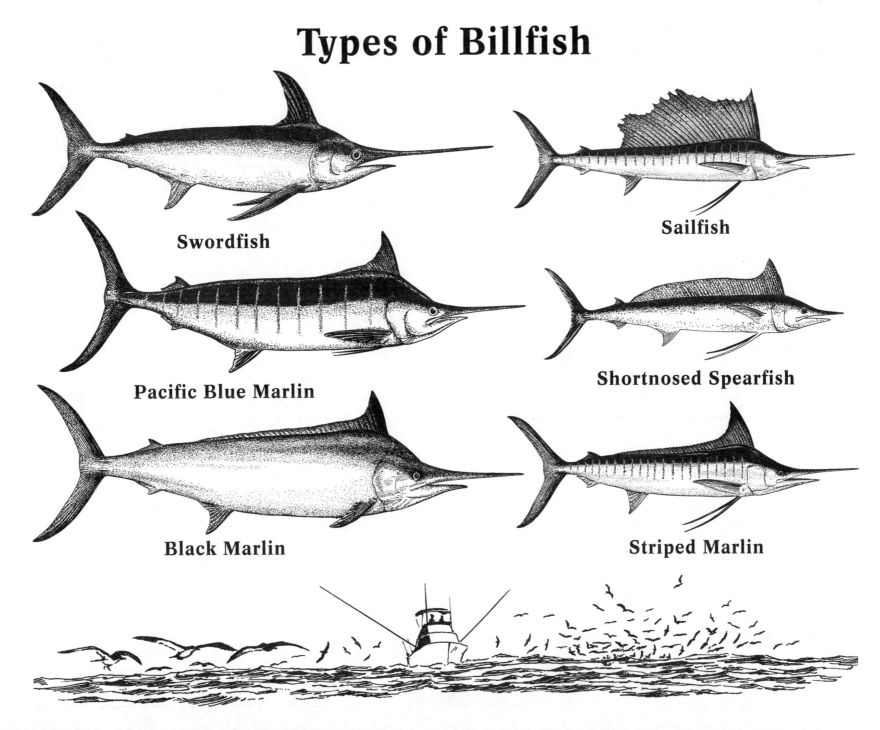

Swordfish

Sailfish

Pacific Blue Marlin

Shortnosed Spearfish

Black Marlin

Striped Marlin

Notes

Mahimahi

Is there anyone who hasn't proclaimed mahimahi, *also known as dolphin fish, the best fish ever after tasting its sweet, tender meat? No matter how much we enjoy succulent snapper, velvety 'ahi, or savory ono, mahimahi deserves its title of "best known ambassador for Hawai'i seafood." Even non-fish lovers devour mahimahi. Its moist, flaky meat is suited to all cooking methods and presentations: sautéed and topped with a fresh fruit salsa; seared in a spicy crust; steamed with vegetables in parchment paper; or dressed in the most elegant manner.*

The constant desire for Hawai'i's fresh mahimahi by residents and visitors makes the fish a high-priced commodity, so frozen or fresh mahimahi from other countries has found its way to the local market. If you are eating out and "won't accept any substitute," ask the waiter whether the mahimahi is fresh and where it was caught. Do the same at your fish market so you can be sure of what you're paying for.

Mahimahi is most abundant in Hawai'i six months of the year, September through November and March through May. The average mahimahi caught weighs in at 15 to 25 pounds.

SUBSTITUTIONS: Drum, Halibut, Lingcod, Orange Roughy and Wahoo.

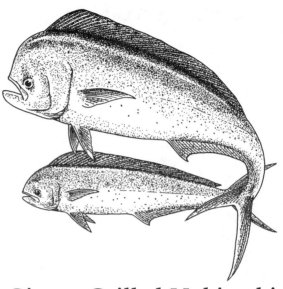

Ginger-Grilled Mahimahi

2 pounds mahimahi, steaked or cut into pieces 1 inch thick
⅔ cup shoyu
¼ cup dry sherry
2 cloves garlic, minced
2 tablespoons minced fresh ginger
¼ cup minced green onion
2 teaspoons sugar
2 teaspoons grated lemon zest
2 tablespoons olive oil

PREPARATION

Place fish in a single layer in a non-reactive pan.

Combine the shoyu, sherry, garlic, ginger, green onion, sugar, lemon zest and olive oil in a bowl. Pour mixture over the fish, and marinate, covered, for 1 hour.

Grill or broil fish for 3 to 4 minutes per side, turning pieces once and basting frequently with the marinade.

SERVES 4

Make-Ahead Mahi

2 pounds mahimahi fillets,
  cut into 8 to 10 pieces
1 tablespoon vegetable oil
1½ cups thinly sliced round onion
½ cup chopped celery
1 clove garlic, minced
½ cup dry white wine
½ cup white wine vinegar
1 bay leaf
1 teaspoon dried thyme
4 whole cloves
  Pinch hot pepper flakes
4 parsley sprigs
10 whole black peppercorns
  Salt and freshly ground pepper to taste
  Lemon slices

PREPARATION

Heat the oil in a saucepan; add the onion, celery and garlic. Cook for 2 to 3 minutes, or until the ingredients are wilted. Add the wine, vinegar, bay leaf, thyme, cloves, hot pepper flakes, parsley, peppercorns and salt to taste. Bring to a boil, lower the heat, and simmer for 10 minutes.

Place the fish in a skillet or pan large enough to hold the fillets in one layer, and sprinkle the fillets with salt and pepper. Pour the hot liquid mixture over the fish through a strainer or see Fishwife's Tip below, and cover the skillet or pan tightly with foil. Bring to a boil, lower the heat, and simmer for 5 minutes. Remove skillet from the heat, and let the fish cool in the liquid. Serve cold on lettuce with lemon slices.

SERVES 8

FISHWIFE'S TIP
Tie up the bay leaf, whole cloves and peppercorns in cheesecloth before adding to the pot.

Suzanne's Mahi With Mac Nuts
courtesy of Suzanne McNaughton

1½ pounds mahimahi
  Salt and pepper to taste
¼ cup flour
2 tablespoons olive oil
2 tablespoons butter
¼ cup minced green onion
½ cup white wine
½ cup chicken broth
2 tablespoons chopped red bell pepper
⅓ cup chopped macadamia nuts
  (salted and roasted)

PREPARATION

Slice mahimahi into serving-sized pieces, ½ to ¾ inch thick. Sprinkle mahimahi with salt and pepper. Dust with flour. Shake off excess.

Heat the olive oil and half of the butter in a large, non-stick skillet over medium-high heat. Add fish in one layer, and cook, turning once, until the fish is done, 5 to 7 minutes, depending on thickness. Remove mahimahi from skillet, and keep fish warm. Repeat until all fish is cooked.

Add onion, wine and chicken broth to the same skillet. Boil over high heat until the liquid is reduced by half. Reduce heat to low. If you only used 1 tablespoon of butter to cook the fish, you may add the remaining tablespoon to the sauce at this point, if you wish. Stir in the red bell pepper and nuts; spoon sauce over fish; and serve.

SERVES 4

Jim's Mahi Dinner With Orange and Celery

1   **pound mahimahi fillet**
¼   **cup flour**
1   **tablespoon oil**
1   **tablespoon butter**
1   **cup slivered celery stalks**
    Dash of salt
1   **teaspoon minced ginger root (optional)**
1   **tablespoon orange zest***
⅓   **cup fresh orange juice**
    Salt and pepper to taste
¼   **cup chopped pecans**

PREPARATION

Cut fish into thin (¼- to ½-inch thick) pieces. Dust them lightly with flour. Heat oil, brown fish pieces quickly on both sides, and remove them from the pan. Set fish on a platter.

Add butter to the frying pan, and melt over low heat. Add celery pieces, a touch of salt and any liquid that has drained off the fish. Stir celery until well-coated; cover; and cook until the celery is tender but still crunchy, about 5 minutes. Remove cover, and add the ginger root, orange zest and juice. Raise heat to medium, and stir, scraping any fish residue from the pan's bottom.

Salt, if you want, and pepper the fish. Return the pieces to the pan with the celery, orange and pecans. Turn mahimahi pieces a few times, and cook until done, probably no more than 2 or 3 minutes. Place fish on a platter, pour sauce over all, and serve.

SERVES 4

*Orange zest is the outer peel without the bitter white parts below. Use a vegetable peeler to remove the zest, or buy one of those neat zesters sold in stores.

Mahi Burritos

2   **cups cooked, flaked mahimahi**
8   **corn or flour tortillas**
⅛   **teaspoon cumin**
½   **cup low-fat sour cream**
1   **small can green chilies, minced**
1   **tomato, chopped**
¼   **cup black olives, chopped or sliced**
2   **tablespoons cilantro**
    Salt and pepper to taste
1   **cup grated jack or sharp cheddar cheese**

PREPARATION

Preheat oven to 375°. Prepare tortillas (see Fishwife's Tips). Oil an oven-proof baking dish, and set aside. Combine the cumin and sour cream in a large bowl. Add all remaining ingredients except the cheese, and mix well. Spoon mixture into the tortillas, fold each one up, and place it seam side down in the baking dish. Sprinkle the burritos with the grated cheese. Bake for 10 minutes, and serve.

SERVES 4

FISHWIFE'S TIPS

1. The tortillas will fold easily if you steam them first. If you prefer to fry them, do so only for a moment on each side, and remove them before they begin to brown, or they will harden and crack.

2. To use fresh fish, cube ½ pound of fish, and sauté it briefly in ½ tablespoon olive oil. Sprinkle with ⅛ teaspoon cumin. (Add another ⅛ teaspoon cumin to the sour cream.)

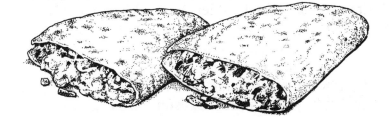

Mahimahi With Coconut-Curry Sauce

courtesy of Paul and Mary Barthelemy

2 pounds mahimahi fillets
Rice flour
Oil to deep-fry (oil need not cover the fish
but should come halfway up the skillet)

CURRY PASTE
2 small red chili peppers, deveined and seeded
2 cloves garlic, peeled
4 scallions, chopped coarsely
1 walnut-sized piece ginger
2 tablespoons chili paste (Indonesian sambal
oelek or Chinese chili paste with garlic)
½ teaspoon galangal powder (Thai ginger)
¼ cup peanuts
3 kaffir lime leaves

SAUCE
1 tablespoon oil (preferably peanut)
2 tablespoons curry paste
½ cup unsweetened coconut milk
1½ tablespoons Nam Pla
1½ tablespoons raw or brown sugar
Fresh Thai basil (or sweet basil)

PREPARATION

To prepare the curry paste, combine all the curry paste ingredients in the bowl of a food processor. (The ingredients will make more paste than necessary for this recipe, but the paste keeps well in the refrigerator. Set aside the 2 tablespoons needed for the sauce, and refrigerate the rest.)

To prepare the sauce, heat the 1 tablespoon oil in a wok or iron skillet until near smoking temperature. Fry the curry paste in the oil for a minute or two. Then add the coconut milk, and bring to a boil. Add the Nam Pla, sugar and basil, and continue to simmer the sauce, reducing it until it thickens somewhat.

Just before frying the fish, dip the fillets in the rice flour, coating them thinly. Heat the oil until it is smoking, and then quickly fry the fillets, turning them once, until they are cooked, about 8 minutes per inch of thickness.

Remove the fillets to waiting plates, and pour the Coconut-Curry Sauce over fish. Garnish with basil leaves, and serve with rice and a green salad.

SERVES 6

Barbecued Mahi With Honey-Lime Sauce

1½ pounds mahimahi steaks, 1 inch thick
¼ cup olive oil
¼ cup fresh lime juice
1 tablespoon white wine, or water
1 tablespoon shoyu
2 teaspoons sesame oil
2 teaspoons honey
1 tablespoon sesame seeds
2 tablespoons minced green onion

PREPARATION

Place fish in a shallow pan. Combine the oil, lime juice, wine or water, shoyu, sesame oil, honey, sesame seeds and green onion, and pour the mixture over the fish. Marinate fish in the refrigerator for 1 hour.

When your coals are ready, remove fish from marinade and cook for no more than 8 minutes. While fish is cooking, turn steaks once and baste with the leftover marinade. Do not overcook.

SERVES 4

Moroccan-Flavored Mahi

1⅓ pounds mahimahi, cut into serving-sized
    pieces ¾ inch thick
    Salt and pepper to taste
¼ cup minced green onion

SAUCE

2 tablespoons sesame seeds, crushed or minced
    for best flavor
2 tablespoons honey
2 tablespoons freshly squeezed orange juice
⅛ teaspoon cinnamon
1 teaspoon ground cumin
1 tablespoon shoyu
1 tablespoon olive oil
2 tablespoons freshly squeezed lemon juice
½ teaspoon Szechwan chili sauce or paste
    Salt and pepper to taste

PREPARATION

Sprinkle mahimahi with salt and pepper, and place fish in a baking pan that will hold pieces in one layer.

Combine all sauce ingredients in a bowl. Blend well. Pour over fish, and marinate 30 minutes on each side.

Preheat broiler for 10 minutes. Place the baking pan on a rack as close to the coils as your oven allows. Broil for 5 to 6 minutes, or until almost done. Turn off broiler, and leave pan in the oven for another minute or so. Remove from oven, and sprinkle green onion on top of mahimahi pieces.   SERVES 4

Mark's Mahi Miracle

courtesy of Mark Lee
The baking time is longer than the prep time–a miracle!

1½ pounds mahimahi fillet
1 cup water
1 teaspoon Korean barbecue sauce
1 tablespoon white flour
¼ cup chopped green onion
¼ cup chopped round onion
½ cup chopped mushrooms
¼ cup chopped fresh parsley
2 cloves garlic, chopped

PREPARATION

Preheat oven to 425°.

Put water, Korean barbecue sauce and flour into a baking dish. Mix well. The mixture will be thick.

Place the mahimahi fillet in the liquid. Top with the remaining ingredients. Bake, covered, for 20 minutes, or until done. Serve with rice. (Spoon the cooking liquid over your rice.)

    SERVES 4

Note: If you aren't watching your fat intake, Mark suggests you sauté the vegetables in a tablespoon of olive oil before putting them in the baking dish. He also pointed out that the barbecue sauce is salty enough, so you needn't add more salt.

Mahimahi With Charred Jalapenos

courtesy of Mark Lee

2 pounds mahimahi fillets
1 teaspoon peanut oil
1 whole jalapeno pepper, medium-hot, diced
½ cup fresh mushrooms
1 green onion stalk, cut into thirds
1 tablespoon olive oil
1 tablespoon flour
¼ cup 2-percent milk
¼ cup water
¼ teaspoon lemon zest

PREPARATION

Heat the peanut oil in a skillet over medium heat. Add diced jalapeno, and cook until burned black with a hard texture. Remove blackened pepper pieces, and put them in a bowl.

Preheat oven to 375°.

Chop the mushrooms and green onion in a food processor. Set aside.

In the same skillet used to blacken the jalapeno pieces, heat the olive oil and sauté the mushrooms and green onion. Add the flour, and cook until it has absorbed most of the moisture in the skillet. Add the milk and water, and cook, just until sauce thickens a little. Add the lemon zest, and remove skillet from heat.

Place the fish in a baking dish, and cover with the sauce. Sprinkle the charred jalapenos on top. Bake for 15 to 18 minutes, depending on thickness of the fish.

SERVES 6

Clay Pot Mahimahi With Tomato Caper Sauce

courtesy of Mary Kleschen, Dededo, Guam

1½ pounds mahimahi fillets
(or any mild, firm fish fillets)

TOMATO CAPER SAUCE
3 tablespoons olive oil
4 cloves garlic, pressed
4 shallots, minced
2 anchovy fillets, sliced (optional)
1 teaspoon capers
4 ripe tomatoes, chopped
¼ cup dry red wine
Freshly ground pepper, to taste

PREPARATION

Heat olive oil in a large skillet, and cook the garlic and shallots until soft. Add the anchovies (if you choose to use them) and the capers. Cook for a few minutes. Add the tomatoes and red wine. Simmer 5 to 10 minutes.

Lay the fish in the bottom of a clay cooker (see Fishwife's Tip). Layer the fillets, if needed. Pour the sauce over and around the fillets.

Put the clay cooker into a cold oven. Bake at 400° for 15 minutes, or until the fish is done. Remove the clay cooker from the oven, and place it on a towel or a wooden board. (Clay containers don't tolerate sudden temperature changes.)

SERVES 4

FISHWIFE'S TIP
If you don't have a clay pan, use any oven-proof baking dish. Preheat the oven.

Mahimahi Genoa-Style

1½ pounds mahimahi fillets
　　Salt and pepper to taste
　　Flour
2　tablespoons oil
3　tablespoons oil
2　cloves garlic, minced
2　tablespoons chopped capers
　　Juice of 2 lemons
¼　cup parsley (Italian, if available)

PREPARATION

Cut the fillets crosswise into pieces ½ to ¾ inch thick. Mix salt and pepper with the flour, and dredge the fish. Shake off excess flour. Heat the 2 tablespoons oil in a heavy skillet (more may be necessary if the skillet is not non-stick) over medium heat. Add the fish to the hot oil, and cook quickly, 2 to 3 minutes per side. Remove from the heat, and set aside.

Heat the 3 tablespoons oil in a small saucepan over medium-low heat; add the garlic, and cook until it begins to turn golden brown. Add the capers, lemon juice and parsley. Cook for a minute, and pour over the fish. SERVES 4

'You'd Think It's Fried' Mahi Bake

1½ pounds mahimahi, cut into pieces
　　1 inch thick
1　tablespoon olive oil
1　cup fresh bread crumbs (I use sourdough)
2　cloves garlic, minced
2　tablespoons grated Romano, Parmesan or
　　Gruyère cheese
1½ teaspoons crushed dried basil, tarragon or
　　oregano
¼　cup minced parsley
¼　teaspoon lemon-pepper seasoning
　　Salt to taste

PREPARATION

Preheat oven to 450°.

Pat fish dry, and brush with the olive oil; set aside. Combine the bread crumbs, garlic, cheese, herb, parsley, lemon-pepper seasoning and salt in a shallow bowl. Mix well.

Dip fish pieces into the bread crumb mixture. Coat both sides of the pieces, and place them in a baking dish. Bake fish, uncovered, for 8 to 10 minutes, or until done. Do not turn. SERVES 6

Craig's Steamed Mahimahi With Black Beans

1½ pounds mahimahi fillets
½ teaspoon coarse salt
1 stalk green onion, cut into 1-inch long strips
2 tablespoons julienned or minced ginger root
2 tablespoons sake, or dry sherry
2 tablespoons fermented Chinese black beans, rinsed and drained
1 tablespoon shoyu
1 teaspoon sesame seed oil
½ teaspoon sugar

PREPARATION

Cut the fish into serving-sized pieces, if you wish. Rub both sides of the fillets with the salt.

Put half of the green onion and ginger root in the bottom of a shallow bowl or platter that will fit into a steamer. Place the fish on top, and cover with the remaining green onion strips and ginger.

Combine the sake, black beans, shoyu, sesame oil and sugar in a small bowl. Pour the mixture over the mahimahi, cover, and refrigerate for an hour. Turn fillets once.

Place bowl or platter on a steamer rack over rapidly boiling water. Steam for 10 to 15 minutes, depending on thickness of fillets, until the fish is opaque. Remove from heat, and serve with cooking liquid.

SERVES 6

FISHWIFE'S TIPS

1. This dish microwaves well. Cover dish with plastic wrap.

2. If you use a small, whole fish (sea bass, snapper, papio) in this recipe, score the fish on both sides and rub the salt (increase amount to 1 teaspoon) into the cuts.

Smoke Infused Marinated Mahimahi With Oriental Shiitake Mushroom Salsa
courtesy of Chef Douglas Lum, Sunset Grill at Restaurant Row, Honolulu

3 pounds fresh Hawai'i mahimahi
1 cup Ginger Vinaigrette (see recipe on page 167)

SALSA
1 pound fresh shiitake mushrooms, chopped
2 medium red onions, finely diced
6 Roma (plum) tomatoes, finely diced
1 bunch Chinese parsley (cilantro), chopped
1 bunch green onions, sliced into rings
2 tablespoons toasted sesame seeds
Sherry

PREPARATION

Cut the mahimahi into serving-sized pieces (see Chef's Notes). Marinate in ¾ cup of the Ginger Vinaigrette for 30 minutes. Smoke using apple wood in a barbecue kettle or smoker for 2½ minutes. Set aside to grill later.

To prepare the salsa, lightly sauté the mushrooms in olive oil (just enough to keep them from sticking). Add the onions, and cook for 1 minute Add the remaining ¼ cup of vinaigrette, and remove the pan from the heat. Mix in tomatoes, Chinese parsley, green onions and sesame seeds. Add sherry (just enough to give it an interesting flavor) to taste.

Grill mahimahi, and top with salsa. SERVES 5

CHEF'S NOTES:

The number of pieces you cut from the fillet is optional. We serve 3 pieces per person, or 15 pieces for this recipe. Enjoy this dish with sautéed vegetables and a crisp/dry Chardonnay or chilled Beaujolais!

Mahimahi Grill
With Cranberry Chutney

2 pounds mahimahi fillets
3 tablespoons olive oil
⅔ cup white wine
1 tablespoon Triple Sec
   Salt and freshly ground pepper to taste

CHUTNEY

1¾ cups fresh cranberries
1 large orange, peeled and seeded
1 large green apple (tart), peeled and cored
2 tablespoons brown sugar
1 tablespoon orange juice
1 tablespoon minced ginger root
2 tablespoons minced onion
2 tablespoons orange zest

PREPARATION

Combine the olive oil, wine and Triple Sec in a non-reactive container large enough to hold the fish in one layer. Salt and pepper the fish, and put it in the marinade for 30 minutes. Turn fish once.

To make the chutney, coarsely chop the cranberries, orange and apple. Put the fruit in a large bowl, add the remaining ingredients, and mix well. Let stand for 1 to 2 hours before serving.   MAKES 2½ cups

Grill the fish over hot coals. Turn mahimahi once during cooking, and baste frequently. Do not overcook. Serve with chutney.   SERVES 6

Nellie's Mango
and Mahimahi Delight

courtesy of Neljane Rizzuto

2 pounds mahimahi fillets
¼ cup orange juice
1 tablespoon sliced, peeled ginger root
½ cup low-fat yogurt, sour cream, or mayonnaise
   Sliced or chunked mango or papaya (or fruit in season: ripe peaches; nectarines or apricots; oranges; grapefruits; et cetera)
⅓ cup flaked coconut (optional)

PREPARATION

Place fish in a pan with water to cover; add the orange juice and ginger root. Poach until half-cooked. Immediately remove fish from the pan, and place fillets in a lightly oiled baking dish.

Spread a thin coating of yogurt, sour cream or mayonnaise over the fish, and place the fruit slices around it. Sprinkle fish with coconut, if you wish.

Broil until the fish has finished cooking. Serve immediately.   SERVES 6

Sheila's Poached Mahimahi in Aromatic Broth
courtesy of Sheila Cadwallader

1½ pounds mahimahi, cut to fit in a deep skillet
Salt and freshly ground black pepper
⅔ cup seeded, diced tomato, canned or fresh
(drain if using canned)
2 tablespoons minced fresh chives
Fresh thyme sprigs, or minced parsley

AROMATIC BROTH
2 cups white wine, or vermouth
1 cup water
1 cup vegetable stock (canned is OK)
3 cloves garlic, sliced in half
2 pieces ginger root, each ¼ inch thick
2 bay leaves, broken in half
½ teaspoon dried thyme, crumbled
2 pieces orange peel, about ½ inch by 2 inches
(orange part only)

PREPARATION

Combine broth ingredients in a large, deep skillet. Bring to a boil over medium-high heat, reduce heat to medium-low, and simmer for 5 minutes.

Season the mahimahi with salt and pepper. Add it carefully to the broth. Cover skillet, and simmer gently until fish is done, about 8 minutes. Remove mahimahi from the skillet, and cover fish to keep it warm.

Strain the liquid from the skillet into a saucepan. Remove the orange peel and cut it into small strips. Boil the broth over medium-high heat until it has reduced to 1½ cups. Add the orange peel to the broth with the tomatoes and chives. Remove the saucepan from the heat.

Serve this meal in shallow soup bowls or in a shallow platter. Spoon the broth over the fish, and garnish with thyme sprigs or parsley.

SERVES 4

Hickory-Smoked Mahi

2 pounds mahimahi, steaked
⅓ cup shoyu
2 tablespoons oil
1 tablespoon liquid smoke
1 clove garlic, minced
1 tablespoon chopped fresh ginger,
or ½ teaspoon ground ginger

PREPARATION

Place fish, cut in pieces of even thickness, in a single layer in a shallow baking dish. Combine the remaining ingredients, and pour over fish. Let fish stand for 30 minutes. Turn steaks once. Remove mahimahi from the pan, and reserve sauce for basting. Place fish in a well-greased, hinged wire grill. Cook 4 inches from moderately hot coals for no more than 10 minutes per inch of thickness of fish. Turn once and baste often during cooking.

SERVES 6

Spicy Mahi Salad

1 pound mahimahi, cut into 1-inch chunks
1 tablespoon olive oil
1 clove garlic, minced

MARINADE

3 tablespoons olive oil
3 tablespoons fresh lemon or lime juice
2 large garlic cloves, crushed or minced
¼ teaspoon salt
   Black pepper to taste
¼ cup white wine vinegar, or 2 tablespoons each white wine vinegar and balsamic vinegar
2 tablespoons Dijon mustard
1 medium tomato, chopped
2 tablespoons minced jalapeno pepper (or to taste)
2 tablespoons chopped parsley or cilantro

PREPARATION

Heat 1 tablespoon olive oil in a large skillet. Sauté the garlic and mahimahi until the fish turns opaque, about 6 minutes. Remove from heat.

Combine marinade ingredients in a non-reactive bowl or dish. Add cooked mahimahi, and toss until it is well-coated. Cover bowl, and refrigerate for 2 to 12 hours.

Serve salad in lettuce cups or in the center of a papaya half. Sprinkle with more parsley, if you wish.

SERVES 8

FISHWIFE'S TIP

Before serving, toss well, and then drain off excess marinade. This recipe also works well with shrimp, either boiled or steamed.

Mahi-Mango Ceviche

2 pounds mahimahi, cut into 1½-inch cubes
   Juice of 4 limes
1 jalapeno pepper, seeded and minced
¼ cup chopped green onions
¼ cup minced cilantro
2 tablespoons minced or shredded peeled ginger root
2 ripe mangoes, peeled and diced
1 ripe avocado, peeled and diced
   Salt and freshly ground pepper

PREPARATION

Place the mahimahi in a non-reactive container. Add the juice of 3 limes; mix well. Cover, and refrigerate for 4 hours, or until mahimahi is opaque. (Marinate overnight, if you wish.)

When ready to serve, drain the fish. Place in a serving dish. Add the juice of the remaining lime, the jalapeno, green onions, cilantro and ginger root. Mix well. Gently mix in the mangoes and avocado; season with salt and pepper. Serve immediately.

SERVES 8

FISHWIFE'S TIP

If mango is not in season, substitute ripe papaya.

Notes

Ono

The torpedo-shaped ono, also known as wahoo, is one of the fastest swimmers in the ocean and, once cooked, disappears as fast from your table. Although other fish of the mackerel family have red, strong-flavored meat, the ono's pale, white flesh is sweet and moderately mild. Some favor it for sashimi for this very reason, and a plate of ono's white slices alternated with the red of 'ahi is particularly pleasing.

Ono is second only to mahimahi in Hawai'i's restaurants, as chefs offer ono as a delicious alternative to fresh mahimahi. Ono is wonderful no matter how it is cooked but is a disaster if overcooked even a bit. As with all fish, time carefully, undercook rather than overcook, and marinate before using any cooking method (like grilling and broiling) that will dry it out.

Look for ono from May to October, but don't expect to find it whole in your market—average catches are 30 to 40 pounds.

SUBSTITUTIONS: Mahimahi, Halibut, Lingcod, Kingfish and Swordfish.

Broiled Ono Steaks With Marmalade Glaze

2 pounds ono steaks, 1 inch thick
2 tablespoons olive oil
1 tablespoon shoyu (or to taste)
½ teaspoon sesame oil (or to taste)
   Pepper
1 cup fresh orange juice
1 cup fresh lemon juice
2 tablespoons green onion, chopped
3 tablespoons orange marmalade
2 tablespoons minced ginger root
¼ cup olive oil

PREPARATION

Combine the 2 tablespoons olive oil, shoyu and sesame oil in a non-reactive pan. Place ono steaks on top. Turn steaks once so both sides are coated. Season with pepper. Set aside.

Meanwhile, combine the orange and lemon juices, green onion, marmalade and ginger root in a pan. Boil mixture over medium-high heat until it has thickened and reduced to approximately ½ cup. Remove mixture from the heat, and let it cool a bit. Add the olive oil slowly until the mixture is of a good spreading consistency; you may choose not to use the whole amount of oil, or you may add a bit more than is called for.

Place the fish on a broiler pan (line it with foil first—the glaze will make a mess), and brush the tops of the steaks with half of the glaze. Broil ono for 3 or 4 minutes, turn the fish over, brush fish with remaining glaze, and broil until the fish is done (about another 4 minutes, depending on thickness of steaks). Remove steaks from pan, and serve.

SERVES 4

Ginger-Flavored Fish

1   pound ono or white-meat fish fillets, no more
    than ¾ inch thick, at room temperature
2   cups fish stock
    (or 1 cup clam juice plus 1 cup chicken broth)
2   tablespoons minced ginger root
1   tablespoon ginger juice
    (put peeled ginger root through a garlic press)
2   cloves garlic, minced
1   teaspoon coarse salt
    Pepper to taste
1   cup chopped tomatoes
    (peeled and seeded, if you wish)
2   tablespoons unsalted butter
1   small stalk green onion, minced
    (about 3 tablespoons)
2   tablespoons sake
1   tablespoon cilantro (optional)

PREPARATION

Place the fish stock in a pan large enough to hold the fillets in one layer. Bring to a simmer. Add the ginger root, ginger juice, garlic, salt and pepper, and simmer for 2 minutes. Remove pan from heat, and add the fish. Cover, and let sit for 10 minutes. Place fish on a warm platter, cover, and set aside.

Bring the fish stock to a boil, and reduce by half. Add the tomatoes, butter, green onion and sake, and boil for 10 minutes, or until sauce has thickened a bit. Add cilantro. Pour sauce over fish, and serve; or pass the sauce with the fish.

SERVES 4

FISHWIFE'S TIP

It is difficult to skin ono. But if the fish is first filleted, chunked or steaked, the meat is easily cut away from the skin.

Poached Ono
With Tomato-Butter Sauce

1½ pounds ono, cut into 4 serving-sized fillets,
    ¾ to 1 inch thick
SAUCE
1   pound plum tomatoes, seeded and chopped
    (if using canned, use 16-ounce size, drain well)
¼   cup minced onion or shallots
2   small cloves garlic, minced
2   tablespoons fresh lime juice
4   tablespoons butter, cut into pieces
1   cup dry white wine
2   teaspoons dried oregano or basil
8   lime slices
4   teaspoons fresh, minced parsley
    (or use parsley with chopped fresh basil or
    fresh oregano)

PREPARATION

Purée the tomatoes, onions or shallots, garlic and lime juice together in a blender or food processor. Transfer the purée to a small saucepan, and cook over medium heat for 10 minutes, or until the mixture is thick. Stir occasionally. Reduce the heat to low. Whisk in the butter, one piece at a time, until well-blended. Cover pan, and remove from the heat.

Combine the wine, dried herbs and lime slices in a skillet or pan large enough to hold all the fish. Heat to a simmer. Add the fish, cover, and poach for 6 to 8 minutes, or until done. Remove fish from the liquid with a slotted spoon. Transfer ono to a platter. Spoon the tomato sauce over each fillet, top with lime slices, and sprinkle with fresh herbs.

SERVES 4

Wahoo Baloise
Hans Peter Hager, Edelweiss Restaurant

6   10-ounce slices ono fillet
    Corn oil for deep-frying
3   medium Bermuda onions, peeled and
    thinly sliced
1   cup cream
1   whole egg, beaten with a fork and blended
    with the cream
1   cup flour
    Salt and pepper to taste
½   pound butter (2 sticks)
1   tablespoon Worcestershire sauce
3   lemons
1   tablespoon chopped parsley
    Lemon wedges (garnish)

PREPARATION

Heat corn oil to 350° in a deep-fryer.

Prefry the sliced onions in the deep-fryer, slowly in order to dry the onions before they get too much color. If dried too fast, the onions will be brown and soggy. Set the onions aside when crisp, and dry on paper towels.

Dip the fish slices in the cream/egg mixture, dust with flour, and season with salt and pepper.

Preheat half of the butter in a large frying pan over medium-high heat. When butter bubbles merrily, lay the fish in the pan and cook evenly on both sides. Transfer the fish to a platter. Sprinkle each slice with Worcestershire sauce and lemon juice.

Add the remaining butter to the frying pan, stir, and brown. The butter will be ready when it stops foaming. Put all the onions in the hot brown butter, and immediately pour the contents of the frying pan over the fish. Garnish with chopped parsley, and serve with lemon wedges, if you like.
SERVES 6

Hans Peter Hager

Edelweiss Restaurant recently celebrated its 10th birthday, but Owner/Chef Hans Peter Hager is coming up on 30 years in Hawai'i. He answered a "Cooks wanted in Hawai'i" advertisement that appeared in a Switzerland newspaper and was hired by the Mauna Kea Beach Hotel. He left the Mauna Kea Beach Hotel to work in New York City, Colorado Springs, and at Caneel Bay before returning to the islands to open Kapalua Bay Hotel on Maui in 1978, and finally back to the Big Island to open the Mauna Lani. In November 1983, Edelweiss opened its doors, just 3½ weeks after Chef Hagar received the key to the building. He does not advertise; word of mouth keeps Edelweiss packed during lunch and dinner the 5 days a week it is open. Chef Hagar's commitment to his customers keeps him at the stove from early morning to closing. Why not hire assistants to relieve him on occasion? "Because my creativity is here, in my heart," he says. "You can't teach that to others."

Ono Poke With Thai Spices
courtesy of Chef Paul Heerlein
The Gallery, Mauna Lani Bay Hotel

1   cup diced ono
¼   teaspoon finely chopped ginger root
1   teaspoon finely chopped kaffir lime leaf
1   small Hawaiian chili, finely chopped
2   tablespoons diced onion
1½ teaspoons fish sauce
3   tablespoons lime juice
2   tablespoons chopped green onions
¼   teaspoon kosher salt, or to taste

PREPARATION

Mix all ingredients together, and serve.
SERVES 2

Baked 'Ono-licious Ono

2 pounds ono fillets
Salt and pepper to taste
Juice of 1 lemon
2 tablespoons olive oil
1½ cups sliced leeks
3 cloves garlic, minced
1 green pepper, diced
¼ cup chopped parsley
½ cup dry white or red wine
1 large can (28 ounces) tomatoes
1 teaspoon dried oregano
1 teaspoon dried thyme

PREPARATION

Cut ono into serving-sized pieces no more than 1 inch thick, and sprinkle them with salt, pepper and lemon juice. Set aside.

Add oil to a large skillet (oven-proof if you have one), and sauté the leeks, garlic, green pepper and parsley until the peppers are tender. Add the wine and tomatoes. Break up the tomatoes with a spoon, and bring the mixture to a boil. Add the oregano and thyme, and mix well. Add the ono, place the skillet in the oven, and bake until the fish is done (8 to 10 minutes per inch of thickness of fish). If your skillet is not oven-proof, transfer everything to a baking dish before baking fish.

SERVES 6

FISHWIFE'S TIP
You can chunk the ono, add it to the skillet and complete the cooking on top of the stove.

Braised Ono Steaks Niçoise

1⅓ pounds ono steaks or fillets,
cut into 4 serving-sized pieces
1 tablespoon olive oil
2 cloves garlic, minced
¼ cup minced round onion
¼ cup white wine, sake or vermouth
¼ cup stock (fish, chicken, or vegetable)
2 tablespoons pitted black olives
(preferably Niçoise), chopped
2 tablespoons capers, drained and rinsed
1 teaspoon anchovy paste
1 teaspoon dried basil
1 teaspoon dried oregano
¼ teaspoon dried red pepper flakes
1 cup crushed canned tomatoes
2 tablespoons chopped fresh parsley

PREPARATION

Heat oil in a large, deep skillet over medium heat. Add the garlic and onions; sauté until softened. Stir in wine and stock, and simmer until the mixture is reduced by a third, about 5 minutes. Add the olives, capers, anchovy paste, basil, oregano and red pepper flakes; blend well. Add the tomatoes. Lower heat to medium-low, and simmer sauce until it thickens slightly, 8 to 10 minutes. Add more liquid if the sauce is too thick.

Place the fish over the sauce. Cover the pan tightly, and simmer for 10 minutes, occasionally spooning sauce over the fish. Garnish with parsley.

SERVES 4

Ono and Tofu Stir-Fry

1   pound ono, cut into ¾-inch cubes
2   tablespoons shoyu
1   tablespoon ginger root, minced
12 ounces firm tofu, cut into
     ¾-inch cubes
1   tablespoon dry sherry, white wine, or sake
3   tablespoons oil
3   cups raw vegetables of your choice, cut
     into bite-sized pieces (try broccoli, carrots,
     zucchini, pea pods, et cetera)
1   medium onion, chunked
1   cup bean sprouts
2   cloves garlic, cut in half
2   tablespoons oyster sauce (or shoyu)

PREPARATION

Combine the shoyu and ginger root, and pour over tofu. Marinate tofu for 10 or 15 minutes. Remove the tofu carefully; drain, saving the shoyu-ginger mixture. Combine shoyu-ginger mixture with the sherry, and marinate the fish in the mixture for 10 or 15 minutes.

Meanwhile, heat 1 tablespoon of the oil in a skillet or wok. Stir-fry the tofu for 2 minutes, or until light brown. Remove from wok. Add another tablespoon of oil to the wok, and stir-fry the hard vegetables (broccoli, carrots, pea pods) for 2 or 3 minutes. Add the onions and the softer vegetables, and cook for 2 minutes. Add the bean sprouts, and cook 1 minute. Then remove all vegetables from the wok.

If more oil is needed, add another tablespoon. Sauté garlic for a minute, and remove. Add the fish in its marinade to the pan, and cook for a few minutes, or until the fish is half-cooked. Add the oyster sauce, the vegetables and tofu, and heat everything through. Remove from heat, and serve.

SERVES 6

'Ono Broiled Ono

1½ pounds ono, steaked or filleted into serving-
     sized pieces ¾ inch thick
¼   cup honey
2   teaspoons lime juice (lemon juice will do)
2   tablespoons olive oil
     Salt and pepper to taste
     Pinch red pepper flakes, or dash hot pepper
     sauce

PREPARATION

Combine the honey, lime juice, oil, salt, pepper and pepper flakes in a small saucepan, and heat slowly to liquefy the honey a bit. (Don't expect the ingredients to bind into a smooth, well-blended mixture. They won't.)

Brush the mixture on the fish pieces, and broil them about 4 inches from the heat source. Baste fish frequently. Time the cooking for 5 to 6 minutes per inch of thickness, but watch the fish carefully so it doesn't overcook.

SERVES 4

FISHWIFE'S TIP
Broiling can dry fish out quickly, so watch it carefully and remove it before it is completely cooked. It will continue to cook after it is removed from the oven.

Cured Gravalox-Style Ono With Lemon and Garlic Mustard Sauce

Richard DeWitt, Royal Waikoloan
Executive Sous Chef

2 to 3 pounds ono fillet
1 cup salt
1 cup sugar
1 cup fresh basil (crushed)

LEMON GARLIC MUSTARD SAUCE
½ cup mayonnaise (store bought or homemade)
1 teaspoon Dijon mustard
1 teaspoon fresh lemon juice
1 tablespoon fresh parsley, chopped
1 teaspoon yellow part of lemon peel, blanched and finely chopped
1 teaspoon garlic, finely chopped

SAUCE PREPARATION

Combine all ingredients, and adjust thickness with a little white wine or water.

ONO PREPARATION

Combine the salt and sugar, and then add the crushed basil. Coat the ono fillet completely, top and bottom, with the mixture. Place in an appropriate pan (*not* aluminum), and cover. Place in refrigerator for 1 day.

Remove fish from the pan, and brush or scrape off basil. The salt and sugar will be gone or absorbed into the fish. Pour a little peanut oil over fish just to coat the fillet. This will prevent it from drying out and will make it easier to slice.

Slice fillet into ¼-inch thick slices, and place each slice between 2 sheets of plastic wrap or wax paper. Pound fish lightly to make nice, thin pieces of ono. Serve as an appetizer with the Lemon Garlic Mustard Sauce. SERVES 10

Grilled Ono With Ginger-Pear Chutney

1½ pounds ono, cut into serving-sized pieces
3 tablespoons olive oil
Salt and pepper to taste
½ teaspoon mustard seeds, crushed

GINGER-PEAR CHUTNEY
¼ cup sugar
2 tablespoons white wine vinegar
2 tablespoons balsamic vinegar
¼ teaspoon mustard seeds (or to taste)
⅛ teaspoon dried red pepper flakes (or to taste)
1 tablespoon minced ginger (or to taste)
1¾ cups diced pears (2 small, firm pears)
2 tablespoons minced fresh mint or green onions

PREPARATION

To prepare the chutney, stir sugar and vinegars together in a saucepan over medium heat. Bring mixture to a boil, reduce heat, and simmer for 5 or 10 minutes. Add the mustard seeds, red pepper flakes, ginger and pears, and bring to a boil again. Reduce heat, add the minced mint or green onions, and simmer mixture, uncovered, until it thickens, about 30 minutes. Let stand at room temperature until your fish is cooked, or refrigerate for up to 2 weeks. The ginger flavor gets stronger over time. (Serve the chutney warm, at room temperature, or cold.) MAKES 1½ cups

While chutney is simmering, brush ono with olive oil. Sprinkle with salt, pepper and crushed mustard seeds, and let stand until the chutney is cooked. Place the fish on a grill or under a broiler. Do not overcook. Serve with chutney. SERVES 4

FISHWIFE'S TIP
If you wish, add the mint or green onion after the chutney is cooked, but while it is still hot. I've split the chutney into serving bowls and added mint to one and green onions to the other.

Ono With Peppers and Onions

2 pounds ono (or any white-meat fish) steaks,
   cut into 1½-inch pieces
2 tablespoons olive oil
2 onions, peeled and coarsely chopped
2 garlic cloves, minced
2 tomatoes, seeded and chopped
1½ teaspoons crushed, dried basil
4 bell peppers (green and yellow), sliced
¼ cup water
   Salt and pepper to taste
¼ cup minced fresh parsley

PREPARATION

Heat oil in a large skillet, and sauté the onions and garlic over medium-low heat. Stir until the onions are limp, 3 to 4 minutes. Add the tomatoes, basil, peppers, water and salt and pepper, and cook, stirring frequently, for 10 minutes.

Add the ono and parsley, cover, and cook for 6 to 8 minutes, or until fish is just cooked. Remove the fish from the skillet to a serving dish. Cover ono, and refrigerate for 1 hour.   SERVES 6

Thyme-Topped Ono

2 pounds ono, cut into serving-sized pieces
   1 inch thick
2 tablespoons olive oil
   Juice of one lemon
1 teaspoon dried thyme, crushed
   Salt and freshly ground pepper
¼ cup white wine
1 tablespoon butter

PREPARATION

Combine the olive oil, lemon juice and ½ teaspoon of the thyme in a non-reactive container. Sprinkle the ono with salt and pepper, and coat both sides of the fish with the lemon-oil mixture. Cover, and refrigerate for an hour. Turn fish once.

Heat a large, non-stick skillet, and pan-fry the ono over medium-high heat. Turn fish once during cooking. Remove fish to a platter when done. Add the white wine and remaining ½ teaspoon of thyme to the skillet. Scrape the bottom of the pan to release bits of fish and flavor. Add the tablespoon of butter, stir to blend well, and pour over the fish.   SERVES 6

Spicy Almond-Coated Ono

1½ to 2 pounds ono fillets
   (or use any small, mild fish fillets)
   Salt and pepper to taste
⅓ cup almonds
1 tablespoon prepared mustard
2 teaspoons lemon juice
1 teaspoon shoyu
1 teaspoon sugar
4 tablespoons low-fat, plain yogurt

PREPARATION

Preheat oven to 425°. Pat fillets dry, and sprinkle them with salt and pepper. Place fillets on an oiled baking sheet or pan. Grind the almonds in a blender, and then mix them with remaining ingredients. Spread the mixture on the fillets, and bake until done.   SERVES 4

FISHWIFE'S TIP
Because almonds have a high oil content, do not blend or process them too much, or you'll end up with a paste.

Broiled Ono With Avocado-Cilantro Salsa

1½   pounds ono, cut into serving-sized pieces
¼   cup olive oil
2   tablespoons lime juice
    Salt and freshly ground pepper to taste

SALSA
1   ripe avocado (firm), diced
2   tablespoons olive oil
2   tablespoons fresh lemon juice
¼   cup chopped green onions
2   cloves garlic, minced
¼   teaspoon salt
    Freshly ground pepper to taste
3   tablespoons minced fresh cilantro
½   teaspoon Szechwan Chili Sauce, or
    2 tablespoons minced jalapeno peppers
    (optional)

PREPARATION

Combine the olive oil and lime juice in a small bowl. Brush both sides of the ono with the mixture, and then season with salt and pepper. Let ono marinate while you prepare the salsa.

Combine all salsa ingredients in a glass container. Let stand at room temperature until ready to serve.

Remove the fish from the marinade. Grill or broil until done. Serve with salsa.   SERVES 4

Ono With Tomatoes and Fresh Herbs

2   pounds ono steaks, about 1 inch thick
2   pounds tomatoes (mix and match–plum, cherry and "regular")
3   tablespoons balsamic vinegar
3   tablespoons olive oil
3   cloves garlic
½   cup fresh herb leaves, firmly packed (basil, oregano, thyme, or parsley)
    Salt and pepper to taste
3   tablespoons olive oil for basting fish

PREPARATION

Cube the tomatoes into large (1-inch) pieces, and put them in a non-reactive bowl with balsamic vinegar and 3 tablespoons olive oil. Marinate for at least 30 minutes, but no more than 2 hours.

Just before cooking, mince the garlic and the fresh herbs and add them to the tomatoes with the salt and pepper. Brush the ono on both sides with the 2 to 3 tablespoons olive oil, and grill, turning ono only once after 3 or 4 minutes. Remove the fish from the heat before it is cooked through, about 8 minutes total. Serve with tomato mixture on top.   SERVES 6

Grilled Ono With Tangy Salsa

2 pounds ono steaks or fillets
1 cup fresh grapefruit juice
1 teaspoon Dijon mustard
2 tablespoons minced fresh mint
1 tablespoon minced fresh chives

SALSA
2 oranges, peeled, sectioned and diced
1 grapefruit, peeled, sectioned and diced
1 small onion (or Maui onion) finely chopped
1 tablespoon chopped fresh mint
½ teaspoon crushed red pepper flakes

PREPARATION

Combine the grapefruit juice, mustard, mint and chives in a non-reactive pan or dish. Add ono, and marinate fish, covered, in the refrigerator, for 30 to 60 minutes. Turn steaks occasionally.

Meanwhile, combine salsa ingredients, cover, and refrigerate until you are ready to serve.

Prepare your coals. When they are medium-hot, oil or use an oil spray on your grill. Place the ono 5 inches away from heat. Turn ono once during cooking, but cook for no more than 8 minutes per inch of thickness of fish; when fish is opaque, it is done. Serve with the cold salsa.
SERVES 4

Ono Kabobs With Pineapple

2 pounds ono cut into 1¼-inch cubes
2 onions, chopped
4 cloves garlic
2 teaspoons ginger root, chopped
½ small dried hot pepper, seeded
2 tablespoons lemon or lime juice
¼ cup oil
¼ cup white wine
Salt and pepper to taste
Fresh pineapple chunks

PREPARATION

Cut the ono into 1¼-inch cubes, and set in a shallow dish. Combine all remaining ingredients except the pineapple in a blender or food processor, and purée. Pour over the fish, and let marinate for 1 hour.

Thread the ono and pineapple chunks on skewers. Cook 4 inches from the coals, 3 to 6 minutes per side, depending on thickness of pieces. Baste kabobs often during cooking. (If you want to serve the marinade with the fish, bring it to a boil and then pour over the fish.)
SERVES 6

Ono Chinese Salad

3 cups chunked, cooked fish (see Fishwife's Tips)
¼ cup unsalted cashew nuts
3 green onion stalks, cut into 1-inch pieces
1 red bell pepper, chopped or cut into strips
2 stalks celery, chopped
¼ cup minced fresh cilantro
½ head of lettuce, shredded and placed on
    a platter

DRESSING
½ teaspoon dry mustard, mixed with
    1 teaspoon water
1 tablespoon shoyu
3 tablespoons rice wine vinegar
2 tablespoons hoi sin sauce
½ teaspoon ground allspice (optional)
1 teaspoon sugar
1 teaspoon toasted sesame seeds
¼ cup olive oil
1 teaspoon sesame oil (optional)

PREPARATION

Combine the fish, cashews, green onions, red pepper, celery and cilantro in a bowl. Toss together, set aside.

To make the dressing, whisk together the mustard mixture, shoyu, vinegar, hoi sin sauce, allspice, sugar and sesame seeds. Add the olive and sesame oils slowly, whisking until the mixture is smooth and well-blended. Add the dressing to the fish salad. Mix well.

Mound the fish salad on the lettuce, and serve. (To add more crunch to the salad, cut won ton squares into strips, deep-fry in hot oil, drain well, and sprinkle on salad before serving. Or, use cellophane noodles in place of won ton.)   SERVES 8

FISHWIFE'S TIPS

Grilled fish is especially good in this recipe. Try this.
1. Double the amount of dressing, and use half to marinate your fillets (20 minutes).
2. Grill the fillets over hot coals. Turn once, baste, and remove when done (8 minutes per inch of thickness of fillets).
3. Let the fish cool; refrigerate until ready to serve.
4. Proceed as above.

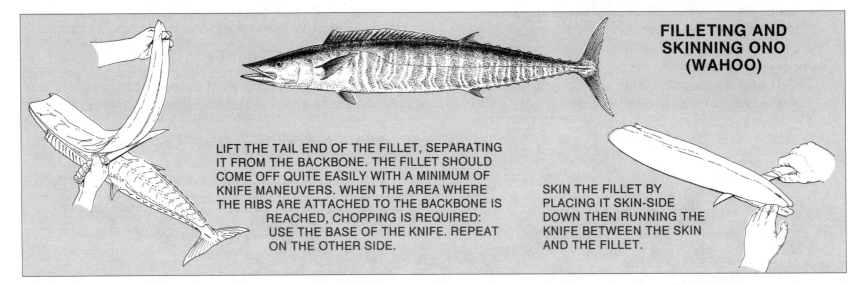

FILLETING AND SKINNING ONO (WAHOO)

LIFT THE TAIL END OF THE FILLET, SEPARATING IT FROM THE BACKBONE. THE FILLET SHOULD COME OFF QUITE EASILY WITH A MINIMUM OF KNIFE MANEUVERS. WHEN THE AREA WHERE THE RIBS ARE ATTACHED TO THE BACKBONE IS REACHED, CHOPPING IS REQUIRED: USE THE BASE OF THE KNIFE. REPEAT ON THE OTHER SIDE.

SKIN THE FILLET BY PLACING IT SKIN-SIDE DOWN THEN RUNNING THE KNIFE BETWEEN THE SKIN AND THE FILLET.

Chilled Hawaiian Gazpacho With Marinated Ono

Wendell Rodrigues, the Mauna Kea Beach Hotel

6 ounces ono strips
10 tomatoes, peeled, seeded and chopped
2 red bell peppers, seeded and diced
2 Japanese cucumbers, peeled, seeded and diced
1 medium Maui onion, diced
5 cloves garlic
3 stems green onions, chopped
1 tablespoon cumin
   Worcestershire sauce to taste
   Tabasco to taste
¼ cup red wine vinegar
   Salt to taste
6 cups tomato juice
½ cup olive oil
1 teaspoon crushed black peppercorns
   Lemon juice
   Garnish: cucumber and yellow bell pepper

PREPARATION

Combine tomatoes, peppers, cucumbers, onion pieces, garlic, green onions, cumin, Worcestershire sauce, Tabasco, vinegar and salt in a non-reactive bowl, and let stand for 30 minutes to allow ingredients to blend. Purée in a blender until mixture is smooth. Return mixture to the bowl. Gradually whip in tomato juice, olive oil and crushed peppercorns.

Toss the ono strips with lemon juice (enough to "cook" the fish, as in a ceviche). Marinate 10 minutes.

To serve, place soup in a bowl, lay fish strips on top, and garnish with more diced cucumber and some yellow bell pepper. Serve with taro chips as an appetizer.

SERVES 6

Ono Ceviche With Mustard Dressing

Maha of Kohala, Hawai'i
First-Place Winner, International Category
Sam Choy Aloha Festival Poke Recipe Contest

1 cup cubed ono (½-inch cubes)
2 tablespoons fresh lime juice
1 tablespoon minced onion
1 teaspoon diced tomato (¼-inch cubes)
⅛ teaspoon salt
¼ teaspoon sliced green onion

DRESSING
¼ cup mayonnaise
⅛ cup white vinegar
⅛ cup salad oil
⅛ teaspoon Dijon mustard
⅛ teaspoon sugar
⅛ teaspoon minced onion
⅛ cup honey
⅛ teaspoon minced parsley
   Pinch of salt
   Pinch of ground black pepper

PREPARATION

Mix together lime juice, onion and tomato. Add ono, salt and green onion. Lomi mixture together well, and marinate it in refrigerator overnight.

With a wire whisk, combine all dressing ingredients well until well blended

Place marinated fish on a bed of lettuce. Slowly pour dressing over fish just before serving.

SERVES 2

Notes

Opah

Opah, also known as moonfish, is literally the most colorful fish available in Hawai'i, both inside and out. It has bright red-orange fins, and its body shade ranges from a dark, silvery gray upper body to a rosy pink belly, with white polka dots all over for accent. It has four types of coarse-textured flesh, each a different color: orange along the backbone, pink toward the belly, ruby red inside the breastplate, and dark red from the fish's cheeks! Sometimes called moonfish because of its shape, the opah landed are large–60 to 200 pounds–so it's unlikely you'd ever get to see this fish whole. Opah are caught by commercial longliners exclusively, so your only chance to bring a fillet home for dinner is to buy it at the market. April through August are peak months.

Opah meat is distinctively flavored and best baked, poached or sautéed.

SUBSTITUTIONS: Monchong, Amberjack, Jack Crevalle and Trevally.

Opah With Herbs and Peperonata

1½ pounds opah fillets
 1 tablespoon olive oil
 2 fresh rosemary sprigs, minced
 2 teaspoons minced fresh parsley
 1 large garlic clove, minced
   Salt and freshly ground pepper to taste
PEPERONATA
 3 tablespoons olive oil
 1 large onion, sliced
 1 large garlic clove, minced
 4 medium tomatoes, peeled and chopped
 3 green bell peppers, coarsely cubed
 3 yellow bell peppers, coarsely cubed
 1 unpeeled medium eggplant, cubed
   Salt and freshly ground pepper to taste
 1 small pinch nutmeg
   Minced fresh parsley

PREPARATION

Combine 1 tablespoon olive oil with rosemary, parsley and garlic. Rub lightly on both sides of the fish. Season with salt and pepper. Place fish on a serving platter, or tray, and cover; refrigerate for 2 hours.

To prepare Peperonata, heat 2 tablespoons olive oil in a large, heavy non-stick skillet over medium heat. Add onion and garlic, and cook until onion is translucent, about 8 minutes. Add the tomatoes, bell peppers and eggplant. Season with salt and pepper. Cook until the liquid has evaporated, about 30 minutes, and stir occasionally. Stir in nutmeg; remove from heat. Drizzle with remaining tablespoon olive oil, sprinkle with parsley.

While Peperonata is cooking, cut opah into serving-sized pieces. Sauté quickly in a hot skillet with a drizzle of olive oil. Serve over Peperonata.   SERVES 4

Opah and Zucchini Sauté

1⅓ pounds opah, sliced into serving-sized pieces
   Salt and freshly ground pepper
 1 tablespoon olive oil
 1 to 1¼ cups zucchini, cut in half lengthwise,
   then across into quarters ⅓ inch thick
 1 large clove garlic, minced
 1 tablespoon balsamic vinegar
 1 teaspoon lemon zest
 ¾ teaspoon minced green onion
 2 teaspoons minced fresh mint

PREPARATION

Sprinkle opah with salt and pepper. Heat oil in a large, non-stick skillet over medium-high heat. Sauté the fish quickly on each side. Remove to a plate before the fish is fully cooked.

Lower the heat under the skillet to medium-low. Add the zucchini, garlic and balsamic vinegar, and sauté for a minute. Stir in the lemon zest and green onion. Salt and pepper to taste. Return the fish to the skillet, and cook briefly. Remove from the heat and serve topped with the zucchini and fresh mint.

SERVES 4

Opah Curry Kabobs

 2 pounds opah fillets
 ¼ cup oil
 2 tablespoons lemon juice
 2 tablespoons grated, or minced, onion
 ¼ teaspoon dried mustard
 1 teaspoon curry powder
   Salt and pepper to taste
 ½ teaspoon thyme, dried
   Onion chunks, mushrooms and zucchini
   wheels

PREPARATION

Cut fillets into bite-sized pieces, and place in a non-aluminum bowl or dish. Combine the oil, lemon juice, onion, dried mustard, curry powder, salt and pepper, and thyme and pour over the fish. Marinate fish for 1 hour. Stir mixture a few times during marinating process.

When ready to cook, thread the fish pieces, onion chunks, mushrooms and zucchini wheels on skewers. Cook 4 inches from coals. Baste fish pieces often with marinade, and turn kabobs once while cooking.

SERVES 4

Soused Hawaiian Opah
With Sweet Potatoes and Yogurt
courtesy of Chris Speere and James McDonald
for the Department of Business and
Economic Development and Tourism
Ocean Resources Branch

12 ounces opah fillets, boned, skin on
Juice of ½ lemon
Juice of ½ lime
¾ ounce macadamia nut oil
¼ cup sake, or mirin
1 tablespoon shoyu
2 tablespoons salt
2 tablespoons sugar
2 tablespoons white peppercorns, crushed
2 tablespoons chopped cilantro

YOGURT SAUCE
½ cup plain yogurt
½ cup sour cream
1 tablespoon rice wine vinegar
1 tablespoon finely chopped green onion
¼ teaspoon sweet yellow mustard
Salt and white pepper to taste

SWEET POTATO CAKES
1 large sweet potato, grated
⅓ cup grated onion
2 tablespoons chopped green onion
1 egg
1½ tablespoons flour
¾ teaspoon salt
Pinch black pepper
1 teaspoon Chinese parsley
½ teaspoon lemon juice
1 cup macadamia nut oil

PREPARATION

To prepare the fish, combine liquids and coat fillets. Combine remaining ingredients, and pack on fish. Lay fish skin side up in a pan, cover, and weight fish. Marinate in refrigerator for 2 days. Remove fish, wipe clean and slice thinly.

To prepare yogurt sauce, combine all sauce ingredients and chill until ready to serve.

To prepare sweet potato cakes, combine the sweet potato, onions, egg, flour, salt, black pepper, Chinese parsley and lemon juice. Heat oil in a large skillet. Gently drop 6 portions of sweet potato mixture into the pan, and fry until crisp.

To serve, place a sweet potato cake on each of 6 plates. Arrange sliced opah around each cake, and top with a dollop of sauce.

SERVES 6

FISHWIFE'S TIP
To slice fish, lay fillet skin side down. Slice down to the skin, and then angle your knife so it slides along the skin, taking the slice of fish with it.

Opah Packets
With Curry-Chutney Butter

1½   pounds opah fillets
⅓   cup mango chutney
1½   tablespoons curry powder
3   tablespoons butter
    Aluminum foil and additional butter
1   cup thinly sliced carrot
1   cup thinly sliced zucchini
4   teaspoons water
4   teaspoons grated, or minced, ginger root
    Salt and pepper to taste
¼   cup almonds, macadamia nuts, or peanuts
    (if salted, don't use any other salt)
2   tablespoons flaked coconut

PREPARATION

Preheat oven to 450°. Cut opah into 4 serving-sized pieces ¾ to 1 inch thick. Set aside.

Prepare the butter by combining the chutney (chopped, if mango pieces are large), curry powder and butter in a small bowl.

Tear off 4 pieces of aluminum foil large enough to hold a serving of the fish and vegetables. Lightly butter the center of the foil. To make each packet, place ¼ of the vegetables on the buttered portion of the foil and sprinkle with 1 teaspoon of water. Place a piece of fish on the vegetables, and sprinkle with 1 teaspoon of ginger and salt and pepper to taste. Put ¼ of the butter, nuts and coconut flakes over each piece of fish. Seal each foil packet, and place it on a large baking sheet.

Bake packets for 10 minutes, or until fish is done.
SERVES 4

FISHWIFE'S TIP
You may cut the fish into 8 pieces and use 2 pieces per packet.

Opah 'Rumaki'

½   pound ground opah fillet
1   ounce dried shiitake mushrooms
¼   cup drained, chopped water chestnuts
¼   cup minced round onion
2   tablespoons minced green onion
2   tablespoons minced raw snow peas
1   teaspoon minced ginger root
1½   tablespoons oyster sauce mixed with
    ½ tablespoon water
1   egg white, beaten
    Freshly ground black pepper to taste
12   strips very lean bacon, cut into thirds
    Oil for deep-frying

PREPARATION

Soak mushrooms in warm water until softened, about 20 minutes. Drain, and squeeze out water; blot dry. Discard stems, and mince caps.

Combine all ingredients except the bacon and oil in a large bowl. Mix well, cover, and refrigerate until well-chilled, at least an hour. Shape mixture into 1-inch balls, or ovals. Wrap each with a bacon strip, secure with a toothpick, and place on a platter, or pan. Return rumaki to the refrigerator for 20 to 30 minutes.

Heat oil to 375° in a large saucepan, or deep skillet. Cook the wrapped fish until golden brown, about 3 minutes. Turn rumaki occasionally during cooking. Don't crowd. Remove rumaki, and drain them on absorbent paper towels, or paper bags. Serve immediately.
MAKES 36

FISHWIFE'S TIPS
If you prefer, broil these in the oven, but be sure not to overcook the fish while you're waiting for the bacon to crisp. Try microwaving the bacon until it begins to brown (be sure it's pliable) before wrapping it around the fish.

Broiled Opah
With Cajun Butter Sauce

courtesy of Wallace Nishimura,
Executive Chef
Kauai Coconut Beach Resort

1⅛ pounds opah fillets, cut into 9 2-ounce pieces
6 large shrimp (12/15 size), shelled, deveined
   and butterflied
2 tablespoons olive oil
1 clove garlic, chopped
   Splash sherry wine
2½ ounces daikon curls (about ¼ cup)

CAJUN BUTTER SAUCE

½ teaspoon Worcestershire sauce
   Juice of ½ lemon
½ cup white wine
1 teaspoon minced onion, or shallots
1 teaspoon tarragon vinegar
1/16 teaspoon white pepper
2 tablespoons bottled Cajun spice
¼ cup heavy cream
½ pound butter, cut into 8 pieces per stick

PREPARATION

To prepare the sauce, combine the Worcestershire sauce, lemon juice, wine, onion, vinegar, pepper and Cajun spice in a heavy saucepan. Bring to a boil, and reduce until the mixture is almost gone. Add heavy cream, and reduce until sauce starts to get thick. Reduce heat, and slowly whisk in butter. Strain sauce. Add more spice, if you want your sauce spicier.

To prepare the opah, broil fish until done. Set aside. Heat olive oil in a skillet, and sauté shrimp with the garlic and sherry wine. Remove from heat.

To serve, arrange daikon curls in the center of 3 plates. Place 3 pieces of opah around daikon and put 2 shrimp in between fillets. Garnish with a basil sprig and Cajun Butter Sauce. Sprinkle with black sesame seeds, if desired.
SERVES 3

Wallace Nishimura

Wallace Nishimura has been executive chef at Kauai Coconut Beach Resort for years, but has been a veteran in the culinary field for over 2 decades. When he graduated from Leeward Community College, he received the Award for Excellence from the Hawaii Restaurant Association. His first job was breakfast cook at the Park Shores Hotel in Waikiki; within 3 months he was promoted to dinner cook, and he kept and worked both jobs. Over the years, Chef Nishimura has worked his culinary magic at many of Hawai'i's top restaurants and resorts, including

Don the Beachcombers, Hyatt Regency Waikiki, Michel's Hilton Hawaiian Village, Sheraton Princeville and Kaluakoi Hotel and Golf Resort on Moloka'i. He enjoys such cooking challenges as the Hawaii Seafood Culinary Excellence Competition, and guest appearances on local cooking shows. He has also served as a chef instructor in the Hotel and Restaurant Industry Employment and Training Trust (H.A.R.I.E.T.T.) program and has taught at the Hilton Hawaiian Village and Leeward Community College.

Opah Stir-Fry With Ginger Sauce

½   **pound opah fillet cut into ¾-inch cubes**
⅓   **cup dried shiitake mushrooms**
    Salt and freshly ground black pepper
1   **tablespoon water**
2   **teaspoons shoyu**
12   **green onions**
3   **tablespoons olive oil**
2   **tablespoons cornstarch**

GINGER SAUCE

2   **cups chicken, or vegetable, broth**
1½   **tablespoons sugar**
1   **tablespoon shoyu**
1   **tablespoon Nam Pla**
1   **tablespoon oyster sauce**
1   **teaspoon rice wine vinegar**
½   **teaspoon salt**
3   **tablespoons cornstarch dissolved in 4 tablespoons cold water**
⅓   **cup minced, or slivered, fresh ginger root**
1   **green chili (Anaheim), minced, or slivered**

PREPARATION

Soak mushrooms in warm water until soft, about 20 minutes. Drain, and squeeze mushrooms dry. Discard stems, and julienne caps.

Season fish with salt and pepper; place in a bowl. Combine water and shoyu, and mix into the fish. Let stand 15 minutes. Cut green stalks of onion into inch-long pieces. Finely slice white sections.

Heat 2 tablespoons of the oil over medium heat in a non-stick skillet. Toss fish with the cornstarch; shake off excess. Add half of the fish to the oil. Sauté quickly, and remove when fish is opaque. Repeat, adding the remaining tablespoon of oil, if necessary. Set fish aside.

Combine the broth, sugar, shoyu, Nam Pla, oyster sauce, vinegar and salt in a heavy pan, or skillet, large enough to eventually hold all ingredients. Bring to a boil; reduce heat to medium-low. Stir in the cornstarch-water mixture, blending until the sauce has thickened, about 30 seconds. Add the remaining sauce ingredients and the fish. Stir just until fish is heated through, about 1 minute. Serve over rice.   SERVES 2

Onion-Topped Opah

1⅓   **pounds opah fillets**
4   **tablespoons olive oil**
1   **large leek, washed and sliced**
4   **large cloves garlic, sliced**
10   **green onions, halved lengthwise**
1   **cup fish stock, or bottled clam juice**
    Salt and freshly ground pepper to taste
    Chopped parsley

PREPARATION

Heat no more than 2 tablespoons oil in a large, non-stick saucepan, or skillet, over medium heat. Add sliced leek and garlic, and sauté briefly, 2 to 3 minutes. Add green onions and stock, or clam juice. Boil until liquid is reduced to a thick glaze consistency, 5 to 6 minutes. Stir often. Season with salt and pepper, and set aside.

Heat remaining oil in a heavy non-stick skillet over medium-high heat. Sprinkle fish with salt and pepper. Add to the skillet, and cook until just cooked through, about 4 minutes per side. Remove to a warm platter. Return the onion mixture to the skillet, and stir to just heat through. Top fish with onion mixture before serving. Garnish with parsley.   SERVES 4

Nellie's Opah Fillets With Grapefruit Marinade

1½ pounds opah fillets
1 grapefruit
¼ cup white wine
2 tablespoons chopped parsley
2 tablespoons oil
1 green onion stalk, sliced
1 teaspoon dried marjoram, crushed

PREPARATION

Cut fillets into 4 pieces, and place in a shallow, non-aluminum pan.

Grate (or shred) grapefruit peel, enough to make 1 teaspoon. Then cut the fruit in half, and squeeze out the juice. Combine the grapefruit peel and juice, wine, parsley, oil, onion and marjoram. Pour mixture over the fish, and marinate in the refrigerator for 2 to 4 hours.

Remove fish from the marinade, and use the sauce to brush on the fish several times during cooking. (If your barbecue has a top, cover the fish during cooking. It will stay moister.) Grill fish 4 inches from the coals for 3 to 6 minutes per side, depending on thickness. Cook no more than a total of 10 minutes per inch of thickness.
SERVES 4

Broiled Opah With Rahna's Relish

½ pound opah, cut into 2 servings
2 tablespoons olive oil
1 tablespoon fresh lemon juice
Black pepper and salt

RAHNA'S RELISH
2 plum tomatoes, diced
⅔ cup diced cucumber
4 radishes, diced
1 shallot, minced
3 tablespoons olive oil
3 tablespoons chopped fresh cilantro
1 teaspoon fresh lemon juice
1 teaspoon rice wine vinegar
Pinch sugar
Salt and pepper to taste

PREPARATION

Rub fish on all sides with olive oil and lemon juice. Season with pepper, and let stand.

Combine all relish ingredients in a non-reactive bowl.

Preheat broiler. Season fish with salt. Broil fish, turning pieces once, until just cooked, about 8 minutes per inch of thickness. Serve with relish.
SERVES 2

Marinated Opah
in Tomato-Jalapeno Sauce

1½ pounds opah
½ teaspoon salt
¼ teaspoon freshly ground black pepper
¼ cup fresh lime juice

TOMATO-JALAPENO SAUCE

¼ cup white wine
1 round onion, thinly sliced
3 small tomatoes, seeded and diced
    (about 2 cups)
⅓ cup canned jalapeno peppers, drained and
    diced (alter amount to suit taste, or use
    canned green chilies)
2 tablespoons capers, drained
¼ cup chopped red bell pepper
    (or substitute bottled roasted red peppers)
2 cloves garlic, minced

PREPARATION

Cut the opah into serving-sized pieces. Place in a non-reactive container, and sprinkle with salt, pepper and lime juice. Marinate fish for 15 minutes. Turn opah once.

To prepare the sauce, add wine to a non-stick skillet and bring to a boil. Add the onion; cover, and simmer over medium heat until onion softens, about 5 minutes. Add the tomatoes, jalapenos, capers, red pepper pieces and garlic; cover, and simmer for 10 minutes, or until the tomatoes have cooked down and all ingredients are blended.

Add the opah, cover, and simmer for 5 minutes. Remove the cover, and continue to cook until the fish is done.

SERVES 4

Opah Pitas

2 pounds opah, cut into small cubes
2 tablespoons olive oil
1 medium onion, diced
4 cloves garlic, minced
1 red bell pepper (about ½ pound), seeded and
    cut into ¼-inch cubes
6 plum tomatoes, cut into ¼-inch cubes
½ cup golden raisins
10 stuffed green olives, drained and halved
2 tablespoons capers, drained
1½ teaspoons dried thyme
1½ teaspoons ground ginger
½ teaspoon ground allspice
    Salt and pepper to taste
½ cup chopped parsley
5 pitas, cut in half

PREPARATION

Heat olive oil in a large casserole, or skillet. Add the onion and garlic, and sauté until onion is limp, about 8 minutes. Add the red pepper, and cook for 2 to 3 minutes. Add the tomatoes, raisins, olives, capers, thyme, ginger, allspice, salt and pepper. Reduce heat, and cook, stirring frequently, until all ingredients are hot. Carefully stir in the fish. Remove from the heat, and let sit. Stir occasionally until the fish has cooked, 5 to 10 minutes. Stir in parsley. Fill pitas and serve immediately.

SERVES 5

FISHWIFE'S TIP

To seed tomatoes, slice the tomato as you would in preparation for dicing, and run your fingers down both sides of the center core, releasing the seeds.

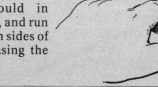

Opah Terrine
courtesy of Wong F. Keng

3   **pounds fresh opah, skinned, deveined and ground**
1   **pound diced fresh opah**
2   **ounces orange tobiko (flying fish eggs), frozen or fresh**
½   **cup heavy cream**
1   **egg white**
½   **tablespoon salt**
½   **tablespoon chopped fresh dill**
    Pinch ground white pepper
1   **green papaya, julienned**
¼   **pound ocean salad (seaweed salad)**
1   **cup Red Peppers Mint Vinaigrette (recipe follows)**
1   **cup chopped macadamia nuts**

PREPARATION

Heat oven to 350°. Refrigerate ground opah/tobiko and cream until well-chilled. Process ground opah and egg white in food processor to a fine paste. Add cream, salt, dill and white pepper, and pulse until mixed.

With a chilled mixing bowl, fold diced opah and tobiko into opah mousseline. Line terrine molds with plastic wrap, distribute mousseline evenly between molds, cover with additional wrap, and press down to get out the air.

Place terrines in a bain-marie. Fill with hot water to cover two-thirds of the molds. Place bain-marie in oven, reduce oven temperature to 275°, and bake until the temperature of the center of each terrine reaches 145°. Remove terrines from bain-marie, remove plastic from tops, let cool, and chill overnight.

Wong F. Keng

Originally from Kuala Lumpur, Malaysia, Sous Chef Wong Keng received most of his culinary experience in Oregon prior to joining the Vanda Court Cafe at the Ilikai Nikko Waikiki staff. He creates his dishes with fresh island fish, meats and produce, combining his high standards with European and Asian techniques and flavors to produce award-winning recipes.

After finishing high school, Chef Keng worked at a Malaysian restaurant where one of the cooks was departing for the adventure of working and traveling around the world on a merchant ship. Chef Keng saw the combination of cooking and traveling as an exciting career.

Prior to joining the Ilikai, he worked as lead cook/ sous chef at Jake's Famous Crawfish Restaurant and as banquet chef/gardemanger at Atwaters Restaurant in Portland.

Red Peppers Mint Vinaigrette

1   **cup granulated sugar**
2   **cups water**
1   **cup rice wine vinegar**
5   **garlic cloves, minced**
1   **tablespoon crushed red peppers**
2   **tablespoons chopped mint**

PREPARATION

Combine sugar and water in saucepan, bring to a boil, and continue boiling until the mixture has the consistency of syrup. Remove from heat. Add vinegar, garlic and red peppers, and stir well. Add chopped mint, and serve at room temperature or chilled.   MAKES 1 cup

To serve, toss papaya and ocean salad with Red Peppers Mint Vinaigrette. Place a portion of the salad in the middle of a plate with 1 ounce of vinaigrette on the bottom of the plate. Arrange sliced terrine alongside the salad mixture. Sprinkle chopped macadamia nuts over entire dish. Serve as an appetizer.

SERVES 8

Sautéed Opah With Ginger-Chili Sauce
courtesy of Marjorie Lincoln

1⅓ pounds opah fillet or steak, sliced into
    ¾-inch pieces
  5 dried shiitake mushrooms
  2 tablespoons shoyu mixed with
    2 tablespoons water
  3 tablespoons cornstarch
    Salt and freshly ground black pepper
  2 tablespoons olive oil

SAUCE
  2 cups chicken broth
1½ tablespoons sugar
  1 tablespoon shoyu
  1 tablespoon fish sauce
  1 tablespoon oyster sauce
  1 teaspoon distilled white vinegar
  ¼ teaspoon salt (or to taste)
  2 tablespoons cornstarch mixed with
    2 tablespoons water
  6 stalks green onions, cut into 1-inch lengths
  ⅓ cup slivered ginger root
  1 green chili (mild to medium hot),
    thinly sliced

PREPARATION

Soak mushrooms in hot water until soft, about 20 minutes. Drain, and squeeze out water. Discard stems, and julienne caps. Set aside.

Place fish in a shallow container with the shoyu-water mixture. Let stand 20 minutes. Turn once. Remove fish from shoyu mixture, and dust pieces lightly with cornstarch. Season with salt and pepper. Place on a cake rack until ready to cook.

Heat oil in a non-stick skillet over medium heat. Cook the fish for 3 minutes, or until golden brown. Turn pieces, and continue cooking for 2 to 3 more minutes, or until done. Remove to a serving dish; cover to keep warm.

To prepare the sauce, combine chicken broth, sugar, shoyu, fish sauce, oyster sauce, vinegar and salt in a heavy saucepan over medium-high heat. Bring to a boil, and reduce heat to medium-low. Add the cornstarch-water mixture; blend until thickened, about 30 seconds. Add the green onions, shiitake mushrooms, ginger and chili. Serve immediately over fish.   SERVES 4

FISHWIFE'S TIP

Recipes often instruct us to use only the stalks of green onions, but that doesn't mean we should discard the white bulb end. Use them in soups, or stews, or simply mince them up and add to the dish you are making!

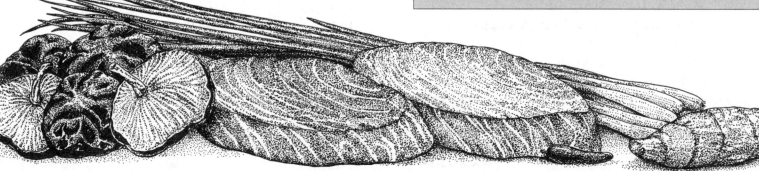

Opah Poached With Thyme and Sun-Dried Tomatoes

1½ pounds opah
1 tablespoon olive oil
2 tablespoons minced garlic
1½ teaspoons minced fresh thyme
½ teaspoon salt
¼ teaspoon black pepper
⅓ cup dry white wine
2 small shallots, minced
8 sun-dried tomatoes, julienned
1 lemon, thinly sliced

PREPARATION

Preheat oven to 375°. Rub opah with olive oil and garlic, sprinkle with fresh thyme, salt and pepper. Place fish in a single layer in a baking dish. Add wine, sprinkle with shallots and sun-dried tomatoes, and place lemon slices on top. Cover the dish, and bake until the fish is cooked, 8 to 10 minutes per inch of thickness. Spoon pan juices over the fish before serving.   SERVES 4

Opah Salad With Szechwan Sesame Sauce

1 pound opah fillet or steak, poached
   Mixed greens of choice (lettuce, spinach)
   Cilantro sprigs for garnish
SZECHWAN SESAME SAUCE
2 cloves garlic, minced
2 tablespoons tahini
2 tablespoons chili oil
2 tablespoons minced fresh ginger
2 tablespoons light soy sauce
2 tablespoons sesame oil
2 teaspoons sugar
1½ teaspoons rice wine vinegar
¼ teaspoon ground Szechwan peppercorns

PREPARATION

Cool opah, and break into pieces. Combine all Szechwan Sesame Sauce ingredients. Divide greens between 2 or 3 plates. Top with opah. Spoon dressing over the salad. Garnish with cilantro.   SERVES 2

Art's Special Poke
courtesy of Art Kamisugi, especially for those who think they don't like raw fish

1 **pound opah, or any white-fleshed fish, diced**
2 **lemons**
1 **small Maui onion, thinly sliced**
½ **teaspoon coarsely ground black pepper**
½ **teaspoon Hawaiian salt**
1 **teaspoon crushed red chili peppers**
1 **tablespoon capers (with brine)**
1 **tablespoon peanut oil**
1 **teaspoon dill weed**

PREPARATION

Place the diced fish in a non-metal container, and squeeze the juice of the 2 lemons over the fish. Mix well. Let sit for 5 minutes. Drain well.

Add all remaining ingredients to the fish. Mix well; serve chilled as an appetizer.   SERVES 6

Notes

Snapper

Snapper are a colorful family, providing moist, mild meat to consumers, creative challenges for chefs, and high prices for fishermen, particularly around the holidays.

'Opakapaka, in Hawai'i, is the most popular fish of the family. Its bright pink skin and manageable size (average 3 to 10 pounds) makes the 'paka perfect for spectacular whole-fish presentations by Hawai'i's fine chefs.

The onaga, with its red skin and long, graceful tail, has become more popular over the years. Onaga's flesh is slightly softer than its pink relative, and it has a higher fat content, particularly in the winter. Like 'paka, onaga is most often enjoyed steamed or as sashimi, but it is as delicious baked, poached or sautéed.

Uku is prettier on the inside than the outside. The moderately firm flesh of this family member makes it better for broiling than the 'paka or onaga.

SUBSTITUTIONS: Lingcod, Sea Bass, Ocean Perch, Rock Cod, Rock Fish and Whiting.

Snapper are often cooked in their skins, so be sure to scale them carefully. The white meat takes well to most cooking methods, especially steaming. Snapper blend well with other seafood, like scallops, shrimp and crab. August and September are the only months snapper are scarce.

Sautéed Snapper With Gremolata

2 pounds snapper, sliced into pieces or chunks 1 inch thick
1 clove garlic
2 teaspoons olive oil
Salt and freshly ground pepper
⅓ cup minced fresh parsley (may use mixture of curly-leafed and Italian flat-leafed parsley)
2 cloves garlic
2 tablespoons green onion
1 tablespoon minced lemon zest

PREPARATION

Cut 1 clove of the garlic in half lengthwise. Rub the fish with the garlic, and then brush with 1 teaspoon olive oil. Season with salt and pepper.

To prepare the gremolata, mix together the parsley, garlic, green onion and lemon zest, and set aside.

Heat the remaining oil in a non-stick skillet over medium heat. Quickly sauté the fish on both sides. When fish is almost cooked through, add half of the gremolata to the skillet, making sure the fish gets coated on all sides as you finish the cooking. Remove fish from the heat, and serve with remaining gremolata.

SERVES 6

Simmered Snapper, Japanese-Style

2 small, whole fish (such as snapper or papio), or one large fish (up to 3 pounds)
1½ cups water
½ cup sake
7 tablespoons shoyu
2 tablespoons mirin
2 to 3 tablespoons sugar
1 thumb ginger root, sliced
3 shiitake mushrooms, soaked in warm water, squeezed, and cut into thin strips

PREPARATION

Score the fish (on one side if fish is small, or on both sides if large) with deep diagonal cuts. Set aside.

Combine the water, sake, shoyu and mirin in a pot or wok large enough to hold the fish in a single layer. Bring mixture to a boil over high heat. Add the ginger, and boil for 30 seconds. Add the fish and the mushrooms, and bring the water back to a boil if necessary. Immediately lower the heat to a simmer. Simmer the fish until it is done (see Fishwife's Tip). Baste fish frequently with the sauce as it cooks. Remove the fish to a serving plate, and spoon cooking liquid over it.

SERVES 4

FISHWIFE'S TIP

Remember to cook the fish for no more than 10 minutes per inch of thickness. If the fish is large, turn it over when it is halfway done. If the fish is small and relatively flat, there is no need to turn it.

Poached Orange Roughy in Carrot-Orange Sauce

1 pound snapper fillets, cut into 4 pieces
1 medium cucumber
2 teaspoons shredded or grated orange peel
1 cup orange juice
2 tablespoons balsamic vinegar
1 small carrot, shredded (about ½ cup)
Salt and pepper to taste
2 teaspoons candied ginger root
1 tablespoon cornstarch
1 tablespoon water

PREPARATION

Chop a portion of the cucumber to make ½ cup. Set aside. Thinly slice the rest of the cucumber, and place slices in a thin layer on the bottom of a serving dish.

Combine the orange peel, orange juice, vinegar, carrot, salt and pepper and candied ginger in a skillet large enough to hold the fish in 1 layer. Bring the mixture to a boil. Carefully add the fish, and bring the sauce to just below the boiling point. Reduce the heat, cover, and simmer fish until done (about 8 minutes per inch of thickness of the fish). Remove fish from the sauce with a slotted spoon, drain a bit, and place the fish on the cucumber bed. Cover to keep the fish warm.

Mix the cornstarch and water together in a small bowl, and stir it into the sauce in the skillet. Cook, stirring constantly, until the mixture thickens and bubbles. Continue to cook and stir for another 2 minutes. Stir in the chopped cucumber, and remove pan from the heat. Pour the sauce over the fish.

SERVES 4

Baked Snapper With Fennel

2 pounds snapper fillets
1 2-pound fennel bulb with 1-inch stalks
    (see Fishwife's Tip)
2 tablespoons olive oil
3 tablespoons butter
1 large Maui onion
    Salt and pepper to taste
¼ cup freshly grated Romano or
    Parmesan cheese
    Lemon wedges

PREPARATION

Cut fennel bulb lengthwise into ½-inch slices (makes about 8 slices). Heat the oil and 2 tablespoons of the butter in a skillet. Sauté the fennel until it is browned and slightly softened, about 10 minutes. Place in a buttered baking dish.

Preheat oven to 400°. Cut snapper fillets into 6 pieces, and place them on the fennel layer. Cover fish with onion, dot with the remaining butter, and sprinkle with salt and pepper and some of the fennel leaves, if you have them. Bake snapper for 8 minutes per inch of thickness of fish. Sprinkle cheese on top. Place the pan under the broiler, and brown lightly. Garnish with lemon.

SERVES 6

FISHWIFE'S TIP

When you buy fennel at the store, it might not have its stalks and leaves attached. If it does, for this recipe, cut the stalks off an inch or so above the bulb, slice and sauté only the bulb.

Broiled Snapper With Orange-Basil Sauce

1 pound snapper fillets
1 cup orange juice
2 teaspoons dried basil
2 tablespoons butter
½ cup diced tomato
½ teaspoon salt
    Pepper

PREPARATION

Marinate the fillets in ½ cup orange juice and basil for 15 minutes per side. Pour remaining orange juice into a saucepan, place over high heat, and reduce to ¼ cup. Add the butter and the tomato pieces, and cook until the butter coats the tomato pieces. Remove from heat.

Preheat broiler. Remove the fish from marinade; allow excess liquid to drip off. Place fillets on a cold, lightly oiled broiler pan. Broil 2 to 4 inches from the heat source for 3 to 4 minutes, or until the fish is cooked. Remove from heat. Serve with the orange sauce.

SERVES 4

Baked Snapper, Mediterranean-Style

2 pounds snapper (fillets or large pieces)
  Salt and pepper to taste
4 teaspoons olive oil
  Juice of one lemon
3 cloves garlic, minced
2 pounds ripe tomatoes, chopped
  (peel first, if you wish)
½ teaspoon thyme
½ teaspoon oregano
⅛ teaspoon dried red pepper flakes
2 onions, sliced
2 tablespoons pine nuts
2 tablespoons raisins (optional)

PREPARATION

Preheat oven to 400°. Place the snapper fillets or pieces in a baking dish in a single layer. Rub the fish with salt and pepper, 2 tablespoons of the oil and the lemon juice. Cover the dish (foil is OK), and bake until fish is almost done (7 or 8 minutes per inch of thickness—remember, it will continue cooking after you remove it from the heat). Keep fish warm.

Sauté the garlic in a non-stick skillet over medium-high heat until garlic begins to turn yellow. Add the tomatoes, herbs and red pepper flakes, and simmer gently for 20 minutes, or until the tomatoes have thickened and broken down. Meanwhile, sauté the onions in the remaining tablespoon of oil in another pan until they are golden. Add the pine nuts and raisins, and cook until the raisins plump up.

To serve, spoon the tomato sauce over the fish and top with the fried onion mixture.　　SERVES 6

Snapper With Three-Citrus Butter

1½ pounds snapper fillets
 1 quart water
 ¼ cup fresh lemon juice
 6 parsley sprigs
12 black peppercorns
 2 bay leaves
 1 2-inch piece ginger root, smashed
1½ tablespoons orange juice
1½ tablespoons lime juice
 1 teaspoon lemon zest
1½ tablespoons butter
 2 tablespoons minced green onion

PREPARATION

Combine the water, lemon juice, parsley, peppercorns, bay leaves and ginger root in a large fish steamer. Bring mixture to a boil over high heat. Reduce heat, and simmer gently for 5 to 10 minutes.

Add the snapper fillets; return broth to a simmer; and cook for 10 minutes, or until the fillets are done. Remove the fish to a serving platter.

Combine the orange juice, lime juice and lemon zest in a small bowl or cup. Melt butter over medium heat in a small saucepan or skillet. As butter begins to brown, add the juices and minced green onion, and let sizzle for half a minute. Pour over the fish, and serve.

SERVES 6

FISHWIFE'S TIP
If you don't have a steamer or pot large enough to hold the whole fillets, cut the fish into pieces.

Spicy Hunan Fish

1 small snapper (2½ pounds), or two smaller ones, cleaned and scaled
1 teaspoon coarse salt
¾ cup sliced green onions (green and white parts)
3 cloves garlic, minced
3 tablespoons minced ginger root
1 teaspoon dried red pepper flakes
6 dried Chinese mushrooms
1 large carrot, thinly julienned
3 ounces Chinese snow peas, cut lengthwise into strips
  Oil for frying (peanut or corn is best)
¼ cup cornstarch

SAUCE
½ cup hot water
2 tablespoons shoyu
2 tablespoons sugar
1½ teaspoons balsamic vinegar or Chinese black vinegar

PREPARATION

Using a sharp knife, score the fish on both sides at 1-inch intervals, beginning below head and continuing to the tail. Make deep gashes about three-fourths of the way to the bone. Sprinkle the fish, inside and out, with coarse salt. Rub salt into the score marks, as well. Set fish aside.

Combine the green onions, garlic, ginger root and red pepper flakes in a small bowl, and set aside. Soak the mushrooms in warm water until they are soft. Rinse well; remove and discard stems. Cut the mushrooms into thin strips. Put in a bowl with the carrot and pea pod strips. Set aside.

Prepare the sauce by combining all sauce ingredients and stirring well until the sugar is dissolved. Set aside.

Heat oil to 375° in a wok or a large, deep skillet. While the oil is heating, pat cornstarch on the fish, including its head and in the score marks. Shake off any excess. When the oil is at the right temperature, gently lower the fish, headfirst, into the oil. Fry the fish on both sides until it is brown on the outside and the flesh of the score marks is white. Baste fish with oil as snapper cooks. Remove fish, drain off excess oil, and place on a warm platter.

Heat another skillet or wok over high heat. Add 2 tablespoons of oil, and coat bottom of pan. Then lower the heat to medium-high. Add the green onions, garlic, ginger and red pepper flakes. Adjust heat if necessary so the ingredients do not brown. Cook for 20 or 30 seconds. Then add the mushrooms, carrots and snow peas, and cook for another 30 seconds, or so. (If mixture begins to stick, drizzle a small amount of oil into the pan.) Stir sauce ingredients before adding them to the pan. Bring entire mixture to a slow simmer. Stir constantly. When mixture is heated through, pour it over the fish, and serve.
                                                    SERVES 4

Grilled Snapper Oriental

2¼ pounds snapper fillets cut into 6 pieces
½ cup rice vinegar
¼ cup chopped round onion, or shallots
1 clove garlic, minced
3 tablespoons fresh lime juice
2 tablespoons shoyu
2 tablespoons minced ginger root
1 teaspoon sugar
¼ cup olive oil
   Salt and pepper to taste
½ cup minced parsley
½ cup diced water chestnuts
   Olive oil (for basting fish)
   Freshly ground pepper
¼ cup toasted sesame seeds

PREPARATION

Combine the rice vinegar, onion, garlic, lime juice, shoyu, ginger and sugar in a saucepan. Gradually whisk in the ¼ cup oil, and season with salt and pepper to taste. Cook over medium heat until heated through. Add the parsley and bell pepper, and set aside; keep warm until the fish is cooked.

Brush the fillets lightly with olive oil, and season with pepper. Place fish on a grill or in a preheated broiler, and cook for 3 minutes per side.

Remove fish from the heat. Pour the sauce on a serving platter, place fish on top, sprinkle with sesame seeds, and serve.

SERVES 6

Rahna's Fish Curry With Fruit

2 pounds snapper fillets
2 tablespoons butter
1 small onion, chopped
2 cloves garlic, minced
1 teaspoon minced ginger root
2 teaspoons hot curry powder
1 firm apple, diced (peel first, if you wish)
1 banana, diced
¾ cup vegetable broth
1 small, ripe papaya, diced
¼ cup soft tofu
½ teaspoon salt

PREPARATION

Slice or chunk fillets into 1-inch pieces. Set aside.

Melt 1 tablespoon of the butter in a saucepan over medium heat, and sauté the onion pieces until they are soft. Add the garlic and ginger root, and sauté for another minute. Add the curry powder, and stir well. Add the diced apple and banana, and sauté for a minute or 2. Pour in the vegetable broth, and cook the mixture over low heat for 10 minutes. Add half of the diced papaya and the soft tofu. Stir mixture well, and remove from the heat. Let curry sauce stand until it is cool enough to purée in a food processor or blender.

Melt the remaining tablespoon of butter in a large non-stick skillet. Add the fish and salt and sauté over medium heat until the fish is almost cooked. Add the sauce to the skillet, and simmer it with the fish for a minute or 2. Top with remaining papaya.

SERVES 6

FISHWIFE'S TIP
To create a sauce of smoother consistency, put the tofu in a blender before adding it to the sauce.

Manicotti Surprise
courtesy of Mark Lee

2 cups raw fish, cut into 1-inch cubes
2 tablespoons olive oil
2 tablespoons Italian salad dressing
 (use no-fat type, if you prefer)
2 tablespoons fresh lemon juice
½ teaspoon grated lemon rind
 (do not include white pith)
¼ teaspoon black pepper
¼ cup chopped fresh parsley
1 package manicotti shells (8) for stuffing
¼ cup green onions
½ cup fresh mushrooms
1 medium tomato, quartered
½ teaspoon liquid smoke
2 cloves garlic, minced

FISHWIFE'S TIP

The Lee family loved this dish prepared as described above. Mark suggested topping the manicotti with tomato sauce or marinara before baking *if* you want to. I suggest you try it as is the first time you make it.

PREPARATION

Preheat oven to 375°.

Combine olive oil and salad dressing in a bowl, and mix well. Pour half of the mixture into a skillet, and set the skillet aside.

To the mixture that remains in the bowl, add the lemon juice and rind, black pepper and chopped parsley. Add the fish, and let it marinate.

Prepare the manicotti shells according to package instructions. Drain, or pat dry.

Meanwhile, heat the skillet with the oil/salad dressing mixture. Put the green onions, mushrooms and tomato pieces into a food processor, and process briefly until the veggies are chopped. Add the liquid smoke and minced garlic, and pour the mixture into the heated skillet. Sauté briefly, and remove from the heat.

Add the contents of the skillet to the bowl of marinating fish. Blend well, and stuff the cooked manicotti shells with the mixture. Place in a lightly oiled baking dish. Top with tomato sauce or marinara, if you wish. (See Fishwife's Tip.) Cover, and bake for 15 to 18 minutes.

SERVES 4

Sauté 'Opakapaka, Thai-Style
courtesy of the Kona Surf Resort

4 5-ounce 'opakapaka fillets
¾ cup dark soy sauce
1 cup water
6 tablespoons vinegar
2 tablespoons minced ginger
6 tablespoons sugar
8 shiitake mushrooms, julienned
½ red bell pepper, julienned
2 tablespoons finely chopped spring onion
3 small chili peppers, seeded and chopped
2 tablespoons cornstarch
   Salt and white pepper
   Clarified butter
¼ cup pickled ginger

PREPARATION

Bring soy sauce, ¾ cup water, vinegar and ginger to a boil. Stir in the sugar, and allow to simmer 15 minutes. Add the mushrooms, bell pepper, spring onion and chili peppers, and cook until vegetables are tender. Mix the cornstarch and remaining ¼ cup of water together to form a thin paste. Slowly stir paste into sauce. Allow to simmer for 5 minutes. Reserve sauce, and keep it warm.

Season 'opakapaka fillets with salt and white pepper. Heat clarified butter in a sauté pan. Add fish fillets, and sauté till just firm.

Arrange fish in center of plate, spoon sauce over fillets, and garnish with pickled ginger. Serve Oriental sticky rice on the side.   SERVES 4

Grilled Snapper With Raspberry-Mint Sauce

1½ pounds snapper
    Salt and freshly ground pepper
2   tablespoons olive oil

SAUCE
¾   cup whole raspberries, fresh or frozen (about 3 ounces)
1   tablespoon balsamic vinegar
3   tablespoons minced shallots or onions
¼   cup vegetable stock
1   teaspoon Dijon mustard
2   teaspoons minced fresh mint
½   teaspoon fresh rosemary, broken into small pieces
¼   teaspoon ground ginger
    Salt and freshly ground pepper

PREPARATION

Season fish with salt and pepper. Brush fish with olive oil, and let stand while you prepare the sauce.

Purée the berries in a food processor. If they are frozen, they'll be the consistency of small pearls when you're done.

Put balsamic vinegar in a saucepan over medium heat. Sauté the shallots or onions in the vinegar until the liquid is reduced by half (2 minutes). Add the vegetable stock and mustard, and bring to a boil before adding the raspberry purée, mint, rosemary, ginger and pepper. Bring to a boil again, lower the heat, and cook, stirring, until the sauce thickens.   MAKES ½ cup

Grill or broil the snapper, and serve with the sauce.
SERVES 4

Steamed 'Opakapaka With Shiitake Mushroom and Butter Shoyu

courtesy of Chef Sam Choy,
Sam Choy Restaurants of Hawai'i,
presented at the Hawaiian Harvest Reception
First Annual Big Island Bounty

4   6-ounce 'opakapaka fillets
¼   cup oil
3   tablespoons soy sauce
1   teaspoon minced ginger
2   tablespoons butter
2   cups fresh shiitake mushrooms
¼   cup chopped cilantro
     Salt and pepper to taste
     Fresh ti leaves

PREPARATION

Marinate 'opakapaka fillets for 1 hour in a combination of oil, 2 tablespoons soy sauce and ginger.

Conventional Preparation

Steam fillets 8 to 10 minutes, or until fish flakes easily when tested with a fork. Set fish aside on a heated platter.

Melt butter in a heavy skillet; add shiitake mushrooms, and sauté until mushrooms are just limp. Add the remaining 1 tablespoon soy sauce and cilantro. Season to taste with salt and pepper. Pour shiitake mushroom mixture over fillets.

Laulau Method

Take 2 ti leaves, and lay them across each other. Place 1 'opakapaka fillet in the middle, top with shiitake mushrooms, and pour 1 tablespoon of the butter sauce on it; top with cilantro. Tie ti leaves together to form a basket. Steam 8 to 10 minutes.   SERVES 4

"When I prepared this dish at the Big Island Bounty, I was so happy to see that it was well-received. The fresh shiitake really make this dish. I add the butter-soy sauce to give it an Oriental flair. To prepare it laulau style is to prepare it the old Hawaiian way. This is truly a dish where East meets West in Hawai'i. Enjoy!"
                                              . . . Sam

Snapper Wrapped in Spinach With Fennel Cream and Pineapple-Mango Relish

courtesy of Executive Chef Stafford T. DeCambra, American Hawaii Cruises

6 5-ounce snapper fillets
1 pound spinach leaves, cleaned and blanched
   Salt and pepper to taste
4 tablespoons olive oil
6 tablespoons julienned fennel, blanched

PINEAPPLE-MANGO RELISH

¼ cup finely diced pineapple
¼ cup finely diced mango (or substitute papaya)
1 teaspoon finely chopped red bell pepper
1 teaspoon finely chopped green onion
¼ teaspoon finely chopped Chinese parsley (cilantro)
¼ teaspoon rice wine vinegar
   Pinch minced garlic
   Pinch minced ginger
¼ teaspoon kiawe honey (or any mild honey)
   Salt and white pepper to taste

FENNEL CREAM

1 tablespoon finely chopped shallot
2 cups fish stock
   (may substitute vegetable stock)
½ cup chopped fennel bulb
2 cups heavy cream
   Salt and pepper to taste
1 cup butter, cut into cubes

PREPARATION

To prepare relish, combine all ingredients in a non-reactive bowl. Cover until ready to use.

To prepare fennel cream, place shallot, fish stock and fennel in a saucepan. Bring to a boil, and reduce to half. Add heavy cream. Simmer until reduced by half, about 6 minutes. Place mixture in a blender, and quickly blend. Strain through a fine sieve. Return to pan, and place in a bain-marie (see Chef's Note). Adjust seasoning with salt and pepper. Whisk in fresh butter. Keep warm.

To prepare snapper, pat spinach leaves dry after blanching, and set them aside. Preheat oven to 325°. Pat fillets dry. Season with salt and pepper. Heat oil in a sauté pan. Sauté fish on all sides until evenly browned. Remove from heat. Wrap each fillet in spinach leaves. Arrange on a serving plate, and place in preheated oven for 3 minutes. Remove plate from oven, and garnish with the relish and fennel julienne. Add sauce.

SERVES 6

CHEF'S NOTE:

A bain-marie, widely used in professional kitchens, consists of a tray or container for water that is kept anywhere from warm to hot. Sauces can stay warm in a bain-marie without risk of curdling because the water temperature doesn't reach the boiling point. You can use a double boiler, your own version of a bain-marie, or keep your burner temperature very low.

Stafford T. DeCambra

As executive chef for American Hawaii Cruises, Stafford DeCambra creates seafood dishes on the high seas. Chef DeCambra has been testing his culinary talents at award-winning, fine dining resorts and restaurants since 1975 and has received more awards and honors for culinary excellence than we have space to mention (over 30 in American Culinary Federation competitions alone!).

He served as president of the American Culinary Federation, Kona-Kohala Chapter, and was recipient of the Chapter Presidents Award in 1988 and 1991. In addition, Chef DeCambra won the ACF Chapter Chef of the Year Award in 1984, 1986, 1987 and 1991. He is involved in numerous community, state and nationwide organizations, volunteering time and energy to promote the culinary arts.

Baked Onaga in Rock Salt Crust

courtesy of George Mavrothalassitis, executive chef, Halekulani Restaurant

1 whole onaga, approximately 2 pounds
3 pounds spinach leaves
3 cloves garlic, finely chopped
3 tablespoons butter

SALT CRUST DOUGH
2 pounds flour
1 pound rock salt
3 egg whites
1 cup water

SAUCE
3 tablespoons olive oil
2 pieces shallots, finely chopped
3 cloves garlic, finely chopped
½ cup white wine
1 tomato, peeled, seeded and diced
1 sprig tarragon, finely chopped
1 sprig chervil, finely chopped
1 sprig chive, finely chopped
2 tablespoons finely chopped green onions
1 tablespoon butter
Salt and pepper to taste

PREPARATION

To prepare the dough, sieve the flour into a mixing bowl. Add the rock salt and egg whites with ½ cup of the water. Mix; add enough of the remaining water to form a stiff dough. Roll out to wrap the fish.

Preheat oven to 325°. Debone the onaga without removing the head and tail from the fish. Keep the skin on. Sauté the spinach with garlic and butter. Season to taste, and cool in the refrigerator for a few minutes. Fill the fish with spinach, wrap with the rock salt dough, and shape the dough like a fish. Bake for 25 minutes.

To prepare the sauce, heat olive oil in a saucepan and sauté the shallots for a few minutes. (Do not color the shallots.) Add the garlic and white wine, and reduce to half. Add tomato pieces, herbs and green onions. Finish with butter. Season with salt and pepper to taste.

To serve, at tableside, cut the crust lengthwise and remove only the top of the crust. (Caution should be taken so that no salt crystals fall onto the fish.) Remove the skin from the fish, and serve immediately on individual plates. Place the spinach on top of the fish, and place the sauce around the fish. SERVES 2

George Mavrothalassitis

Cooking is not work to George Mavrothalassitis, executive chef at the Halekulani. "It is an expression of the individual," he explains. "Creativity is very important." Chef Mavro, as he is called by almost everyone, oversees daily operations of Halekulani's 3 restaurants, catered functions and menu creations at La Mer. No recipe is introduced to the public until he is certain it is perfect: some recipes may take 3 months to perfect; others work right away. Chef Mavro, one of the nation's most respected French chefs, has masterfully created a menu for the Halekulani that is a tasteful combination of sophisticated regional Hawai'i cuisine with the cooking of Provence. Under his direction, La Mer has set the standard for Hawai'i Regional Cuisine with its innovative menus and harmonious use of fresh local products along with exotic herbs, spices, fish and poultry. Halekulani and La Mer have received worldwide recognition in the lodging and restaurant categories for pursuing excellence and standards of the highest quality.

Grilled Snapper With Apricot-Onion Sauce

2 pounds snapper fillets
Salt and freshly ground pepper
3 tablespoons olive oil
Juice of half a lemon

SAUCE

1 tablespoon butter
1 tablespoon olive oil
1 large onion, coarsely chopped (1¼ cups)
1 tablespoon sugar
½ cup dry vermouth, or white wine
2 tablespoons cider vinegar
2 teaspoons balsamic vinegar
½ cup chopped canned apricots, drained well
1 teaspoon shoyu
2 teaspoons chopped fresh mint
2 teaspoons butter
Salt to taste
Slivered mint leaves for garnish

PREPARATION

Season snapper with salt and a generous amount of pepper. Place in a non-reactive pan. Combine olive oil and lemon juice; brush mixture on both sides of the fish, and let it stand while you prepare the sauce.

To prepare sauce, melt the tablespoon of butter with the olive oil in a large saucepan over medium-low heat. Add onion pieces and sugar. Cover, and cook, stirring occasionally, until the onions are soft and golden brown, about 15 minutes. Remove cover.

Blend in the vermouth and cider and balsamic vinegars. Increase heat to medium-high, and boil until the liquid is reduced by half, 5 to 7 minutes. Reduce heat to medium-low. Add the apricots and mint, and cook until the liquid is reduced by half again, about 5 minutes. Blend in the 2 teaspoons butter. Add salt, if you wish. Remove from heat.

Grill or broil the snapper fillets. Serve fish with sauce; garnish with slivered mint.   SERVES 6

Sautéed Snapper With Black Olive Relish

1½ pounds snapper fillets
(cut into serving-sized pieces)
1 tablespoon olive oil
Salt and freshly ground pepper
Pinch of minced fresh rosemary (optional)

RELISH

⅓ cup minced black olives (about 18 olives)
2 tablespoons minced shallots, or sweet onions
1 clove garlic, minced
1 tablespoon minced parsley

2 teaspoons red wine vinegar
1 teaspoon oil
2 teaspoons lemon zest
½ teaspoon shoyu
Salt and freshly ground pepper

PREPARATION

Combine all relish ingredients in a bowl. Let stand while you prepare the fish.

Heat the olive oil in a non-stick skillet over medium-high heat. Season fish with salt, pepper and rosemary. Sauté fish quickly on both sides; remove to a platter when done. Top each piece with a portion of the relish.
SERVES 4

FISHWIFE'S TIP
Relish ingredients can be adjusted to suit your taste.

'Opakapaka With Leeks, Fresh Herbs and Lobster Butter, Baked in Parchment Paper

courtesy of Beverly Gannon,
Hali'imaile General Store, Hali'imaile, Maui

1   1-pound 'opakapaka fillet
2   leeks, white part only, split and thinly sliced
2   carrots, thinly sliced on the diagonal
¼   cup minced ginger
2   teaspoons chopped chives
2   teaspoons lemon thyme
2   teaspoons chopped parsley
½   cup sliced fresh shiitake mushrooms
8   tablespoons Lobster Butter
     Salt and pepper to taste
4   pieces parchment paper

LOBSTER BUTTER

6   ounces cooked lobster meat
12 ounces unsalted butter, softened
1   tablespoon chopped parsley

PREPARATION

To prepare Lobster Butter, place lobster, butter and parsley in food processor bowl fitted with a metal blade, and process until smooth. Place on piece of plastic wrap, and roll into a log. Freeze.

Preheat oven to 375°. Fold each sheet of parchment paper in half. Using as much of each whole sheet as possible, cut out half a heart shape so that when you open the paper, you have a large heart-shaped piece of paper. Place the 4 open pieces of parchment paper on a counter. Place a few leek and carrot slices, some ginger, chives, thyme and parsley on each piece of parchment– on 1 side of the fold only.

Slice the 'opakapaka fillet into 4 pieces. Place a fillet on top of the vegetables and herbs. Place a few slices of shiitake mushrooms on top of each piece of fish. Cut 2 tablespoons of lobster butter per piece of fish, and place on top of the mushrooms. Season with salt and pepper. Fold over parchment to cover the fish, and crease the edges to seal the package.

Place packages on a baking sheet, and bake in preheated oven for 20 minutes. Open the packets, and serve on or off the paper.

SERVES 4

Beverly Gannon

Born and raised in Dallas in the era of canned, packaged and overcooked foods, Beverly Gannon has come a long way. As chef/co-owner of Hali'imaile General Store, Beverly creates innovative menus featuring eclectic American cuisine full of international flavors and island-fresh ingredients. She suspects her upbringing in the Jewish tradition of "eat, eat" piqued her interest in food and its preparation, which eventually took her to London's Cordon Bleu, followed by classes with Marcella Hazan and Jacques Pepin. She returned home, started her own catering company, met and married Joe Gannon, and together they made Maui home. In 1985, she established Fresh Approach Catering, which continues to grow every year. Two years later, Beverly and Joe opened Hali'imaile General Store, which was to be a gourmet eat-in, take-out deli/catering headquarters/ general store. But Maui residents wanted more, which they proved by waiting patiently in line for a seat at 1 of 5 tables and 30 chairs that the Gannons set up. It is now a restaurant, and seats are still in heavy demand.

Quick Snapper Escabeche

2 **pounds snapper fillets, sliced or cubed**
   Salt and pepper
1 **tablespoon olive oil**
1 **small round onion, thinly sliced**
1 **teaspoon dried thyme**
½ **cup Kalamata olives, chopped**

DRESSING

2 **tablespoons olive oil**
4 **tablespoons fresh lemon juice**
4 **tablespoons orange juice**
2 **tablespoons white wine vinegar**
2 **cloves garlic, pressed**
½ **teaspoon dry mustard**
   Zest from half a lemon
2 **tablespoons balsamic vinegar**
1 **lemon, thinly sliced**
2 **tablespoons minced parsley**

PREPARATION

Sprinkle fish with salt and pepper. Heat ½ tablespoon of oil in a large, non-stick skillet. Sauté the fish for 2 or 3 minutes per side until done, and remove. Drain on paper towels. Discard oil, and wipe skillet with a paper towel. Heat remaining ½ tablespoon of oil in the skillet, add the onion slices, and cook until caramel-colored. Remove onion slices from the pan, and drain on paper towels.

Place the fish and onions in a large, non-reactive dish or bowl. Sprinkle with thyme and olives. Set aside. Combine the 2 tablespoons olive oil, lemon juice, orange juice, white wine vinegar, garlic, dry mustard, salt and pepper and lemon zest in a small bowl. Blend well.

Pour the dressing over the fish. Let stand for 1 hour before serving. Garnish with lemon slices and parsley.
SERVES 6

Bird's Snapper Salad

2 **pounds fish fillets, cut into 1-inch cubes**
   (or use leftover fish)
1 **round onion, chunked**
1 **bay leaf**
4 **cups torn lettuce leaves**
   (Boston, butter, romaine, et cetera)

MARINADE

¼ **cup balsamic or red wine vinegar**
2 **tablespoons olive oil**
2 **tablespoons chicken stock**
1 **tablespoon chopped fresh dill, or**
   1½ teaspoon dried dill weed
1 **yellow or red bell pepper, cut into thin strips**
1 **small Bermuda (red) onion, thinly sliced**

PREPARATION

Place fish in a skillet. Add water just to cover, and add the onion chunks and bay leaf. Simmer 5 to 7 minutes, or until the fish pieces are opaque. Drain.

Combine the vinegar, olive oil, chicken stock, dill, bell pepper strips and sliced onion in a large bowl. Add fish, and toss until well-mixed. Cover bowl, and marinate fish in the refrigerator for 1 hour. Before serving, toss the fish mixture with the romaine, add salt and pepper to taste, and spoon over the lettuce.   SERVES 4

FISHWIFE'S TIP
1. This tastes better if you roast the peppers first.
2. If you use leftover fish, skip the poaching step.
3. If you'd like to use roasted pimento peppers that come in a jar, delete the 2 tablespoons olive oil from the recipe, because the bottled peppers are coated in oil.

Types of Snapper

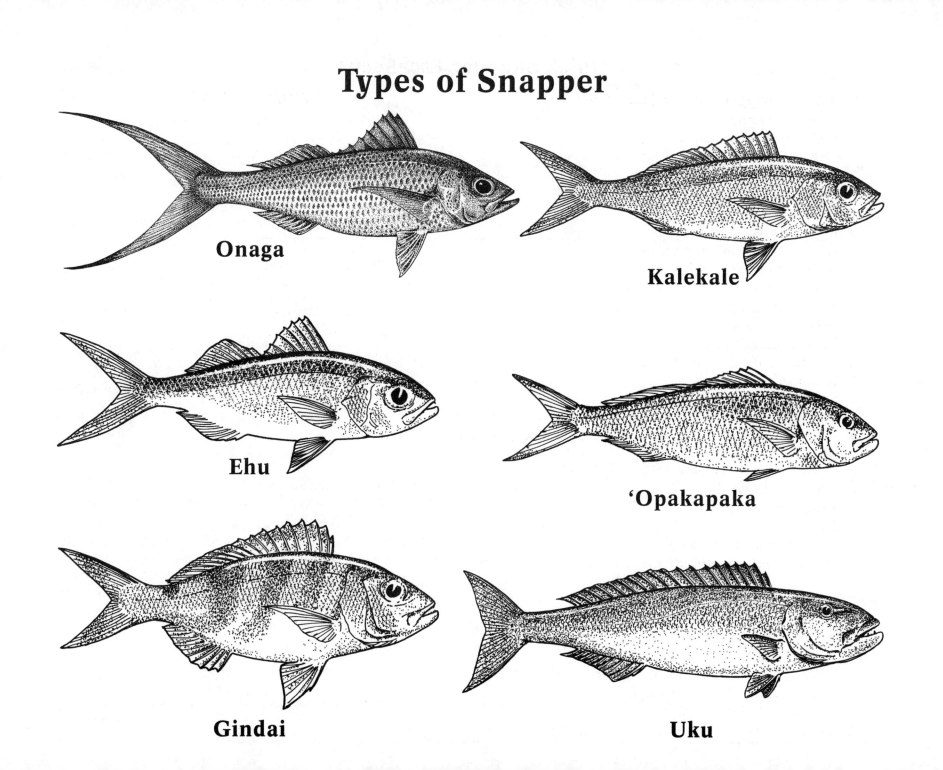

Onaga

Kalekale

Ehu

'Opakapaka

Gindai

Uku

Notes

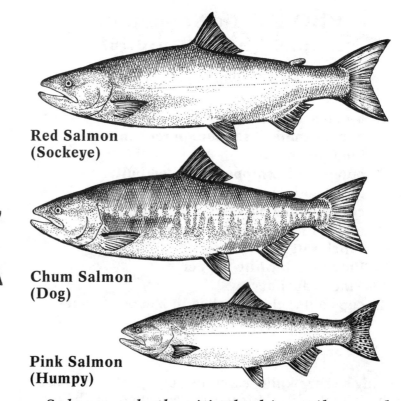

**King Salmon
(Chinook)**

**Silver Salmon
(Coho)**

**Red Salmon
(Sockeye)**

**Chum Salmon
(Dog)**

**Pink Salmon
(Humpy)**

Salmon

Salmon, whether from the Pacific or Atlantic oceans, probably graces more restaurant menus worldwide than any other single species of fish.

The Fishwife, after considering the many sport fishing adventures HAWAII FISHING NEWS publisher Chuck Johnston and staff made to Alaska and Canada, opted to include this selection of recipes. Many wonderful meals have been prepared for Chuck and his staff from their day's catch by salmon-wise chefs of the North country. We proudly share with you and your guests these recipes so you may also experience the wild salmon cuisine of the Northwest.

Salmon, whether it's the king, silver, red or pink variety, is very similar in its distinctive taste and texture, even though there are subtle differences among the various species.

During the summer months when salmon are migrating, they are one of the best price values you will find in your local markets.

Because salmon is high in natural oil content, it lends itself to a wide variety of preparations including being baked, barbecued, blackened, smoked, pickled and even casseroled. Each method can lend itself to making many distinctive taste sensations. Here are a few of our favorites.

BBQ Pacific Salmon in Smoked Salmon Butter

Chef Peter Staufer of Eagle Pointe Lodge,
Wales Island, British Columbia, Canada

6   6-ounce salmon fillets, skin left on
4   ounces smoked salmon, puréed in a
     food processor
8   ounces soft whipped unsalted butter
1   tablespoon vegetable oil
¼   cup chopped chives
1   ounce finely chopped capers
     Pinch salt
     Pinch fresh white pepper
     Pinch cayenne
2   cups alder chips soaked in 2 cups of water
     for 1 to 2 hours

PREPARATION

Using a sharp knife, carefully cut a pocket into each of the salmon fillets. Blend smoked salmon with butter and vegetable oil, and then add chives, capers, salt, pepper and cayenne. Mix together until well-combined. Use a spoon to stuff salmon pockets with half of smoked salmon butter. Arrange salmon fillets, skin side down, into a tight-fitting roasting pan. Evenly divide the rest of the salmon butter over salmon fillets.

Preheat barbecue to 350°, and add water-soaked alder chips to the coals. Place salmon in a pan on middle rack, close lid, and let fish smoke for 8 to 10 minutes, or longer depending on thickness of salmon. Remove salmon from pan to serving dish. Spoon 2 tablespoons of salmon butter over salmon.

Serve with fresh lemon, wild rice and seasonal vegetables, or a cool cucumber salad.   SERVES 6

Shelter Island Lodge Barbecued Salmon

Shelter Island Lodge, Juneau, Alaska

6   salmon steaks, cut 1 inch to 1½ inches thick
     (critical)
     Salt and pepper to taste
3   stalks green onion, chopped

SAUCE
5   tablespoons cornstarch
½   cup water
½   cup granulated sugar
½   cup soy sauce
4   dashes Tabasco
2   teaspoons sesame seed oil

PREPARATION

To prepare sauce, mix cornstarch in water thoroughly. Add sugar, soy sauce, Tabasco and sesame seed oil. Cook over low heat in saucepan stirring frequently until mixture thickens and becomes translucent.

Salt and pepper fish. Place steaks in a fish basket and cook over coals for about 10 minutes, or until meat begins to separate from bone. Coat fillets on both sides with sauce and cook another 5 minutes per side. Total cooking time will be 20 minutes.

Garnish with chopped green onion.   SERVES 6

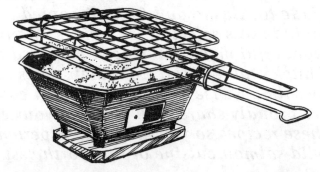

Salmon Wellington

Cape Fox Lodge, Ketchikan, Alaska

1   pound cooked, flaked salmon
¼   cup chopped green pepper
¼   cup chopped green onions
1   tablespoon lemon juice
2   tablespoons dill weed
¼   teaspoon salt
¼   teaspoon pepper
2   eggs
1   cup soft bread crumbs
1   sheet puff pastry
1   egg yolk (lightly beaten)
1   tablespoon water

PREPARATION

Preheat oven to 425°. Mix together first 9 ingredients, and shape into a loaf. Place loaf on puff pastry sheet, fold, and place on a cookie sheet, seam side down. Brush top and sides with egg yolk mixed with water. Bake for 25 minutes.   SERVES 4

Slice, and serve with Dill Celery Sauce.

Dill Celery Sauce

1   (10¾-ounce) can cream of celery soup
½   can milk
1   tablespoon lemon juice
1   tablespoon dill
1   ounce of Sherry (optional)

PREPARATION

Mix all ingredients together. Heat, and serve over Salmon Wellington.

SERVES 4

Baked Salmon (Pink)

Shelter Island Lodge, Juneau, Alaska

4   pounds salmon fillets (skin removed)
     Salt, pepper and garlic powder
2   medium brown onions (sliced thin)
2   cups mayonnaise
4   chopped green onions
     Cayenne pepper (to taste)

PREPARATION

Place salmon in a baking dish. Season with salt, pepper and garlic powder. Top with a layer of brown onions, followed by a generous layer of mayonnaise. Sprinkle with chopped green onions and cayenne pepper. Bake for 45 minutes at 350°.   SERVES 8

Sake No Kasu Salmon Eggs 'Caviar'

Anchor Point Lodge, Juneau, Alaska

SALMON EGG PREPARATION

Boil salted water (approximately 2 tablespoons non-iodized salt per 1 cup water). Put salmon roe sacks in colander. Slowly pour salt water mixture over salmon roe while swirling eggs in colander. Membrane will shrink. Remove membrane from roe and set aside. *Do not rinse or clean roe in fresh water.*

PASTE MIXTURE

2   pounds sake no kasu
1   pound miso
1   cup sugar

PREPARATION

Mix paste ingredients together. Spread one half of paste mixture on bottom of pan. Lay cheese cloth over mixture. Place salmon eggs on top of cheese cloth. Lay another layer of cheese cloth over salmon eggs. Spread remaining paste mixture on top. Cover with plastic wrap. Ferment in refrigerator for 10 days.   SERVE ON CRACKERS

Shirley's Stuffed Salmon in Wine Marinade

by Shirley Reaume, chef of the Kenai Peninsula's Famous Great Alaska Fish Camp

1   **whole salmon, approximately 10 pounds (head removed, if preferred)**

MARINADE

2   **cups white wine**
¾   **cup lemon juice**
¾   **cup oil**
1   **large onion**
4   **cloves garlic, finely minced and crushed**
3   **tablespoons dried parsley**
1½ **teaspoons ginger**
1   **teaspoon thyme**
½   **teaspoon Tabasco sauce**
1   **teaspoon paprika**
1½ **teaspoons salt**
⅓   **teaspoon white pepper**

RICE STUFFING

2   **cups rice, cooked**
½   **cup wild rice, cooked**
½   **cup minced onion, sautéd till soft**
⅓   **cup parsley**
¼   **cup finely chopped nuts**
¾   **teaspoon salt**

PREPARATION

Combine all marinade ingredients, and bring them to a boil. Set aside immediately to cool.

Score the fish on both sides with diagonal cuts about 3 inches apart, ¼ inch deep and 6 to 8 inches long. Place the salmon in a large roasting pan, and pour the cooled marinade over the fish. Turn the salmon several times to saturate it.

Allow the salmon to marinate 2 to 3 hours; baste several times. Meanwhile, prepare the stuffing. Mix all ingredients and warm thoroughly. Set aside.

About 1 hour before serving, fill the salmon with the slightly cooled stuffing. Bake at 375° until done. Garnish with lemon slices and fresh parsley.   SERVES 12

Salmon Balls

Great Alaska Fish Camp

4   **cups smoked salmon**
1   **8-ounce package cream cheese**
1   **cup sour cream**
1   **teaspoon salt**
1   **teaspoon pepper**
1   **teaspoon sweet basil, crushed**
⅓   **cup minced onion**
1   **tablespoon lemon juice**
    Chopped nuts and chopped parsley for garnish

PREPARATION

Blend all ingredients except nuts and parsley together, and shape into bite-sized balls. Roll balls in chopped nuts and parsley. Serve as an appetizer with crackers.
SERVES 20

Great Alaska Fish Camp Salmon

4 6-ounce salmon steaks or fillets
½ red onion, sliced
2 peaches, peeled and sliced
2 ounces honey
1 ounce red wine vinegar
2 shakes curry powder
1 shake ground ginger
   Cornstarch to thicken

PREPARATION

Bake salmon with onion and peach slices at 325° for 15 minutes. Remove fish from pan. Transfer drippings into a saucepan, and add honey, vinegar, curry powder and ginger. Blend well. Thicken with cornstarch mixed with cold water, and serve over salmon.   SERVES 4

Seared Salmon With Mustard Sauce

4 6-ounce salmon steaks or fillets
1 teaspoon diced garlic
1 teaspoon diced shallots
4 ounces white wine
2 ounces Dijon mustard
6 ounces heavy cream
   Cornstarch to thicken

PREPARATION

Preheat oven to 325°.

Quickly pan-fry salmon with garlic and onions. Turn the fish to sear both sides. Remove salmon from frying pan, place in a baking dish, and bake fish for 15 minutes.

Add white wine and mustard to the frying pan, and reduce the mixture by half. Add cream, and reduce again. Thicken sauce with cornstarch mixed with cold water. Serve over salmon.   SERVES 4

Pickled Salmon

Loui Stamm, Luckey Strike Charters, Ketchikan, Alaska

2 pounds salmon fillets, skinned, rinsed,
   dried and cut into bite-sized pieces
1 cup water
1 cup distilled white vinegar
3 tablespoons granulated sugar
½ teaspoon salt
1 small white onion, thinly sliced or
   1 cup peeled whole tiny onions
1 lemon, thinly sliced
1 tablespoon mustard seeds
1 teaspoon black peppercorns, cracked
2 bay leaves
¾ cup firmly packed fresh dill sprigs

PREPARATION

Combine the water, vinegar, sugar, salt, onion, lemon, mustard seeds, peppercorns and bay leaves in a saucepan. Bring to a boil over medium-high heat. Stir until the sugar melts. Remove from the heat, and cool.

Put the fish and dill sprigs in a glass container and pour in the cooled vinegar solution, covering all the pieces. Cover, and refrigerate for at least 24 hours, or up to 5 days.

To serve, pour off the brine, and arrange the salmon with the pickled onion and lemon in a bowl. Serve as an appetizer with toothpicks for spearing.   SERVES 12

Notes

Shrimp

Shrimp is unquestionably the most popular seafood in the United States. We consume more than 500 million pounds per year. Even folks who don't like fish love shrimp, which is odd because shrimp's strong flavor is far more distinctive than many species of fish. Shrimp is caught or farmed all over the world, but most of what we consume is tropical shrimp caught off the Gulf of Mexico and South Atlantic coasts.

To protect the quality of the shrimp and because shrimp is shipped all over the world, commercial boat handlers flash-freeze it immediately upon catching. So, unless the shrimp you buy is raised or caught nearby, assume the shrimp arrived at your supermarket or fish store frozen.

Don't be too concerned about the color of your raw shrimp because they vary in color depending where they are from. They can be white, pink, brown, gray-green or striped.

Shrimp is marketed by size (count per pound), so pick the size that suits the meal you've planned and the number of people you're serving. When stuffed shrimp is on the menu, you'll purchase extra-jumbo or colossal shrimp. Shrimp curry for the family? Medium or medium-large might work. How to decide on size? Here's what you'll get, per pound:

SHELL ON

Extra-Colossal	Colossal	Extra-Jumbo	Jumbo	Extra-Large
less than 10	10 to 15	16 to 20	21 to 25	26 to 30
Large	**Medium-Large**	**Medium**	**Small**	**Extra-Small**	**Tiny**
31 to 35	36 to 42	43 to 50	51 to 60	61 to 70	70+

PEELED AND DEVEINED

Extra-Colossal	Colossal	Extra-Jumbo	Jumbo	Extra-Large
less than 14	14 to 19	20 to 25	26 to 31	32 to 38
Large	**Medium-Large**	**Medium**	**Small**	**Extra-Small**	**Tiny**
39 to 44	45 to 53	54 to 63	64 to 74	76 to 88	85 to 95

FISHWIFE'S TIPS

1. Assume the shrimp at your store has been frozen. Because shrimp are very perishable, in most cases they're immediately frozen on board the shrimping vessels to maintain quality.
2. Once you buy the shrimp, use it right away because you don't know how long it's been in the fish counter display case. If you can't use it immediately, poach it (for a curry, soup, spring rolls, et cetera) or marinate it for use the next day.
3. It's best to purchase shrimp raw and in their shells. You want shrimp that smells mild and fresh, with shiny shells that cling to the meat. If the shrimp has pulled away from its shell, it's old. The meat should be firm and springy, not mushy and soft.
4. If the odor is strong and unpleasant, don't buy it.
5. In the batch of shrimp you buy, it's possible that one or a few might be "off." Don't assume they are all bad. Examine and smell each one; discard those that you question.
6. If the shrimp is frozen when you buy it, look carefully for signs of freezer burn before you purchase it. Keep it frozen until you are ready to cook it. Defrost it in the refrigerator. If you are desperate, run part of the frozen block under cold water; carefully break off only what you need. Rewrap the remainder, and stick it back in the freezer.

Grilled Shrimp With Cajun-Spiced Butter

25 large shrimp, cleaned, shelled and deveined
 1 teaspoon black pepper
½ teaspoon cayenne pepper, or according to taste
½ teaspoon ground cumin
½ teaspoon dried rosemary, crumbled
½ teaspoon dried thyme, crumbled
¼ teaspoon dried oregano, crumbled
 2 tablespoons butter
 2 tablespoons olive oil
 2 cloves garlic, minced
 1 teaspoon Worcestershire sauce

PREPARATION

Combine the peppers, herbs and spices in a small bowl. Melt the butter in a saucepan over low heat. Add the olive oil and garlic, and cook for 3 or 4 minutes. The garlic should not get dark or burn. Add the Worcestershire and the herb mixture. (If you make this ahead, rewarm before using.)

Thread the shrimp on skewers (see Fishwife's Tip). If you want, score the shrimp lightly along the sides to speed cooking time. Brush the shrimp with the herb butter as you cook them over hot coals, about 2 minutes per side. SERVES 4

FISHWIFE'S TIP

Soak the bamboo skewers in water for about an hour before using so they won't burn while over the coals.

Pepper Shrimp

2 cups small shrimp, deveined
1 tablespoon butter (or olive oil)
1 green pepper, chopped
½ cup minced shallots, or minced round onion
2 cloves garlic, minced
⅓ cup chopped green onions
2 teaspoons ground or crushed green peppercorns (dried)
 Salt to taste

PREPARATION

Heat the butter or olive oil in a skillet. Add the green pepper and shallots, and sauté them until they are tender. Add the shrimp, garlic, green onions, peppercorns and salt. Cover, and cook slowly until shrimp are done (about 3 minutes). SERVES 4

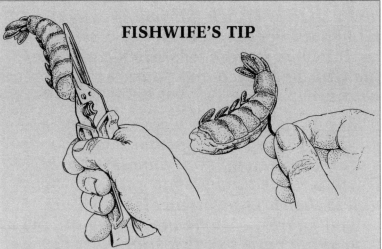

FISHWIFE'S TIP

To clean shrimp without peeling, take a sharp knife and slice through the shell and a bit of the meat on the backside of the shrimp. Remove the black vein that runs along the center of the back. Rinse quickly, and pat dry. If the shrimp is large, the shell will be tougher and you may have to snip the shell with kitchen shears.

Hot and Spicy Asian Shrimp

25 large shrimp, shelled and deveined
1½ cups orange juice
¼ cup shoyu
2 tablespoons peanut oil
2 tablespoons grated orange peel
1 tablespoon sugar
1 tablespoon minced ginger root
4 garlic cloves, minced
3 green onions, minced
¾ teaspoon dried red pepper flakes

PREPARATION

Combine all ingredients in a non-reactive bowl or container. Stir to cover shrimp well. Marinate for 30 to 45 minutes. Stir occasionally. Thread shrimp on skewers, if you wish, and grill until done, about 2 minutes per side.   SERVES 4

Shrimp in Beer

1 pound unshelled shrimp (medium-sized)
1 12-ounce can of beer
½ teaspoon dried dill weed
2 cloves garlic, minced
  Pinch of thyme
1 bay leaf
  Salt and pepper to taste

PREPARATION

Combine all ingredients except shrimp in a large pot. Bring to a boil, and cover. Simmer for 10 minutes. Add the shrimp, bring to a boil again, and simmer shrimp for 30 seconds. Remove shrimp, and drain. Serve with melted garlic or herb butter.   SERVES 4

Skewered Shrimp With Spicy Pesto
courtesy of Terri Gedo

1½ pounds shrimp, shelled and deveined
2 tablespoons peanut oil
2 tablespoons finely chopped, seeded jalapeno chilies
2 tablespoons finely chopped fresh basil
2 tablespoons minced fresh ginger root
2 cloves garlic, minced
2 teaspoons sake, dry sherry, or vermouth
1 teaspoon salt
1 teaspoon Oriental sesame oil
½ teaspoon freshly ground pepper
2 teaspoons sesame seeds

PREPARATION

Rinse shrimp, pat dry, and thread on skewers.

Mix remaining ingredients (except the sesame seeds) in a blender or food processor until a paste forms. Spoon half of the mixture into a pan (preferably large enough to hold the skewers in one layer). Add skewers, sprinkle with sesame seeds, and top with the remaining paste. Cover, and refrigerate for an hour.

Barbecue the shrimp, turning once, cooking until pink (2 to 3 minutes per side).   SERVES 6

Shrimp Spring Rolls

1   pound large shrimp, shelled and deveined
½   cup distilled white vinegar
     Pinch of salt
1   small onion, chopped
2   cloves garlic, minced
¼   teaspoon dried red pepper flakes
¼   teaspoon sugar
2   teaspoons Nam Pla, or shoyu
1   tablespoon fresh lime juice
     Rice paper wrappers
     (rounds, 6½-inch diameter)
5   lettuce leaves, washed, patted dry,
     ribs removed
2   tablespoons black sesame seeds
3   tablespoons chopped fresh cilantro
3   tablespoons chopped fresh mint
4   ounces bean sprouts

PREPARATION

Cut shrimp in half lengthwise. Combine the shrimp, vinegar and salt in a glass or ceramic bowl. Let shrimp soak for 5 minutes. Remove the shrimp, and squeeze them to remove excess vinegar. Pour off the vinegar, and return the shrimp to the same bowl. Add the onion, garlic, red pepper flakes, sugar, Nam Pla, or shoyu, and lime juice. Mix well, cover, and refrigerate for an hour or 2 until the shrimp are "cooked" (opaque).

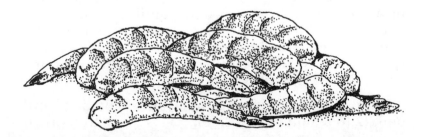

PREPARATION OF SHRIMP SPRING ROLLS

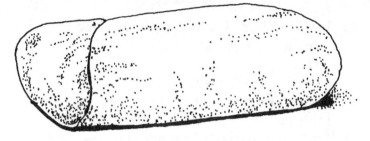

To assemble spring rolls:

1. Tear the lettuce leaves in half or in pieces that will "cradle" the shrimp. Break the bean sprouts into shrimp-length pieces.

2. Put lukewarm water (about 110°) in a bowl. Using a pastry brush, brush both sides of a rice paper wrapper with the water. (You may have to brush each side more than once.) Set the wetted wrapper on a flat working surface until it is soft and pliable. When it appears crinkled with no stiff surfaces, it is ready to use. (Prepare 2 wrappers at first. After you complete the first spring roll, rehydrate another wrapper so it will be ready when your second spring roll is completed.)

3. Center the lettuce leaf on the bottom third of the wrapper, leaving an inch or 2 at the edge. Place the shrimp in the center of the lettuce leaf. Sprinkle lightly with black pepper. Add a pinch of sesame seeds, and a scant teaspoon each of cilantro and mint on top. Top with bean sprouts (roughly 1 tablespoon).

4. Fold up the bottom of the wrapper snugly and completely over the filling. Fold the right edge, and then the left edge of the rice paper over the filling. Continue rolling, as tightly as possible without tearing the paper, until you have an enclosed cylinder. Place the spring roll, seam side down, on a platter or tray. Cover with a damp towel.

5. Repeat process until all are completed. Serve with your favorite dipping sauce.

MAKES APPROXIMATELY 15 SPRING ROLLS

HOW TO ASSEMBLE SPRING ROLLS

1. Rice paper spring roll wrappers come in several diameters and may be found in the Oriental Food section of your market. Until you rehydrate them, they are very brittle and will crack if you drop or mishandle them.

2. The wrappers are fully cooked and, once rehydrated, can be eaten as is. The rice flavor is delicate and barely discernable. If you prefer, you can fry, boil, broil or bake them.

3. To rehydrate, brush them with warm water, about 110°. If the water is too hot, the wrapper will disintegrate. If not warm enough, the wrapper will remain brittle.

4. The wrappers will not soften instantly. Depending on the temperature of the water, they could take 2 minutes or so to soften. If the wrappers don't soften, brush them with more warm water.

5. Softened wrappers will stick together, which is great for keeping them in the shape you want. But if your spring rolls touch each other, they'll stick together and will tear as you separate them.

6. Taste these spring rolls "as is" the first time, without cooking them further. The translucence of the wrapper lets the colors of your ingredients show through, making them as lovely to look at as they are tasty to eat.

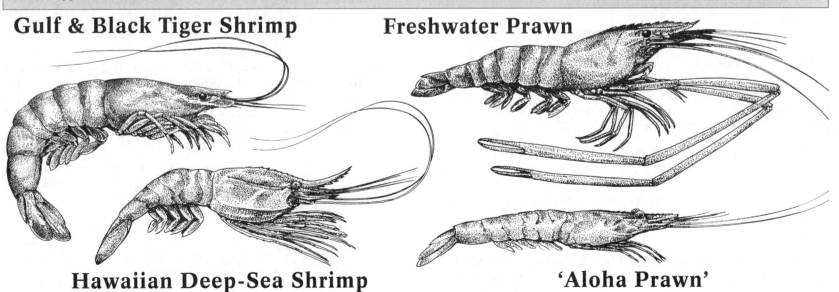

Gulf & Black Tiger Shrimp

Freshwater Prawn

Hawaiian Deep-Sea Shrimp

'Aloha Prawn'

Shrimp and Papaya Quesadillas

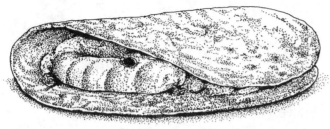

½ **pound large shrimp, shelled and deveined**
3 **tablespoons minced fresh cilantro or American parsley**
4 **tablespoons minced fresh mint leaves**
1 **clove garlic, minced**
1 **tablespoon minced ginger root**
1 **lime**
 Salt and freshly ground black pepper
8 **flour tortillas (6-inch diameter)**
1 **large ripe papaya, peeled and thinly sliced (about 1½ cups)**
3 **green onions, sliced**
½ **cup farmer's cheese, shredded**

PREPARATION

Poach shrimp; cool. Slice shrimp in half lengthwise, place in a shallow bowl, and add the cilantro, mint and ginger. Mix to coat shrimp well. Squeeze half a lime over the shrimp. Toss gently. Cover, and refrigerate until ready to use. (May be kept overnight.)

To assemble quesadillas, place the shrimp and papaya over half of each tortilla. Sprinkle with green onions and cheese (reserve some for topping the tortillas). Fold the plain half of the tortilla over the filled half, and place on an ungreased baking sheet. Top with a light sprinkling of cheese.

Bake at 350° for 7 to 10 minutes, or until light brown. Serve plain to enjoy delicate flavors or with your favorite salsa.   MAKES 8

Spicy Shrimp

½ **pound small or medium shrimp, shelled and deveined**
2 **tablespoons olive oil**
¼ **cup finely chopped onion**
2 **cloves garlic, minced**
1 **teaspoon flour**
1 **teaspoon paprika**
¼ **cup tomato sauce**
¼ **cup dry white wine**
¼ **cup fish stock, or clam juice**
½ **dried red chili pepper, seeded (or 1 teaspoon dried pepper flakes)**
¼ **teaspoon thyme**
1 **tablespoon minced parsley**
 Salt and pepper
 Pinch of sugar

PREPARATION

Sauté the onion and garlic in 1 tablespoon of the oil until the onion is soft. Stir in the flour and paprika. Add the tomato sauce, wine, stock, chili pepper, thyme, parsley, salt and pepper and sugar. Cover, and simmer slowly for 20 minutes. Heat the remaining tablespoon of oil in another skillet. When oil is very hot, add the shrimp, and stir-fry over high heat for 1 minute. Add the shrimp to the tomato sauce mixture, and cook until shrimp is done (4 to 5 minutes). Serve hot or cold.

SERVES 4

FISHWIFE'S TIP

Isn't parsley confusing? Coriander, cilantro and Chinese parsley are the same herb—flat leaves, pungent flavor. American parsley has curly leaves and a milder flavor.

Shrimp and Leek Stir-Fry

1   **pound shrimp, shelled and deveined**
1   **pound whole leeks**
3   **tablespoons chicken broth**
1   **tablespoon sake, or sherry**
2   **tablespoons shoyu**
1   **teaspoon salt**
¾   **teaspoon sugar**
¼   **cup vegetable oil**
1   **1-inch piece of ginger root, peeled and minced**
2   **cloves garlic, minced**

PREPARATION

Clean and trim the leeks by removing any discolored or damaged outer leaves. Cut off and discard the green leaves at the point where the dark green begins to lighten. Cut leeks into thin diagonal rounds or julienne into 1½-inch strips.

Combine the broth, sake or sherry, shoyu, ½ teaspoon salt and ¼ teaspoon sugar, and set aside.

Heat the oil in a wok or deep-sided skillet or pan. Quick-fry the shrimp, a few at a time, until they whiten and blister–a minute or so. Remove the shrimp from the oil, drain and set aside. Drain all but 2 tablespoons of the oil from the pan. Reheat the oil, and add the leeks. Season with ½ teaspoon salt, and stir-fry for 1 minute. Add ½ teaspoon sugar, and stir for another 2 minutes. Add ginger and garlic, and sauté for less than a minute. Return shrimp to the pan with the sake/shoyu mixture. Cover, and cook for 1 minute. Uncover, and continue to cook for 1 or 2 minutes more until shrimp are pink and done.

SERVES 4

Shrimp and Scallion Stir-Fry

¾   **pound unshelled large shrimp**
4   **tablespoons peanut oil**
1   **bunch green onions, cut into 1-inch lengths**
½   **teaspoon salt**
2   **tablespoons shoyu**
2   **tablespoons sake, or dry sherry**
1½   **teaspoons sugar**

PREPARATION

To clean shrimp, slit the back of each shell with scissors. Remove shell, and devein. Rinse shrimp, drain, and dry with paper towels.

Add 1 tablespoon of the oil to a hot skillet, and sauté the green onions and salt for 30 seconds. Remove onions from pan, and place them on a plate. Add the rest of the oil to the skillet, and heat. Add the shrimp, and stir-fry until they turn pink, about 2 minutes. Add the shoyu, sake and sugar, and stir-fry for a few seconds more. Return the green onions to the skillet; stir to heat through; and serve.

SERVES 2

Shrimp Risotto Flavored With Thai Curry and Fresh Corn

courtesy of Chef Alan Wong, Le Soleil,
Mauna Lani Bay Hotel and Bungalows

3 16/20 shrimp, peeled, deveined and sliced in half lengthwise
1 cup Risotto Base
½ cup fresh corn kernels
¼ cup peeled and diced fresh water chestnuts
¼ cup Lemongrass Broth
8 Chinese parsley (cilantro) leaves
2 tablespoons grated Provolone cheese

RISOTTO BASE

⅞ cup olive oil
1 10-ounce onion, diced
1 tablespoon minced garlic
2 tablespoons red curry paste
4 cups Arborio rice
2 tablespoons fish sauce
½ cup white wine
¾ cup coconut milk
15 kaffir lime leaves
6 lemongrass stalks, smashed
7½ cups Lemongrass Broth

LEMONGRASS BROTH

1 gallon chicken stock
1 head garlic, cut in half
2 4-inch lengths ginger root (6 ounces)
¼ ounce Chinese parsley (cilantro)
¼ ounce basil
6 lemongrass stalks, smashed
15 kaffir lime leaves
3 tablespoons fish sauce
2 Hawaiian chili peppers
1½ cups coconut milk
Salt and pepper

GARNISH

1 lemongrass stalk
2 kaffir lime leaves
1 Hawaiian chili pepper
1 pinch green onion hairs
1 pinch black sesame seeds

FISHWIFE'S TIPS

Unless you grow lemongrass or have a supermarket that stocks it, you can't always find it when you need it.

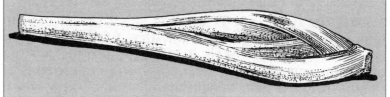

1. Substitute lemon peel - 1 tablespoon of lemon zest has the same flavor intensity as 1 tablespoon of chopped fresh lemongrass.

2. Plan ahead - freeze the bottom 5 or 6 inches of lemongrass, well-wrapped, to use in an emergency.

SHRIMP RISOTTO PREPARATION

To prepare Lemongrass Broth, bring chicken stock to a boil, add all remaining ingredients, and simmer for 20 minutes. Season with salt and pepper. Strain through a fine sieve. (Makes 1 gallon.)

(Note: When preparing risotto, constant attention and stirring is required to avoid burning the rice. Use a stainless steel sauce pot and a wooden spoon.) To prepare Risotto Base, heat olive oil in a large sauce pot. Sauté onion, garlic and curry paste; blend curry paste well. Add rice, and sauté briefly. Be sure to coat the rice well with olive oil. Add fish sauce, white wine, coconut milk, lime leaves and lemongrass.

Stirring constantly, add Lemongrass Broth to rice, ¾ cup at a time. Let rice absorb liquid before adding more. Cooking time is 11 minutes from when the first liquid is introduced to rice. The last amount of broth should be added at 9 minutes of cooking time.

When the rice is finished cooking, turn out into a large shallow pan to cool. Remove lemongrass and lime leaves. Let stand until ready to serve. (Makes 12 cups.)

To prepare the shrimp risotto, place 1 cup Risotto Base, shrimp, corn, water chestnuts and Lemongrass Broth in a sauté pan. Bring to a boil; stir constantly. When liquid is almost fully absorbed by rice, add Chinese parsley and cheese. Stir until cheese is melted; adjust ingredients. Place risotto in a bowl, and garnish.

SERVES 1

Alan Wong

Chef Alan Wong's cuisine spans the Pacific Rim, combining the best elements of several countries to create the dazzling dishes he prepared as restaurant chef of Le Soleil, a signature restaurant of the AAA 5-Diamond Mauna Lani Bay Hotel and Bungalows. His menu highlighted fresh local fish, including many less common species rarely offered in Hawai'i restaurants. La Soleil features East-West cuisine with dishes that reflect Chef Wong's creative blend of influences from the Mediterranean, the Far East and Hawai'i.

Chef Wong was named Most Outstanding Student in Kapiolani Community College's 2-year culinary program and was accepted into a 2-year apprenticeship program at the prestigious Greenbriar in West Virginia. He then became chef de partie at Lutece, one of New York City's most acclaimed restaurants. He now has his own restaurant in Honolulu.

In addition, he has garnered extensive media acclaim–as a guest on the "Today Show" and with features in Bon Appetit *and* Food & Wine*–for his lively cuisine.*

Chef Wong has participated in the James Beard Foundation's Rising Star of American Cuisine series, has received several gold medals from the American Culinary Federation and was a 1994 nominee for Best Regional Chef by the James Beard Foundation.

FISHWIFE'S TIPS

Chef Wong prepared large quantities of the Risotto Base and Lemongrass Broth at Le Soleil, which means this dish is extremely popular! Home cooks may suit their needs by cutting down the amounts of Risotto Base and Lemongrass Broth they prepare.

You will notice that Chef Wong specifies ¼ ounce cilantro and basil. Most home kitchens lack a sensitive scale, so here's how to determine the correct amount of each.

Six sprigs of cilantro with stems that are between 3 and 4 inches long equal ¼ ounce. If you have leaves only, ¼ cup loosely packed will equal ¼ ounce. If you push leaves down, they will measure ⅛ cup and equal ¼ ounce.

For basil, 3 to 5 large leaves will equal ¼ ounce.

Shrimp in Peanut Sauce
courtesy of Terri and Andy Gedo

1   pound shrimp, shelled and deveined
4   green onions, bias-cut into 1-inch pieces
1   6-ounce can straw mushrooms
8   ounces bean sprouts

PEANUT SAUCE
½   cup water
¼   cup guava jelly
2   tablespoons shoyu
2   tablespoons peanut butter
2   teaspoons cornstarch
¼   teaspoon hot chili paste

PREPARATION

Cut each shrimp in half, rinse, and pat dry. Set shrimp aside.

Combine sauce ingredients–water, jelly, shoyu, peanut butter, cornstarch and hot chili paste–in a small pan. Set aside.

Preheat a wok or non-stick skillet over medium-high heat. Add half of the shrimp to the wok. Stir-fry for 2 minutes, or until shrimp turn pink. Remove cooked shrimp, and set aside. Repeat with remaining shrimp.

Whisk sauce over medium heat, and cook until it has thickened and is bubbly. Cook, stirring constantly, for 2 minutes. Lower heat if necessary. Remove from heat.

Sauté the green onions, mushrooms and bean sprouts in the wok or skillet until tender-crisp. Add the shrimp, and heat through, mixing gently. Serve over rice and top with a generous portion of peanut sauce.

SERVES 4

Fishwife's Note: No oil is necessary in this recipe.

Garlic Shrimp
courtesy of Terri and Andy Gedo

1   pound large shrimp, shelled and deveined
1   large head garlic
1   bunch cilantro
1   tablespoon peanut oil
½   teaspoon freshly ground pepper
1   cup water
4   tablespoons black bean sauce with garlic
2   tablespoons sugar
1   small onion, chopped
2   stalks celery, chopped

PREPARATION

Separate the cloves of garlic, and peel. Put cloves in a food processor with the cilantro, and process until finely minced. Set aside.

Heat the peanut oil in a wok or heavy skillet over medium-high heat. Add the garlic-cilantro mixture and the black pepper, and sauté until the garlic is light brown. Be careful not to burn it. Add the shrimp; sauté briefly. Add the water, black bean sauce and sugar, and bring to a boil. Add the onion and celery, and remove the pan from the heat. (If you prefer, add the onion and celery with the garlic and cilantro.) Serve immediately.

SERVES 4

FISHWIFE'S TIP

How To Butterfly Shrimp:
  Cut along the outside curve of the shrimp, from the large end to the beginning of the tail. Cut almost through to the other side; devein; spread shrimp open. Lightly score the flesh, if you wish.
  Note: if the shell is on, you will need sharp scissors to make the initial cut through the shell. Do not cut through the underside of the shell when you cut through to the small curved side.

The World's Best–Bistro Scampi

As prepared by the former Bistro Restaurant in Honolulu in the 1970s

1 pound large shrimp, 16/20 size
1 tablespoon light olive oil
2 whole lemons
   Garlic cloves (to taste)
¼ pound butter cube (frozen)
   Linguini pasta
½ cup dry white wine
   Bread crumbs
   Paprika
   Parsley

PREPARATION

Freeze cube of butter ahead of time in a wrapper.

Prepare shrimp by removing heads (if you don't have headless shrimp); leave body shells and legs intact. With a sharp paring knife, carefully butterfly shrimp through top of shell (leave both halves joined). Carefully cut a small slot through body just above the tail with the point of the knife. (This will make the tail stand up when cooked.) Rinse shrimp under cold, running water to remove vein and any sand.

Cutting Shrimp

Grating Frozen Butter

Heat oil in skillet over medium-high heat. Dry shrimp with a paper towel to avoid splatter, and sauté quickly to retain crispness, or snap, of the fresh shrimp.

Slice lemons in half. Peel and mince garlic. Shred frozen butter with a hand grater and then refreeze.

When shrimp have been cooked just enough, pour remaining oil over cooked linguini (while still in strainer) for flavor.

Add garlic (to taste) to shrimp in pan, and sauté briefly while stirring. Next, add white wine and squeeze lemon juice over the sautéing shrimp (about ½ lemon to 4 shrimp). Reduce slightly by continuing to cook. Add bread crumbs to thicken slightly. Add paprika for taste and color.

Finally, add a generous amount of frozen shredded butter. Stir in quickly. Do not overcook or you will lose the creamy effect of the frozen butter.

Arrange a bed of linguini on each serving plate. Spoon shrimp and sauce mixture over linguini; garnish with parsley, and serve.

SERVES 4

Freshwater Prawns, Pohole Fern & Shichimi Roasted Garlic Sauce

courtesy of Amy Ferguson-Ota, The Ritz-Carlton, Mauna Lani

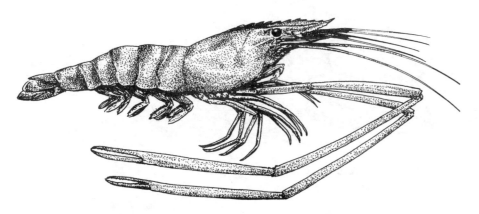

16 freshwater prawns or colossal shrimp, with heads
4 cups fish stock
1 cup Riesling wine
2 stalks lemongrass, crushed
Pinch Hawaiian salt
1 cup Shichimi Roasted Garlic Sauce (recipe follows)
16 pohole fern tops
1 ounce tobiko (flying fish roe)
Ira goma (black sesame seeds) for garnish

PREPARATION

Peel freshwater prawns, but keep heads intact. Combine fish stock, wine, lemongrass and Hawaiian salt in a stockpot; bring to a boil. Turn off heat, and add the prawns. Poach for 2 to 3 minutes, depending on their size. Spoon **Shichimi Roasted Garlic Sauce** onto individual plates. Arrange prawns and fern tops on sauce, and sprinkle with tobiko and ira goma.

SERVES 4

SHICHIMI ROASTED GARLIC SAUCE

2 large shallots, peeled and minced
2 large cloves garlic, peeled and roasted
½ cup Riesling wine
½ cup fish stock infused with lemongrass
¼ cup heavy cream
Shichimi pepper blend to taste
8 ounces unsalted butter, cut into pieces
⅛ lemon to balance flavor
Salt to taste

PREPARATION

Combine shallots, garlic, wine and fish stock in a saucepan. Simmer over medium heat until reduced by two-thirds. Add heavy cream and shichimi pepper blend. Continue to cook until reduction has thickened. Whisking constantly, add butter to reduction. Adjust flavor using lemon, salt and more shichimi pepper blend, if needed. Set aside; keep warm.

MAKES 1 CUP

Amy Ferguson-Ota

Amy Ferguson-Ota is executive chef at The Ritz-Carlton, Mauna Lani. Her specialty is blending Southwestern and Hawai'i regional cuisines with a solid foundation in classic French techniques.

She began her career as executive chef at acclaimed Houston restaurants Che, Chez Lilliane and Charley's 517.

Chef Ferguson-Ota was named one of America's Top Women Chefs at Beringer Vineyard's 1987 Summer Harvest fund raiser for the American Institute of Wine and Food. She studied French at Laval University in Quebec City, Canada, before moving to Paris to continue her education at The American College, the Sorbonne and Le Cordon Bleu.

Shrimp and Broccoli Fry

1 pound medium shrimp, cooked, shelled
  and deveined
1 tablespoon olive oil
4 large garlic cloves, minced
2 small red bell peppers, sliced
1 large onion, sliced
3 cups steamed broccoli pieces (bite-sized)
3 tablespoons coarsely chopped peanuts or
  cashews (unsalted, if you prefer)
  Salt and pepper to taste

PREPARATION

Heat the oil in a large skillet or wok over medium heat. (Use only half the oil if using a non-stick pan.) Add garlic, and sauté until golden, about 1 minute. Do not let garlic brown. Remove garlic, and set aside. Turn heat to high, and, when oil is hot, add the red peppers and onion slices. Stir-fry until vegetables are softened (not limp), no more than 2 minutes. Add the broccoli and nuts, and stir-fry briefly, just until broccoli is heated through. Put shrimp and garlic into the pan, and stir-fry until the shrimp is heated through. Sprinkle with salt and pepper to taste.　　　SERVES 4

FISHWIFE'S TIP

If you prefer to use raw shrimp, sauté it with the red pepper and onion, remove it before adding the broccoli, and return it with the garlic at the end.

Shrimp and Tofu Sauté

1 pound shrimp, shelled and deveined
2 tablespoons olive oil
3 cloves garlic, minced
4 stalks scallions, sliced
1 cup diced or sliced raw vegetables of choice:
  broccoli, carrots, zucchini, beans
1 12-ounce cake firm tofu, in 1-inch pieces
3 tablespoons oyster sauce (to taste)
  Black pepper to taste

PREPARATION

Heat oil in a skillet or wok over medium heat. Add the garlic, scallions and vegetables of your choice, and sauté for 2 to 3 minutes. Add the shrimp, and cook for 1 minute. Add the tofu cubes, and continue to sauté until the shrimp are done (pink). Add the oyster sauce and pepper; simmer for 2 minutes; and serve.　　　SERVES 4

Garlic Shrimp With Nuts

24 large or jumbo shrimp, shelled and deveined
 2 tablespoons olive oil
 3 cloves garlic, minced
 ¼ cup chopped scallions (white and green parts)
 ½ cup chopped nuts (macadamias or cashews)
 1 tablespoon Worcestershire sauce
   Dash of bottled hot sauce
   Dash of cayenne pepper
 ½ cup dry white wine, or vermouth

PREPARATION

Heat olive oil in a skillet or wok over medium heat. Add the garlic, scallions, nuts, Worcestershire, hot sauce and cayenne pepper. Sauté for 1 or 2 minutes. Add the wine and the shrimp, and cook just until shrimp are done (pink).　　　SERVES 4

Sautéed Shrimp With Orange-Honey-Mint Sauce

36 medium shrimp (about 1⅓ pounds), shelled and deveined
1 cup fresh orange juice
  Zest from one orange
2 tablespoons Triple Sec (optional)
¾ cup dry white wine
½ cup honey
2 tablespoons minced ginger root
2 tablespoons olive oil (or 1 tablespoon olive oil plus 1 tablespoon butter)
3 large garlic cloves, minced, pressed, or crushed
⅔ cup slivered almonds, optional
2 tablespoons fresh, sliced mint leaves
  Salt and pepper to taste

PREPARATION

Combine the juice, orange zest, Triple Sec, wine, honey and 1 tablespoon of the ginger in a small bowl. Set aside. Heat oil and garlic in a skillet over medium heat. Add the shrimp and the remaining tablespoon of ginger, and sauté briefly. Stir in the almonds, and continue cooking until the nuts are golden and the shrimp are cooked through, about 2 minutes. Remove the shrimp to a platter. Return the skillet to the burner, and heat briefly. Add the orange juice mixture, and bring to a boil. Reduce heat, and simmer until sauce thickens a bit. (If you want to thicken it further, combine ½ teaspoon of cornstarch with a little sauce in a bowl, stir, and add it to the skillet.) Return shrimp to the skillet, and add the mint and salt and pepper to taste. Heat through, and serve immediately.　　　　SERVES 6

Stir-Fried Shrimp, Spanish-Style

1 pound medium-sized shrimp, shelled
3 tablespoons olive oil
1 green bell pepper, cut into strips
1 cup chopped onion
1 pound mushrooms, sliced ¼ inch thick
3 cloves garlic, minced
⅓ pound ham, cubed
  Salt and pepper to taste
¼ cup dry sherry
¼ cup chicken broth

PREPARATION

Heat 2 tablespoons of the oil in a large non-stick skillet. Briefly sauté the green pepper and onion over medium-high heat. Add the shrimp, and fry, stirring constantly, for 1 minute. Remove shrimp from the skillet. Add the mushrooms, garlic, ham, salt and pepper and remaining tablespoon of oil to the pan, and cook for 2 or 3 minutes. Return shrimp to the skillet. Add the sherry and chicken broth. Stir, and scrape the pan (with a wooden utensil). When shrimp is cooked, serve immediately.　　　　SERVES 4

Shrimp Stir-Fry With Citrus Ginger Sauce on Rice

1¼ pounds medium shrimp, shelled and deveined
1 tablespoon olive oil
2 cups small yellow squash, sliced
2 cups sliced zucchini
1 cup chopped red bell pepper
½ cup sliced celery
1 pound fresh mushrooms, sliced
2 tablespoons cornstarch
1 tablespoon brown sugar
3 tablespoons shoyu
3 tablespoons orange juice
1 cup chicken broth
2 cloves garlic, minced
1 tablespoon grated, or minced, ginger root (or ½ teaspoon ground ginger)
2 tablespoons orange zest
2 tablespoons minced green onion

PREPARATION

Heat oil in a large, non-stick skillet over medium-high heat. Add shrimp; stir-fry 2 minutes; remove shrimp from skillet.

Stir-fry the squash, zucchini, red bell pepper, celery and mushrooms in two batches. Set aside.

Combine cornstarch, brown sugar, shoyu, orange juice and chicken broth in a small bowl. Set aside.

Add garlic and ginger to skillet; sauté briefly. Add cornstarch mixture, and bring to a boil over medium heat. Stir constantly to keep cornstarch from lumping. Cook for 1 minute, or until sauce is thickened.

Return shrimp and vegetables to the skillet, add orange zest and green onions and cook for a minute. Serve over cooked rice.

SERVES 4

Sweet-and-Sour Shrimp

1¼ pounds large or jumbo shrimp, shelled
2 tablespoons coarse Dijon mustard
2 tablespoons white or rice wine vinegar
2 tablespoons oil
2 tablespoons honey
Pinch of freshly ground pepper
1 tablespoon sesame seeds

PREPARATION

Combine the mustard, vinegar, oil, honey and pepper in a bowl large enough to hold all the shrimp. Add the shrimp, and toss until they are coated. Cover, and marinate in the refrigerator for an hour.

Preheat the broiler. Place shrimp on a pan 4 inches from the heat source, and cook for 4 to 6 minutes. Turn shrimp once, and baste often with the marinade. Sprinkle with sesame seeds before serving.   SERVES 4

Shrimp With Sun-Dried Tomatoes

1½ pounds shrimp, shelled and deveined
2 tablespoons olive oil
Salt and pepper to taste
2 cloves garlic, minced
¼ cup sun-dried tomatoes, chopped and rehydrated
¼ cup freshly squeezed lemon juice
1 tablespoon dry white wine
¼ cup minced parsley

PREPARATION

Heat the oil in a large non-stick skillet over medium heat. Add the shrimp, salt and pepper, and stir quickly (don't brown). Add the garlic, tomatoes and lemon juice. Cook and stir for 1 minute. Add the wine and parsley. Cook and stir for another minute, or until shrimp is cooked.   SERVES 6

Fran's Fragrant Shrimp and Rice

1½ **pounds large shrimp, shelled and deveined**
½ **teaspoon cumin seeds**
¼ **teaspoon coriander seeds**
1 **tablespoon olive oil**
¼ **teaspoon cayenne pepper**
  Salt and freshly ground black pepper to taste
2 **shallots, minced**
4 **cloves garlic, minced**
2 **tablespoons minced ginger root**
2 **teaspoons curry powder**
1 **28-oz can plum tomatoes, chopped, with juice**
1 **red bell pepper, sliced**
1 **green bell pepper, sliced**
1 **small zucchini, halved and sliced**
1 **tablespoon cornstarch blended with**
  3 tablespoons water (optional)
½ **cup chopped cilantro**
1 **tablespoon lemon juice**
1 **tablespoon lemon zest**

PREPARATION

Heat a small non-stick skillet over medium-high heat, and toast the cumin and coriander seeds. Shake the pan constantly, for 30 seconds, or until the spices are fragrant. Remove from heat. When the spices are cooled, crush them.

Heat oil in a large, non-stick skillet over medium-high heat. Add shrimp and cayenne, and sauté for 2 minutes, or until shrimp turns pink. Remove from skillet and season with salt and pepper.

Add shallots, garlic, ginger, curry powder and crushed cumin and coriander to the skillet. Sauté until shallots brown lightly. Add tomatoes, bell peppers and zucchini. Cook over medium heat, stirring often, for 10 minutes, or until the sauce is slightly thickened. (If a thicker consistency is desired, add cornstarch mixture, a tablespoon at a time.) Return the shrimp to the skillet with the cilantro, lemon juice and zest; heat through. Serve over rice.

SERVES 6

Chili-Garlic Shrimp & Snow Peas

1 pound medium shrimp, shelled and deveined
3 cloves garlic, minced
1 teaspoon minced ginger
1 tablespoon chili paste with garlic
2 tablespoons tomato paste
3 tablespoons dry sherry, or white wine
1 tablespoon oyster sauce
1 teaspoon red wine vinegar
1 teaspoon sesame oil
½ teaspoon sugar
2 tablespoons peanut oil
4 stalks Chinese cabbage, cut diagonally into 1½-inch pieces
4 ounces Chinese snow peas
3 green onions, cut into 2-inch pieces
2 tablespoons cornstarch mixed with 3 tablespoons cold water

PREPARATION

Cut shrimp in half lengthwise, and set them aside. Combine the garlic, ginger and chili paste in a small bowl. Combine the tomato paste, sherry, oyster sauce, wine vinegar, sesame oil and sugar in another bowl, and set aside.

Heat wok or large skillet to a high heat. Add half the peanut oil and coat cooking surface. When the oil begins to smoke, add the shrimp and stir-fry quickly until shrimp are no longer translucent. Remove the shrimp.

Cover the wok or pan, and return it to a high heat. Add the rest of the peanut oil and coat pan's surface. Add the garlic-ginger mixture, cabbage, snow peas and green onions. Stir-fry until the pea pods are bright green. Pour in the sauce mixture, and add the shrimp to the pan. Pour in the cornstarch-water mixture to thicken. Serve immediately.   SERVES 4

Thai-Style Shrimp Poke

courtesy of Kerry Kakazu, 'Aiea, O'ahu,
Second Place, International Category,
Sam Choy Poke Contest

½ pound large shrimp
2 cloves garlic
1 cup mint leaves
½ cup Chinese parsley (cilantro)
6 tablespoons fresh lime juice
4 tablespoons Nam Pla (fish sauce)
¼ teaspoon red curry paste
3 tablespoons fried onion flakes

PREPARATION

Peel and devein shrimp; cook shrimp in salted boiling water until they are pink (approximately 2 minutes). Cool, and chop into bite-sized pieces.

Mince the garlic, mint and parsley, and combine with the lime juice, Nam Pla and curry paste. Add shrimp and fried onion flakes. Chill well before serving.
SERVES 4

FISHWIFE'S TIPS

1. Do not overcook! Shrimp cook quickly. As soon as they change from translucent to opaque, they're done. If properly cooked, shrimp are juicy, almost crunchy.
2. Do not refreeze frozen shrimp! Use them right away.
3. Keep water off the shrimp. Remove with damp towel if necessary.

Notes

Squid and Octopus

Squid. Ika. Calamari. *No matter what you call it, many local fishermen would rebel if they saw the weird-looking mollusk on their dinner tables. In Hawai'i, "Squid's only good for 'opakapaka bait! No way I'm gonna eat it!"*

But calamari is common fare in many countries, including ours. In California, it's big business, plentiful and considered an underutilized species in southern waters. In 1992, more than 65 million pounds were hauled in by only 24 boats in a small geographic region off the West Coast of the United States.

Squid are strange-looking creatures: short tentacles on one end; a long, bullet-shaped body on the other; and all-seeing eyes in between. Cleaning it could affect your appetite, but don't overlook calamari when planning your menus. You can purchase it cleaned (body only, which is well-suited to stuffing) and skinned in your local market. It's fast and easy to prepare and is one of those high-protein, low-fat food items we're all seeking. *Try it; you'll be pleasantly surprised.*

Squid are caught year-round but are most plentiful in April, May and June. One pound of raw sliced squid makes a little over a cup when cooked.

Octopus is equally interesting to look at and just as good to eat. Large octopuses can grow to a 16-foot spread off the northern coast of Washington state, but common ones we've all seen are usually under 2 feet. Although they can't hear, they do have all-seeing eyes and change color according to their emotions! They camouflage themselves to look like their surroundings when threatened and, if given the chance, can hang on to you with the strong suckers on their tentacles.

FISHWIFE'S TIP

Don't be confused by the difference in cooking instructions with these recipes. As Marcella Hazan said, "Squid is born tender, as anyone who has had it raw knows. To remain tender, it must be cooked briefly over high heat or for a long time over low heat." Otherwise, your calamari will be rubbery.

I've found that small squid can be cooked in seconds, but large or thick squid must be simmered slowly until tender before further preparation.

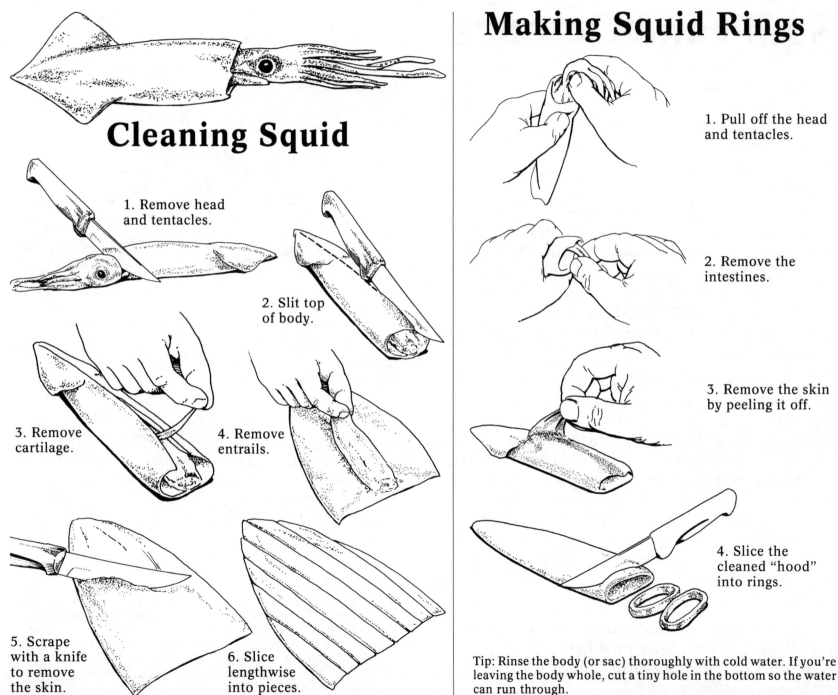

Cleaning Squid

1. Remove head and tentacles.

2. Slit top of body.

3. Remove cartilage.

4. Remove entrails.

5. Scrape with a knife to remove the skin.

6. Slice lengthwise into pieces.

Making Squid Rings

1. Pull off the head and tentacles.

2. Remove the intestines.

3. Remove the skin by peeling it off.

4. Slice the cleaned "hood" into rings.

Tip: Rinse the body (or sac) thoroughly with cold water. If you're leaving the body whole, cut a tiny hole in the bottom so the water can run through.

Cleaning Octopus

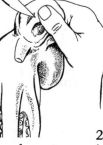

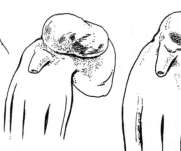

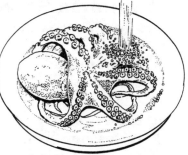

1. Cut tendon at opening of head.

2. Turn head inside out and remove entrails.

3. Remove eyes and any cartilage.

4. Use generous amounts of Hawaiian rock salt or table salt while vigorously massaging octopus to remove slime. Rinse and repeat twice.

5. Rinse thoroughly to remove slime and salt.

Helpful Hint: Freezing helps to tenderize octopus.

Cooking Octopus

1. Use a heavy pot that has a tight-fitting cover. It should be just big enough to accommodate the octopus. Place the octopus in the pot, head side up. Do not add water or any other liquid You will see why in the cooking process.

2. Cover pot and start with a medium heat. As the octopus starts to turn red, lower heat to a slow simmer.

It is important to know that octopus gets more tender the longer it is cooked but if cooked too long, it will get soft and mushy. The larger the octopus the longer it takes. A 2- to 3-pound octopus usually takes about an hour and 15 minutes to an hour and a half.

3. Simmer slowly for about an hour and 15 minutes. By now there will be quite a bit of liquid in the pot and the octopus will have shrunk considerably. Test for doneness, using a pointed chopstick, not the wooden kind you break apart. Poke the thickest portion of the leg. If the chopstick goes in easily, it is probably ready, but the best way to test it is to cut a bite-sized piece off the thick section of the leg and eat it. It should not be chewy or rubbery. If chewy, simmer for another 15 minutes or so and test again by cutting off another piece.

4. Cool and cut into bite-sized pieces. This method of cooking retains the unbelievable flavor of the octopus.

Tip: To clean pot, rub with lemon, let stand and use a scouring pad to clean off stains.

Grandma Saracino's Calamari
courtesy of Dan Saracino, Santa Clara University

    3   pounds squid
    ⅓   cup olive oil
    ¼   cup wine
    ¼   cup dry sherry
    1   tablespoon crushed fresh garlic
        Juice of ½ lemon
    1   teaspoon lemon zest
    1   teaspoon dry or fresh basil
    1   teaspoon dry or fresh oregano
    ¼   teaspoon dried, crushed red pepper
RED SAUCE
    1   pound whole, peeled tomatoes,
        canned or fresh
    1   tablespoon olive oil
    ½   green bell pepper, chopped
    1   stalk celery, chopped
    1   medium yellow onion, chopped
    3   cloves fresh garlic, minced

PREPARATION

To prepare Red Sauce, mash tomatoes and set them aside. Heat oil in a medium-sized pan; add bell pepper, celery, onion and garlic; sauté until onion is translucent. Add tomatoes, and simmer for ½ hour.

Heat ⅓ cup olive oil in a large pan over high heat. Add wine and sherry, and sauté the crushed garlic. Add lemon juice and zest; bring to a boil. Sprinkle in the herbs, and cook the liquid down about 25 percent. Lower the heat to a simmer, and add squid. Simmer for approximately 4 minutes. IMPORTANT: Do not overcook!

Pour Red Sauce over squid, and heat for 1 minute. Serve over a bed of pasta, or rice.

SERVES 8

Stir-Fried Squid With Pork

    2   pounds squid
        (clean, slit body open, and lay flat)
    1   tablespoon sherry, or white wine
    1   tablespoon shoyu
    4   dried shiitake mushrooms
        (soaked in warm water until soft)
    2   teaspoons cornstarch
    1   cup chicken broth
    2   tablespoons oil
    2   cloves garlic, minced
    2   teaspoons grated, or minced, ginger
    1   pork chop, minced
    ¼   cup sliced green onions
    ½   cup sliced bamboo shoots
    ½   teaspoon salt
    ¼   teaspoon pepper
    1   teaspoon white (or rice wine) vinegar

PREPARATION

Cut squid into bite-sized squares, or strips. Place in a bowl, and pour boiling water over; let stand for 1 minute. Drain. Mix sherry and shoyu with the squid, and set aside. Drain and quarter the mushrooms. Mix cornstarch with the chicken broth, and set aside.

Heat oil in a heavy skillet or wok. Add garlic, ginger and pork. Stir-fry until pork is white and garlic starts to brown. Mix in the green onions, bamboo shoots, salt and pepper. Add the chicken broth mixture, and stir constantly while the sauce thickens and heats to a boil. Lower the heat, cover, and cook for 2 to 3 minutes. Add the squid-shoyu mixture, and stir while heating to a simmer. Add the vinegar, and serve.

SERVES 4

Beer-Braised Calamari

1 pound small squid
  Hawaiian salt
2 12-ounce cans beer

PREPARATION

Rub squid bodies with Hawaiian salt, inside and out.

Heat a heavy pot (large enough to hold all of the squid) over medium-high heat. When it is hot, add squid. It will sizzle. When the sizzling stops, add one or two cans of beer (you want enough liquid to cover the squid).

Simmer for 30 to 45 minutes, or until squid is tender.

Remove from heat. Slice squid before serving as an appetizer. SERVES 4

Phyllis' Korean Pupu

3 pounds squid
¾ cup shoyu
  Juice of 1 lemon
1 small onion, sliced
¼ cup sesame oil
3 stalks green onion, chopped
1 tablespoon toasted sesame seeds
½ teaspoon chili powder, or 1 very small red chili pepper, finely minced

PREPARATION

Clean squid, and place in a large, flat container. Pour boiling water over squid. Pour off water. Rinse squid, and slice into strips.

Combine all remaining ingredients. Mix together with squid and serve as an appetizer. SERVES 8

Gary's Birthday Calamari

2 pounds squid
2 tablespoons fresh lemon juice
⅓ cup red wine vinegar
1½ tablespoons balsamic vinegar
1 teaspoon dried oregano, crumbled
2 cloves garlic, minced
1 teaspoon green peppercorns, crushed or ground
⅓ cup olive oil
¼ cup minced celery
¼ cup minced green onions
¼ cup minced round onion

PREPARATION

Cut the squid bodies crosswise into ⅓-inch rings. Add the rings and the lemon juice to a large pot of boiling, salted water. Cook for less than a minute, drain, and rinse under cold water.

Combine the vinegars, oregano, garlic and peppercorns in a bowl. Add the olive oil, whisking it in a thin stream until the dressing is well-blended.

Place the squid in a large bowl; add the minced vegetables, and blend well. Add the dressing, toss, cover, and chill for 4 hours. Stir occasionally. SERVES 6

Crispy Calamari With Curried Dipping Sauce

2 pounds squid, cut into rings
3 cups oil (for deep-frying)
Rice flour
2 tablespoons chopped fresh coriander

CURRIED DIPPING SAUCE
2 teaspoons whole coriander seeds, crushed
2 cloves garlic, minced
2 teaspoons curry powder
¼ teaspoon ground ginger
⅓ cup water
½ teaspoon shoyu
1 rounded tablespoon hoi sin sauce
1 tablespoon fresh lemon juice

PREPARATION

To prepare sauce, heat 1 tablespoon of the oil in a small saucepan over low heat. Add the coriander seeds, garlic, curry powder and ginger; stir occasionally until the garlic is limp, about 3 minutes. Turn heat to high, and add ⅓ cup water. Boil until the mixture is reduced, about 2 minutes. Add the shoyu, hoi sin sauce and lemon juice; bring mixture to a boil. Remove from heat, and strain sauce into a small bowl. Set aside.

Heat remaining oil to 375° in a wok or deep pan.

Toss squid rings with flour until all are lightly coated. Deep-fry squid to a golden brown in batches that fit comfortably in your wok without crowding. Remove rings, drain, and keep them warm in a 300° oven. Repeat until all squid is cooked.

Garnish squid with coriander leaves, and serve as an appetizer with the sauce on the side.

SERVES 6

Spanish Calamari

2 pounds squid, cut into rings
2 tablespoons salt
2 tablespoons dry sherry
1 tablespoon brandy
½ cup white wine
1 tablespoon balsamic vinegar
¼ cup fresh lemon juice
3 tablespoons fresh lime juice
2 tablespoons olive oil
¼ cup chopped red onion
2 to 3 tablespoons minced Kalamata olives
3 cloves garlic, minced
¼ cup chopped mixed parsley and cilantro
1 tablespoon dried oregano
Freshly ground black pepper

PREPARATION

Bring 3 to 4 quarts of water to a boil in a large pot. Add squid and salt, and blanch for 1 minute. Remove squid immediately, and transfer to a bowl of ice water (to stop the cooking). Drain well.

Combine the sherry, brandy, wine, vinegar, lemon juice and lime juice in a non-reactive container. Slowly whisk in the olive oil. Add remaining ingredients.

Add squid rings to the container, mix well; cover, and refrigerate for at least 8 hours.

SERVES 6

FISHWIFE'S TIP

To serve this appetizer as a salad, drain the squid and reserve the marinade for dressing. Serve the squid over salad greens mixed with cucumbers and tomatoes. Top with crumbled feta cheese and sprinkle with additional marinade if desired.

Stewed Squid With Sausage

2 pounds squid (cut bodies into rings no more than ½ inch wide)
3 tablespoons olive oil
1 large onion, chopped
1 stalk celery, chopped
2 large cloves garlic, minced
1 teaspoon dried thyme
1 teaspoon dried red pepper flakes (reduce amount to suit taste)
2 cups tomato purée
½ cup white wine (or water)
½ cup red wine
1½ teaspoons coarse salt (or to taste)
¼ teaspoon sugar
2 links hot Italian sausage, cooked and sliced
¼ cup minced parsley

PREPARATION

Heat oil in a large pot (4-quart capacity), and sauté onion and celery until tender. Do not brown. Add garlic, thyme and red pepper flakes, and sauté briefly until fragrant. Add tomato purée, white and red wine, salt and sugar, and bring to a simmer. Cover, and simmer gently for about 5 minutes.

Stir in cooked sausage, and cover again. Simmer gently, stirring occasionally, for about 15 minutes. Add a little water if mixture seems dry. Stir in the squid and parsley, and heat briefly, just until mixture is very hot.

SERVES 6

FISHWIFE'S TIP

If you need to reheat the stew, do so gently so you don't toughen the squid.

Calamari With Coconut Milk and Papaya

1 pound squid bodies, cut into ½-inch rings
½ cup coconut milk
2 tablespoons lime juice
½ cup chopped celery
¼ cup minced green bell pepper (or use Anaheim pepper)
3 tablespoons minced green onions
Salt and pepper to taste
1 large papaya

PREPARATION

Bring 2 quarts of water to a boil in a large pot. Add the squid. Drain immediately, and transfer the squid to a bowl of ice water. Drain again.

Combine cooled squid with ¼ cup coconut milk, lime juice, celery, green pepper, green onions and salt and pepper to taste. Add more coconut milk if necessary to achieve the consistency you want.

Peel and seed papaya, and cut the fruit into cubes. Fold papaya into squid mixture just before serving.

SERVES 4

Octopus Curry
courtesy of the Captain Cook Hotel,
Christmas Island

The hotel's octopus is extremely tender because it is skinned and cooked longer than it would be for Quick Octopus Pupu, recipe below.

1   **2-pound cleaned octopus**
1   **each, onion, carrot, celery stalk and green pepper, all cut into large chunks**
2   **cloves garlic**
1   **16-ounce can of tomatoes**
     Curry powder
     Salt to taste
     Coconut milk

PREPARATION

Put the octopus in a large pot, and cover octopus with water. Boil it long enough for the skin to soften. You'll know it's done when you can scrape the skin off of the tentacles with a spoon. Remove octopus from the pot and skin it. Cut into 1-inch pieces.

Using a large pan, sauté the onions, carrots and garlic in butter until vegetables are soft. Add the celery and green peppers, and sauté for a few more minutes. Add the tomatoes, curry powder (just for color) and salt, and simmer together. Add the coconut milk (enough to thicken the mixture) and octopus. Simmer until the octopus is heated through. Serve.

SERVES 6

> **IMPORTANT**
> See octopus cleaning and preparation on page 121.

Baked Octopus
courtesy of Mitchell Uyeno, Kahala Caterers

3   **pounds octopus, frozen at least 1 week (and thawed)**
     Rock salt
     Red pepper flakes

PREPARATION

Preheat oven to 350°. *Lomi* (mix) thawed octopus with rock salt and pepper flakes (amounts to suit your taste). Place octopus beak down on a baking tray, or baking dish, and spread tentacles. Bake until tips of tentacles are crisp and curled. When necessary, drain liquid that accumulates in the pan; keep the pan dry. Remove from heat, and thinly slice octopus and serve as an appetizer.

SERVES 10

Quick Octopus Pupu
courtesy of the Captain Cook Hotel,
Christmas Island

1   **whole cleaned octopus**
1   **cup shoyu**
1   **"finger" ginger root**
2   **cloves garlic**
     Sugar to taste
     Tabasco to taste

PREPARATION

Boil the octopus until it turns red. Remove it from the pot, and cut the octopus into small pieces. Put the pieces into a serving bowl, and add shoyu (it should come to the same level as the octopus pieces). Add remaining ingredients, and serve.

SERVES 6

Mike's Calamari, South African-Style

courtesy of Mike Schultz, president of the
South African Deep Sea Angling Association

1 squid, 7 to 9 inches long
   (clean, cut body down one side, and lay flat)
1 lemon
   Milk (enough to cover steak)
   Seasoned flour
   (use herbs and spices of your choice)
   Oil for deep-frying

PREPARATION

Pat the squid steak dry, and place in a shallow container. Squeeze or sprinkle lemon juice over both sides of the steak, and let stand for half an hour. Add milk to cover the steak (don't worry about the lemon juice), and soak for 2 hours. Remove the steak from the milk, and pat it dry with paper towels. Place steak in the refrigerator for about 20 minutes.

Meanwhile, mix flour and seasonings on a plate or in a bag. Heat oil in a deep-fryer until very hot (365° to 385°). Remove the squid from the refrigerator, and dust steak with the flour. Carefully place the steak in the hot oil. Cook for only 24 *seconds*. Remove to a plate, slice, and serve as an appetizer.   SERVES 4

Squid Salad With Mint Dressing

2 pounds small whole squid
1 tablespoon dried thyme
2 bay leaves, broken
1 teaspoon green peppercorns
1 teaspoon black peppercorns
1 teaspoon celery seeds
½ teaspoon mustard seeds
⅔ cup coarse salt
½ cup fresh mint leaves, packed
½ teaspoon dry mustard
2 tablespoons lemon juice
1 tablespoon minced jalapeno pepper
½ teaspoon salt
1 teaspoon sugar
½ teaspoon black pepper
⅓ cup olive oil
   Lemon slices
   Fresh mint leaves

PREPARATION

Bring a large saucepan of water to a boil; add thyme, bay leaves, peppercorns, celery and mustard seeds, salt and squid. Remove the pan from the heat after 1 minute. Let stand for 30 minutes. Pour into a colander and drain.

Combine mint leaves, dry mustard, lemon juice, jalapeno pepper, salt, sugar and black pepper in a food processor. When ingredients are puréed, add the olive oil in a thin stream until blended.

Slice the squid bodies into thin rings. Place in a large bowl, and combine with the dressing. Garnish with lemon slices and mint and serve as an appetizer.
                                                    SERVES 8

Squid Salad Italiano

3   pounds fresh squid, cleaned and washed
4   cups water
2   tablespoons red wine vinegar
1   onion pierced with 4 whole cloves
2   bay leaves
¼   teaspoon hot red pepper flakes
1   teaspoon dried oregano
2   parsley sprigs
1   tablespoon lemon juice
    Salt and freshly ground pepper to taste
½   cup finely chopped onion
1   cup diced plum tomatoes
1   tablespoon drained capers
1   clove garlic, minced
½   cup finely chopped fresh parsley leaves
¼   cup red wine vinegar
2   tablespoons fresh lemon juice
½   cup olive oil
    (start with less, and add as necessary)

PREPARATION

Cut the squid into bite-sized pieces, making rings out of the body. Bring the water to a boil in a saucepan. Add the squid rings (and tentacles, if you want), vinegar, onion, bay leaves, hot red pepper flakes, oregano, parsley sprigs, lemon juice and salt and pepper. Simmer very gently for 25 to 30 minutes, or until tender. Remove the pan from the heat, and cool to room temperature.

Remove the squid from the cooking liquid, drain well, and place in a salad bowl. Add the remaining ingredients, except the olive oil, and toss well. Add the olive oil slowly, mixing lightly before adding more. Use enough to help bind the dressing ingredients together, balance flavors and give you the consistency you want. Serve at room temperature.

SERVES 6

Calamari Lentil Salad
courtesy of Chef Kirby Wong,
Ilikai Yacht Club Restaurant, Honolulu

1¼   pounds squid
1⅓   cups lentils
¼   cup diced celery
¼   cup diced Maui onions
¼   cup diced carrots
¼   cup diced Japanese cucumbers
¼   cup diced red bell peppers
2   tablespoons chopped cilantro
1   cup Red Wine Vinaigrette (¼ cup per serving)

RED WINE VINAIGRETTE
½   cup red wine vinegar
¼   tablespoon Dijon mustard
¼   teaspoon freshly ground black pepper
⅛   teaspoon chopped garlic
⅛   cup sugar
     Juice of 1 lime
     Salt to taste
1   cup olive oil

PREPARATION

Clean squid (see page 120); cut into bite-sized pieces. Cook in salted, boiling water for 10 seconds (do not overcook). Cool squid in ice water; remove; set aside.

Cook lentils in lightly salted water until tender; drain, and cool.

To prepare Red Wine Vinaigrette, whisk together all ingredients except olive oil. Slowly whisk in olive oil.
MAKES 1½ cups

Combine squid, lentils and remaining salad ingredients. Toss with 1 cup Red Wine Vinaigrette.

SERVES 4

Notes

Notes

Seafood Pasta Dinners

Seafood and pasta star in these recipes, a combination that has a lot going for it. First of all, seafood and pasta each begin as low-fat ingredients and, when combined in a recipe, remain that way if you're careful to avoid excessive amounts of butter, cream and cheeses in your sauces. Second, the combination is quick-cooking (the pasta cooks while you prepare the other ingredients), and, finally, pasta pairs well with all types of seafood and sauces!

Simple, easy, delicious–what could be better?

Alan's Shrimp Scampi on Pasta

1   pound raw medium shrimp, shelled
2   tablespoons olive oil
1   red bell pepper, diced
3   cloves garlic, minced
½   teaspoon dried basil
½   teaspoon dried oregano
    Salt and pepper to taste
¼   cup chopped fresh parsley
2   tablespoons butter
2   tablespoons fresh lemon juice
8   ounces spinach fettuccini, cooked and hot

PREPARATION

Heat 2 tablespoons oil in a non-stick skillet over medium heat. Add red bell pepper, and cook, stirring constantly, for 3 or 4 minutes, or until tender. Add the shrimp, garlic, basil, oregano and salt and pepper; cook, turning shrimp once, for 3 to 5 minutes, or until the shrimp are pink. Remove from the heat and stir in the parsley, butter and lemon juice. Toss with the pasta.

SERVES 4

FISHWIFE'S TIPS

How To Cook Pasta:

1. Bring water (at least 4 quarts per pound) to a wild boil over high heat. Add pasta and salt, and lower heat to medium-high or whatever temperature will keep a rolling boil going. Test the pasta frequently; you don't want it so limp that it turns to mush when you bite it, nor should it be crunchy. The Italians say *al dente*, or "to the tooth," which I translate to mean it should still have enough firmness that you know you're biting something.

2. If you must precook your pasta, remember that it will stick together while it waits. Put it in a colander and refresh it in one of two ways: Run tap water over it, and drain before adding it to your sauce. The pasta will be cold. If you want the precooked pasta hot, don't discard the water. Leave it in its pot. Pour it over the pasta before using. (If you have one of those neat pots that includes a pasta strainer, leave the pasta in the strainer and just pop it back into the water for a second.)

'Ahi Pasta Puttanesca

¾ pound 'ahi fillets, or steaks, ½ inch thick
3 tablespoons olive oil
½ teaspoon crushed, dried red chilies
3 cloves garlic, minced
3 cups chopped plum tomatoes (4 large)
¾ cup dry white wine
⅓ cup pitted, chopped Greek olives
1 tablespoon capers, drained
1 teaspoon dried oregano, or 1 tablespoon
   fresh oregano
2 tablespoons chopped anchovy fillets
   (optional)
   Black pepper to taste
¼ cup chopped parsley
   Salt and freshly ground black pepper to taste
1 pound vermicelli, cooked

PREPARATION

Heat half the olive oil in a large skillet over medium heat. Add the chilies, garlic, tomatoes, wine, olives, capers, oregano and anchovy fillets. Cook at a gentle boil, uncovered, until the sauce is thickened, about 15 minutes. Stir occasionally. Add black pepper and parsley; cover, and remove from heat.

Brush the 'ahi with the remaining oil; season with salt and pepper. Broil, pan-fry, or grill fish, turning once, until done, about 4 minutes. Slice 'ahi into bite-sized pieces.

Place pasta on a serving platter; top with the sauce and 'ahi.   SERVES 4

FISHWIFE'S TIP

Cut the 'ahi into bite-sized pieces, and pan-fry while sauce is cooking. Try this dish with ¾ pound medium shrimp, or an 'ahi/shrimp combination.

Seafood Pasta With Tomato Sauce

1 pound fish steak, about ¾ inch thick
1 tablespoon fresh lemon juice
2 teaspoons olive oil
1 teaspoon minced fresh thyme
1 teaspoon lemon zest
1 clove garlic, minced
   Salt and freshly ground pepper to taste
12 ounces small pasta shells, cooked

QUICK TOMATO SAUCE
1 tablespoon olive oil
1 small onion, chopped
3 pounds plum tomatoes, chopped
2 cloves garlic, minced
1 tablespoon fresh lemon juice
1 tablespoon chopped fresh Italian parsley
2 teaspoons chopped fresh thyme
½ teaspoon lemon zest
   Salt and freshly ground pepper

PREPARATION

To prepare fish, combine lemon juice, oil, thyme, lemon zest, garlic and salt and pepper in a small bowl. Coat both sides of steak with mixture, and place fish in a shallow, non-reactive pan. Refrigerate for an hour.

To prepare sauce, heat oil in a heavy pan over medium heat. Add onion; sauté until tender. Mix in tomatoes. Cook for 5 minutes; stir frequently. Continue to cook until the sauce begins to thicken, about 10 minutes. Add next 5 ingredients, and cook until sauce is well-blended, about 2 minutes. Salt and pepper to taste.

Grill, or broil, fish, turning once, until just cooked through. Break, or cut fish into 1-inch chunks.

Combine cooked pasta and sauce in a large bowl. Top with fish.   SERVES 4

Grilled 'Ahi With Veggies on Fettuccini

1¾ pounds tuna fillets, or steaks, 1 inch thick
¼ cup olive oil
1 large garlic clove, peeled and cut into quarters, or crushed
  Salt and freshly ground pepper
1 red onion, chopped
3 plum tomatoes, chopped
1 cup chicken, or vegetable, broth
2 tablespoons fresh lemon juice
2 teaspoons lemon zest
12 ounces fettuccini, cooked
3 cups loosely packed spinach leaves, cut into thin strips
⅓ cup fresh basil leaves, cut into thin strips
3 tablespoons freshly grated Parmesan cheese

PREPARATION

Combine oil and garlic; let stand at least 30 minutes. Or, briefly run oil and garlic through a food processor to blend flavors quickly.

When coals are ready (or broiler is hot), brush 'ahi with garlic oil (about a tablespoon) and season with salt and pepper. Place fish on rack, and cook 'ahi for 4 to 6 minutes. Turn fillets once. 'Ahi should be pink inside. Remove from heat, and break the fish into small chunks. Set aside.

Heat 2 tablespoons of the garlic oil in a large skillet over medium heat. Add onion, and sauté until softened. Mix in tomatoes, ¾ cup stock, lemon juice and zest. Simmer; add fettuccini, and cook until pasta is warmed. Mix in 'ahi and spinach; cook until warmed through. (Add remaining stock, if you wish.) Remove from heat; sprinkle with basil and Parmesan.

SERVES 6

Emily's Shrimp and Asian Noodles

1½ pounds small shrimp, cooked, shelled and deveined
½ pound rice sticks, cooked
2 cups fresh bean sprouts
2 cups shredded cabbage, or bok choy
1 cup minced green onions, or chives
1 cup fresh mint leaves, slivered
1 cup fresh cilantro leaves
1 cup coarsely chopped peanuts
½ cup seeded and chopped fresh green chilies
SAUCE
1 cup fish sauce (nuoc mam)
1 cup water
⅓ cup fresh lime juice
¼ cup sugar
3 fresh red or green chilies, seeded
4 cloves garlic, halved

PREPARATION

To prepare sauce, purée all sauce ingredients in a food processor until smooth. Set aside. (May be refrigerated for 1 week.)

Place rice noodles in a shallow serving dish. Gently mix in the bean sprouts, cabbage, green onions, mint and cilantro. Add sauce, ½ cup at a time, until it coats the noodles well. Place remainder of sauce in a bowl to pass at the table. Top the noodles with peanuts, chilies and shrimp.

SERVES 4

Baked Shrimp and Orzo

1 pound medium shrimp, shelled and deveined
2 teaspoons olive oil
1 small onion, chopped
3 cloves garlic, minced
¼ cup chicken broth
1 28-ounce can plum tomatoes, chopped, with juice
¼ cup minced parsley
1 tablespoon capers, drained and crushed
1 teaspoon dried oregano
1 teaspoon dried basil
Salt and freshly ground black pepper to taste
Dash hot pepper sauce
1 cup orzo (rice-shaped pasta), cooked and drained
½ cup crumbled feta cheese

PREPARATION

Preheat oven to 425°. Heat oil in a deep skillet, or large saucepan, over medium heat. Add onion and garlic, and sauté until onion softens. Add broth, and boil for a minute. Stir in tomatoes and their juice, half of the parsley, the capers, oregano, basil, salt, pepper and hot pepper sauce. Cook for a few minutes. Add shrimp, and cook briefly, stirring, until shrimp are pink. Remove pan from heat. Combine shrimp mixture with cooked orzo in a casserole dish (about 2-quart capacity). Sprinkle with remaining parsley and feta cheese. Bake for 10 minutes, or until the cheese bubbles.

SERVES 6

FISHWIFE'S TIP

Pasta made from 100 percent semolina flour doesn't turn soggy on the plate as quickly as pasta made with softer flours, but it also takes a bit longer to cook.

Hawaiian 'Ahi With Linguini

recipe by Barbara Gray
courtesy of the Department of Business, Economic Development and Tourism

1 pound 'ahi fillet
2 tablespoons olive oil
½ onion, thinly sliced
1 clove garlic, minced
1 tablespoon butter (preferably clarified)
1 tablespoon sun-dried tomatoes, thinly sliced
2 tablespoons capers
¼ cup freshly grated Parmesan cheese
½ teaspoon salt
1 pound linguini, cooked
1 tablespoon minced parsley

PREPARATION

Cut 'ahi into cubes. Heat 1 tablespoon of the olive oil in a skillet, and sauté onion and garlic until golden brown; set aside. Heat the remaining tablespoon oil and the butter in a skillet, and sauté 'ahi for 2 minutes, or until just done. Add onion mixture, sun-dried tomatoes, capers, Parmesan and salt; toss gently. Serve over linguini, and sprinkle with parsley.

SERVES 4

Seafood Pasta With Spinach-Herb Pesto

1½ pounds fish fillets or steaks, cubed (red or white meat)
1 tablespoon olive oil
1 teaspoon dried oregano, or thyme
1 to 2 cloves garlic, minced
   Salt and freshly ground pepper to taste
½ cup chicken broth
12 ounces cooked pasta

PESTO
1½ cups lightly packed fresh spinach leaves (rinsed and drained)
¼ cup lightly packed fresh oregano or thyme
¼ cup grated Parmesan cheese
¼ cup olive oil

PREPARATION

Put all pesto ingredients in a food processor. Process until the spinach is finely chopped (not puréed). Set aside ¼ cup of the pesto and refrigerate, or freeze, the rest in a covered container.

Heat the tablespoon of olive oil in a non-stick skillet over medium heat. Add the fish, dried oregano, or thyme, minced garlic and salt and pepper. Sauté until fish is half-cooked. Remove the fish to a bowl. To the skillet, add the reserved pesto and chicken broth. Cook until well-blended. Add more pesto to sauce as needed. Return fish to the skillet; cook until fish is done, and remove pan from heat. Serve over hot pasta.

SERVES 4

FISHWIFE'S TIP
Don't add oil to the pasta water. If you cook your pasta in an ample amount of water and stir it occasionally, it won't stick together.

Szechwan Seafood Pasta

1¼ pounds fish fillet or steak, cut into 1-inch cubes
3 tablespoons shoyu
1 tablespoon rice wine vinegar
1 teaspoon chili paste (or to taste)
1 tablespoon olive oil
2 cloves garlic, minced
1 tablespoon minced ginger root
1 small red bell pepper, cut into strips
2 ounces snow peas, cut diagonally into thirds
¼ cup green onions, sliced into rounds
12 ounces vermicelli
½ cup coarsely chopped peanuts

PREPARATION

Combine shoyu, rice wine vinegar and chili paste in a small bowl; set aside.

Heat the olive oil in a skillet, or wok, large enough to hold all ingredients, including pasta. Stir-fry the garlic and ginger for 30 seconds. Add the fish; stir-fry briefly, about 2 minutes. Add the bell pepper, snow peas and green onions; stir-fry until fish is opaque. Add shoyu mixture and pasta; remove from heat; blend well. Top with peanuts.

SERVES 4

Sweet and Spicy Shrimp Lo Mein

½ pound shrimp, shelled, deveined and
  cut in half crosswise, if large
3 tablespoons shoyu
1 teaspoon dry sherry
1 teaspoon cornstarch
¼ cup dry sherry
¼ cup chicken broth
¼ cup hoi sin sauce
1 teaspoon brown sugar
2 teaspoons peanut oil
3 cloves garlic, minced
3 teaspoons minced ginger root
¼ teaspoon dried red pepper flakes (or to taste)
¼ cup water
1 small carrot, peeled and thinly sliced
¼ cup sliced green onions
6 ounces snow peas
1 small zucchini, quartered and sliced
1 bell pepper, seeded and cut into thin strips
1 pound lo mein noodles, cooked

PREPARATION

Combine half the shoyu, 1 teaspoon dry sherry and cornstarch in a bowl. Add shrimp, and combine until well-coated. Cover, and refrigerate.

Combine the ¼ cup sherry, chicken stock, hoi sin, remaining shoyu and brown sugar. Set aside.

Heat 1 teaspoon oil in a wok, or large, non-stick skillet over high heat. Add shrimp, and stir-fry until shrimp is opaque, about 2 minutes. Remove shrimp from wok immediately, and set aside. Add the remaining oil with the garlic, ginger and red pepper flakes. Stir-fry briefly (less than a minute). Add water, carrot slices and green onions; stir-fry for 2 minutes. Add the stock mixture and remaining vegetables, and cook for 2 minutes. Stir frequently. Return the shrimp to the pan with the noodles. Stir gently to combine.   SERVES 6

Herbed Shrimp and Pasta With Shallot-Butter Sauce

24 jumbo shrimp, shelled and deveined
3 tablespoons butter
2 tablespoons dried herbs
  Salt and freshly ground pepper to taste
⅓ cup chopped shallots, or minced round onion
1 cup dry white wine
¼ cup heavy cream
2 tablespoons Dijon mustard
¼ cup minced parsley
10 ounces pasta, cooked

PREPARATION

Melt 1 tablespoon butter in a large, non-stick skillet over medium-high heat. Add dried herbs, and sauté briefly. Add shrimp, salt and pepper, and cook for about 3 minutes, or until done. Transfer shrimp to a dish.

Add 1 tablespoon butter to the skillet with the shallots and wine. Bring to a boil, and cook over high heat until the liquid is reduced by half. Add cream and mustard, and cook, stirring, for about 2 minutes. Return shrimp to the sauce, and stir until shrimp are just warmed through. Sprinkle with half the parsley, and stir in all or part of the remaining butter, if you wish. Pour shrimp and sauce over cooked pasta and sprinkle with remaining parsley.   SERVES 4

FISHWIFE'S TIP

Pasta comes in an endless variety of shapes, sizes, colors and "flavors," such as squid ink, tomato, basil, etc. Shelves that used to offer plain, old spaghetti and elbow macaroni now display everything from rice-shaped orzo, wagon wheels and spirals, to giant shells and tubes that hold your favorite filling and everything in between. When trying to decide which to purchase, keep the pasta sauce in mind. Shaped pasta scoops up heavier sauces and the goodies in it, while spaghetti, linguini and orzo are fine with light, simple sauces.

Japanese Noodles With Seafood

2 pounds fish (or small shrimp, shelled and deveined, or combination)
½ cup sesame seeds
1 teaspoon sesame oil
14 ounces dried soba noodles
7 fresh or rehydrated shiitake mushrooms, thinly sliced
1 pound fresh bean sprouts
3 cucumbers, peeled, halved and thinly sliced
6 green onions, sliced

DRESSING
⅔ cup rice wine vinegar
¼ cup shoyu
¼ cup light sesame oil
3 tablespoons mirin
1 teaspoon dry mustard
¼ teaspoon cayenne pepper (optional)
  Salt to taste (optional)

PREPARATION

To prepare dressing, whisk together the vinegar, shoyu, oil, mirin and mustard in a small bowl. Season with cayenne pepper and salt, if you wish. Cover and leave at room temperature. (May be prepared 1 day in advance.)

To prepare the fish, cut it into bite-sized cubes. Toss with sesame seeds to coat; press in sesame seeds, if necessary. Heat sesame oil in a non-stick skillet over medium-high heat. Sauté cubes quickly until opaque. Remove fish from pan, and let cool.

Bring a large pot of salted water to a boil. Add noodles, and boil until tender, about 3 minutes. Drain and refresh in cold water. Drain again, and place in a large bowl. Add a bit of dressing, and toss to coat. (If you prepare this dish in advance, cover and refrigerate bean sprouts and noodles separately. Bring to room temperature before serving.)

Add fish, mushrooms, bean sprouts, cucumbers and onions to the noodles. Drizzle with dressing. Toss gently to combine. Serve over lettuce leaves.   SERVES 12

Lemon Shrimp With Pasta

1½ pounds large shrimp, shelled and deveined
¼ cup rice wine vinegar
3 tablespoons lemon juice
1 tablespoon sugar
1½ tablespoons minced ginger root
1 tablespoon shoyu
12 ounces fettuccini (mix green and white)
1 tablespoon sesame oil
⅓ cup sliced green onions
1 tablespoon lemon zest
  Salt and freshly ground pepper to taste
3 teaspoons black sesame seeds

PREPARATION

Combine vinegar, lemon juice, sugar, ginger and shoyu in a large pot over high heat. Add shrimp when the mixture begins to boil. Remove pot from heat, and cover. Let it stand until shrimp is cooked (stir occasionally). Remove shrimp to a dish (refrigerate if making ahead). Save liquid.

Put cooked pasta on a large platter with the shrimp, reserved liquid, sesame oil, green onions and lemon zest. Toss well. Season with salt and pepper to taste. Top with sesame seeds.

SERVES 6

Prawns With Feta Cheese and Pasta

courtesy of Margo Elliopoulos,
Bluewater Cuisine Catering

16 king prawns, shelled and deveined
 3 tablespoons olive oil
 1 onion, chopped
 4 garlic cloves, crushed
 8 large, ripe peeled tomatoes, roughly chopped
    (or 1 large can with juice)
 2 tablespoons tomato paste
½ cup dry white wine (or retsina)
 1 teaspoon dried oregano
 4 sprigs parsley, chopped
    Salt and freshly ground black pepper to taste
 6 ounces feta cheese, cut into 1-inch cubes
 1 pound fettuccini, cooked

PREPARATION

Heat oil in a large skillet over medium heat. Lightly fry the onion and garlic until the onion pieces are transparent and soft. Add the tomatoes (and liquid, if using canned tomatoes), tomato paste, wine and oregano. Simmer for 20 to 30 minutes until some of the liquid has evaporated and the mixture has the texture of a thick sauce. Add parsley, and season with salt and pepper to taste.

Add the feta and the prawns to the sauce and continue cooking for 2 to 3 minutes, long enough to cook the prawns and heat the feta. If cooked too long, prawns will be tough and feta will melt too much.

Serve hot over fettuccini with French bread. Enjoy with a glass of chilled retsina.

SERVES 4

Margo Elliopoulos

Margo Elliopoulos of Bluewater Cuisine Catering could fuel any fire with her boundless energy. She was featured by Hawaii Business *magazine in 1989 as one of Hawai'i's most successful businesswomen, and Bluewater Cuisine Catering was named number 5 in the nation in* Home Office Magazine's *annual Business of the Year recognition in 1992. After studying at the Cordon Bleu and La Varenne in Paris, she returned stateside, first as pastry chef at Sun Valley Lodge (Idaho), then to open and manage a delicatessen and serve as assistant catering consultant with Caravannere, San Francisco's largest catering company at that time. Chef Elliopoulos moved to Kona in 1979, fired up by her first taste of catering, and Bluewater Cuisine was born, the first endeavor of its kind in the area. It quickly expanded into a booming business with private catering, conventions incentive group marketing, in-flight catering services and a nationally renown 75-seat oceanside restaurant called the Beach Club. To meet the changing demands of the food industry, Bluewater Cuisine has successfully diversified and Chef Elliopoulos continues to find new and creative ways to enhance her business.*

Shrimp With Shiitake Mushrooms on Noodles

1   pound medium shrimp, shelled and deveined
2   teaspoons dry sherry
2   teaspoons cornstarch
12 ounces thin pasta
1   tablespoon sesame oil
3   tablespoons peanut oil
1   bunch green onions, thinly sliced
3   to 4 tablespoons minced, or slivered,
    fresh ginger
12 dried shiitake mushrooms, soaked, drained
    and sliced
6   ribs bok choy, cut into ¾-inch slices
8   ounces snow peas
1   teaspoon ground Szechwan peppercorns
¾   cup chicken broth
2   tablespoons dry sherry
½   cup shoyu

PREPARATION

Combine shrimp, 2 teaspoons dry sherry and cornstarch.

Cook pasta in a pot of salted, boiling water until done. Drain; rinse with cold water. When cool and well-drained, place pasta in a bowl and mix with sesame oil.

Heat 1 tablespoon peanut oil in a heavy skillet over medium-high heat. Add half of the green onions and ginger, and briefly stir-fry (about 30 seconds). Add mushrooms, and stir-fry for 30 seconds. Add shrimp, and stir-fry until they begin to turn pink. Remove shrimp from the skillet immediately.

Add 1 to 2 tablespoons oil to the skillet. When the oil is hot, add the remaining green onions and ginger, and stir-fry for 30 seconds. Add the bok choy, and stir-fry to soften, about 2 minutes. Add the snow peas, and stir-fry until they turn a darker green. Add peppercorns and pasta, and stir-fry briefly to heat through. Return the shrimp to the skillet, and briefly stir-fry. Add broth/sherry/shoyu mixture and stir until the noodles absorb the broth and the shrimp are cooked.   SERVES 4

Oriental Seafood Pasta

¾   pound fish, cut into bite-sized pieces
4   tablespoons peanut oil
½   pound Chinese egg noodles cooked
1   clove garlic, minced
1   teaspoon minced ginger root
4   cups shredded green cabbage
1   bunch green onions, sliced
1   onion, sliced
1   small carrot, peeled and sliced
¼   cup oyster sauce
2   tablespoons shoyu
⅛   teaspoon dried red pepper flakes

PREPARATION

Heat 2 tablespoons oil in a wok or deep skillet over high heat. Add noodles, and stir-fry briefly, 2 to 3 minutes. Remove to a large bowl. Add remaining oil to the pan, and heat until very hot. Add fish, garlic and ginger, and stir-fry until fish is opaque, about 2 minutes. Remove fish. Add cabbage, green onions, onion, carrot, oyster sauce, shoyu and red pepper flakes. Stir-fry 2 minutes; return fish and noodles to the pan, and stir-fry until fish is done and all ingredients are blended, 2 to 3 minutes.

SERVES 4

Shrimp and Veggie Pasta Dinner

- 1 **pound large shrimp (about 20), shelled and deveined**
- 2 **tablespoons butter**
- 2 **tablespoons olive oil**
- 3 **cloves garlic, minced**
- 1 **cup sliced, or diced, eggplant**
- ½ **cup sliced mushrooms**
- ½ **teaspoon dried oregano**
- ½ **teaspoon dried basil**
- ½ **teaspoon dried thyme**
- ¼ **cup chicken broth (optional)**
- 1 **cup sliced zucchini**
- 16 **ounces spaghetti, cooked**
- ¼ **cup grated Parmesan cheese**

PREPARATION

Heat 1 tablespoon each of butter and olive oil in a non-stick skillet over medium-high heat. Add shrimp and half of the garlic; cook until shrimp are pink, about 2 minutes per side. Remove shrimp with a slotted spoon, and set them aside.

If necessary, add remaining butter and oil to the skillet; melt butter. Add the remaining garlic, eggplant, mushrooms, herbs and half of the chicken broth; sauté about 2 minutes. Add the zucchini, and cook until all vegetables are tender. (Add remaining broth, if necessary.) Reduce heat to low. Return shrimp to the skillet, and heat through. Pour over the spaghetti, toss, and sprinkle with Parmesan. SERVES 4

FISHWIFE'S TIP

This recipe originally called for ¾ cup (1½ sticks) of butter, which would have been yummy, but deadly. To reduce the amount of fat, I used a non-stick pan, cut the amount of butter to 2 tablespoons, added 2 tablespoons olive oil and used chicken broth, a bit at a time, to keep the veggies soft and provide some liquid replacement for the missing ½ cup of butter. You may want to add more butter to your version.

Shrimp and Pasta With Basil Purée

- 1½ **pounds large shrimp, shelled and deveined**
- 3 **cups fresh basil leaves**
- 3 **tablespoons olive oil**
- 2 **tablespoons fresh lemon juice**
- ¼ **cup extra-virgin olive oil**
  Salt and freshly ground pepper to taste
- ½ **pound pasta (bow ties, shells)**
- 1 **cup chopped zucchini**
- 2 **tomatoes, chopped**

PREPARATION

To prepare basil purée, process the basil leaves with 2 tablespoons of the oil until smooth. Transfer to a bowl, and whisk in the lemon juice, ¼ cup extra-virgin oil, salt and pepper. Set aside.

Cook pasta with the remaining tablespoon of olive oil in a large pot of boiling water. Drain.

At the same time, bring another pot of water to a boil. Cook the shrimp until they are opaque, about 1½ minutes. Drain, and rinse under cold water; pat shrimp dry.

Combine the pasta and shrimp in a large bowl. Toss with the basil purée, zucchini and tomatoes.

SERVES 8

Seafood Combo Pasta Salad

¾ pound medium shrimp, shelled and deveined, crab meat, or scallops

12 ounces pasta, cooked, drained and tossed in 1 to 2 tablespoons olive oil

1 cucumber, coarsely chopped

2 large tangerines, peeled and sectioned

1 tablespoon tangerine zest

3 green onions, thinly sliced

DRESSING

¼ cup rice wine vinegar

2 tablespoons brown sugar

1 tablespoon Dijon mustard

½ teaspoon red pepper flakes

Salt and freshly ground black pepper to taste

PREPARATION

To prepare dressing, combine ingredients in a non-reactive bowl; set aside.

Cook shrimp in gently boiling water until opaque, about 3 minutes. Remove from heat; drain, run under cold water, and drain again.

Place pasta in a serving dish. Add seafood, cucumber, tangerine sections and zest and green onions. Toss with dressing.   SERVES 4

Ono With Hot Peanut Pasta

1½ pounds ono, cut into 8 serving-sized pieces

Salt and freshly ground black pepper to taste

2 tablespoons olive oil

1 large onion, minced

3 jalapeno peppers, seeded and minced

3 cloves garlic, minced

½ cup dry white wine

1 teaspoon coriander seeds, crushed

2 tablespoons minced ginger root

1 cup dry-roasted, unsalted peanuts, ground

1 tablespoon shoyu

1 tablespoon brown sugar

1 tablespoon lemon zest

10 ounces angel hair pasta, cooked

PREPARATION

Season fish lightly with salt and pepper; set aside.

Heat oil in a large non-stick skillet over medium-high heat. Add onion and jalapenos, and sauté for 3 minutes, or until onion pieces soften. Remove from skillet. Add garlic and fish, and cook fish for 2 minutes per side. Return the onion/pepper mixture to the skillet with the wine, coriander seeds, ginger, ground peanuts, shoyu, brown sugar and lemon zest. Simmer for 2 minutes, or until the fish is done. Remove fish; gently mix sauce with pasta. Top with fish.   SERVES 4

Shell   **Fettuccine**   **Elbow**   **Bow Tie**   **Linguini**

Notes

Soups, Stews and Seafood Combos

Soups and stews are the ultimate comfort foods, and seafood combinations are equally inviting. The savory aroma of a simmering soup and the delightful bursts of flavor in each heaping spoonful of seafood bring back memories of home and family in all of us.

Fortunately, soups and stews aren't "just for family" anymore. Restaurants now offer several soup options on their menus, not just the "soup of the day." As a testament to the growing, universal appeal of steaming soups, hearty stews and creative combinations of seafood, 11 of the recipes in this chapter were created by Hawai'i's top chefs!

Soups and stews are perfect centerpieces for a meal; team with a fresh, crisp salad and crusty bread to complete the wholesome dinner (although in Hawai'i, a little hot rice on the side is a must).

Hawaiian Fish Stew
by Barbara Gray, courtesy of DBEDT, Ocean Resources Branch

1½   **pounds monchong fillets, skinned and cut into 1-inch cubes**
1½   **pounds hapu'upu'u fillets, skinned and cut into 1-inch cubes**
¼   **cup olive oil**
1   **cup coarsely chopped onion**
1⅓   **cups coarsely chopped bell pepper**
1   **clove garlic, minced**
3½   **pounds whole tomatoes, coarsely chopped and drained**
1   **cup dry white wine**
2   **teaspoons salt**
1   **teaspoon fresh thyme, or ¼ teaspoon dried**
¼   **teaspoon black pepper, coarsely ground**
2   **bay leaves**
1   **tablespoon minced parsley**

PREPARATION

Heat olive oil in a large skillet. Sauté onion, bell pepper and garlic until tender, 2 to 3 minutes. Add tomatoes, white wine, 1 teaspoon salt, thyme, black pepper and bay leaves; blend well. Bring sauce to a boil; reduce and simmer, uncovered, for 15 minutes, or until slightly thickened.

Sprinkle fish cubes with the remaining salt. Place fish on top of tomato sauce. Simmer, covered, for 10 to 15 minutes, or until fish is cooked. Sprinkle with minced parsley.   SERVES 8

Gingered Onaga Soup, Flavored With Tamarind
courtesy of Rey Dasalla, executive chef,
Hau Tree Lanai Restaurant

1   **pound onaga fillet, skin on**
½   **cup tomato concasse (see Chef's Note)**
    Fresh vegetables of choice
    (won bok, white stem cabbage, string beans,
    squash blossom, et cetera)
FISH STOCK
1   **round onion, diced coarsely**
1   **tomato, cut into wedges**
2½ **ounces ginger root, peeled and crushed**
2   **pieces tamarind**
3   **stalks green onions, cut into 1-inch lengths**
2   **pounds fish bones**
    Water to cover the bones
    Salt and pepper to taste

PREPARATION

To prepare stock, combine onion, tomato, ginger, tamarind, green onions, fish bones and water in a stock pot. Bring stock to a boil, and simmer for 10 minutes. Skim and strain through double-layered cheesecloth. Salt and pepper to taste.

Cut fresh onaga into ½-ounce portions (about 32 pieces, ¼ inch thick). Poach fish and your choice of vegetables with half of the fish stock. Transfer to a soup tureen with the tomato concasse, and add remaining hot stock.

SERVES 6

Chef's Note: Tomato concasse is a tomato that has been peeled, seeded and sliced. To loosen skin from tomato, bring water to a boil and put tomato into boiling water for 30 to 60 seconds, depending on the size of the tomato.

Rey Dasalla

Competition pays off for Rey Dasalla, executive chef of the Hau Tree Lanai Restaurant at the New Otani Kaimana Beach Hotel. He has been recognized for his culinary expertise at the Annual Hawaii Seafood Culinary Excellence Competition and other culinary events, capturing 1st place in 1991 for his entrée, and 1st and 2nd places in 1992 and 1993 for his soups. As a member of the Chef's de Cuisine, Honolulu Chapter, and the Professional Cooks of Hawaii, he participates in fund raising events to benefit children in the state. The New Otani Kaimana Beach Hotel overlooks the historic San Souci Beach, where writer Robert Louis Stevenson often sat under the hau trees to write and reflect on his life.

Shrimp Broth

1   **pound shrimp shells**
3½ **cups water**
2   **cloves garlic, peeled and crushed**
    Salt and pepper
1   **tablespoon dried thyme**
6   **black peppercorns**
1   **bay leaf**
1   **round onion, chunked**
    Chopped celery and carrots (optional)

PREPARATION

Place all ingredients in a large pot. Bring to a boil; reduce heat, and simmer for 20 minutes. Strain, and set aside to cool. Refrigerate.

MAKES 3 cups

FISHWIFE'S TIP
If you will not use all the broth within a few days, freeze the remainder in ice cube trays. Store the frozen cubes in a Ziploc bag to use as you need them–1 or several at a time.

Striped Marlin Coconut Chowder

courtesy of Chef Kevin Carlson,
Volcano Spice Company

¾ **pound striped marlin, swordfish or ono fillets (cut into ½-inch cubes)**
5 **pounds fish bones to boil for stock ('opakapaka or other white fish)**
1 **large Maui onion, chopped**
2 **medium celery stalks, chopped**
2 **small carrots, chopped**
4 **cloves garlic**
½ **head small cabbage, chopped**
1 **small sweet potato, cut into ½-inch cubes**
1 **small yucca root or white potato, cut into ½-inch cubes**
1 **large "finger" fresh ginger, grated**
¾ **cup canned coconut milk**
½ **cup chopped green onion**
¼ **cup chopped Chinese parsley (cilantro)**
   Juice from 1 small lime, and ½ of the peel
4 **bay leaves**
   Spice blend of your choice for garnish

PREPARATION

Wash off fish bones, remove gills and split the heads. Put into a 6-quart stock pot, and cover with water. Bring to a boil, and cook over medium heat for 45 minutes. Remove bones, and strain liquid. Return liquid to the pot, and continue to cook until liquid is reduced to about 1 quart. Add all other ingredients, except the fish and garnish, and bring to a slow boil. Cook for 15 minutes; then add the fish. Immediately remove chowder from heat. Garnish each portion with 1 tablespoon of the spice blend of your choice, and serve.

SERVES 4

Chef's Note: Canned clam juice may be substituted for fish stock.

Kevin Carlson

Originally from Florida and "born to be a Gypsy" with a father who was "King of the BBQ," Chef Kevin Carlson says his destiny was set before he knew it. The Gypsy blood carried him throughout the mainland, Central and South America, the Caribbean and finally to Maui. He has worked at the unique upcountry restaurant The Hali'imaile General Store for the past 5 years. Kevin has always been liberal with spices in his style of cooking, so the creation of his gourmet spice company has been a natural progression in his career. He feels fortunate that restaurant owners Beverly and Joe Gannon have given him the freedom to "play with his spice blends" while performing his duties as roundsman. Kevin now markets 9 spice blends under his Volcano Spice label.

FISHWIFE'S TIPS

1. Use the freshest fish possible. If you cannot get it fresh, use fish that hasn't been frozen too long.

2. Experiment with combinations of seafood rather than using only one type. Mixtures of red- and white-meat fish with shellfish are especially tasty.

3. Remember to not overcook fish. Unlike beef, fish will not get more tender the longer it cooks. Always lower the heat before adding fish to a soup, stew or seafood combination, and simmer gently until the fish is cooked.

4. Feel free to substitute chicken broth for fish stock in a soup recipe. The soup will be milder, but can be punched up with some clam juice.

5. When you add milk to a soup, chowder or stew, warm it first and then add it slowly to the pot. If you pour cold milk or cream into hot broth, the milk may curdle.

6. When making a soup or fish stock, skim off the foam that rises to the top during cooking.

7. Always throw gills away, They are not made of anything edible–just hard tissue and blood.

Ellen's Favorite Cioppino

3 pounds fish fillets, cut into 1-inch chunks
1 pound shrimp, peeled and deveined
2 pounds other seafood (crabs, scallops, clams)
¼ cup olive oil
2 large onions, chopped
2 green peppers, seeded and chopped
6 celery stalks, chopped
5 cloves garlic, pressed or minced
1 cup minced parsley
1 48-ounce can V-8 juice
1½ cups dry red wine
1½ cups dry white wine
1 8-ounce bottle clam juice
1 6-ounce can tomato paste
3 teaspoons dried oregano
3 teaspoons dried basil
4 bay leaves
1 teaspoon crushed red pepper flakes
2 teaspoons sugar
   Salt and pepper to taste

PREPARATION

Heat olive oil in a heavy pot over medium-high heat. Add the onions, peppers, celery, garlic and three-quarters of the parsley, and sauté until the vegetables are soft (do not overcook). Add all other ingredients except the seafood, stir until well blended and bring to just below the boiling point. Reduce the heat and simmer the stock for one-half hour. Stir frequently.

Add the seafood in given order: fish, shrimp, crab and scallops and fresh clams last. Cook only until the seafood is done, approximately 10 to 15 minutes. Serve in bowls topped with remaining parsley.   SERVES 6

FISHWIFE'S TIP
The stock can be made ahead of time and frozen with only the seafood to be added at a later date.

Ticia's 'Hot-Stuff' Chowder

1 pound ono fillets, cut into ½-inch cubes
1 tablespoon butter
1 tablespoon olive oil
2 tablespoons minced fresh ginger
2 teaspoons cumin seeds
2 cloves garlic, minced
1 large onion, chopped
2 tablespoons curry powder
6 cups broth (chicken, fish or vegetable)
1 pound potatoes, peeled and cut into
   ½-inch pieces (approximately 3 medium)
1 small green bell pepper, cut into
   ½-inch pieces
1 small carrot, peeled and cut into
   ½-inch pieces (optional)
1 tablespoon lemon zest
1 teaspoon crushed red pepper flakes
   (alter to taste)
¼ cup thinly sliced green onions
1 cup plain, low-fat yogurt
6 lemon wedges

PREPARATION

Combine butter, oil, ginger, cumin seeds, garlic and onion in a large pot (6-quart) over medium-high heat. Sauté until onion has softened, about 5 minutes. Add curry powder, and stir until well-blended. Slowly add the broth with the potatoes, green pepper, carrot, lemon zest and red pepper flakes. Bring to a boil, cover, and lower heat. Simmer soup until potatoes and carrots are tender enough to pierce (not soft), 15 to 20 minutes.

Add fish; cover, and simmer until pieces are opaque, 2 or 3 minutes. Remove from heat, and add 1 tablespoon green onions. You may add the remaining green onions and yogurt to the soup before serving, or pass them with lemon wedges at the table.   SERVES 6

Green Chili Ono Chowder

courtesy of Jean W. Hull, CCE,
University of Hawaii, West Hawaii Campus

1 pound ono fillet, skinned and cut into
  1-inch pieces
1 onion, chopped
2 tablespoons butter
1 red bell pepper, seeded and diced
1 pound green Anaheim chilies, seeded
  (approximately 6)
½ cup flour
3 cups fish stock
2 cups 2-percent milk, hot
1 teaspoon salt
½ teaspoon cracked black pepper
2 pounds potatoes, peeled, minced and cooked
  (approximately 6 medium)
1 cup frozen corn, thawed
  Parsley for garnish

PREPARATION

Using a large saucepan, sauté onion in butter for 3 to 4 minutes. Add red bell pepper and chilies, and sauté for 2 minutes. Sprinkle flour over vegetables, and cook them over medium heat for 1 minute. Add fish stock, and simmer, stirring frequently, for 10 to 15 minutes. Add milk, salt and pepper, and continue to simmer, stirring occasionally, for 10 to 15 minutes. Add ono, cooked potatoes and corn, and simmer, stirring occasionally, for 5 to 8 minutes. Keep chowder on low heat or in a hot water bath until ready to serve. Taste, and correct seasonings. Garnish with finely chopped parsley. Suggest 6-ounce servings.

SERVES 8

Chef's Note: Chicken stock plus clam juice makes an excellent substitute for fish stock. However, the following recipe is easy to make and freezes well.

Fish Stock

1 pound fish trimmings (head and bones,
  washed) minus gills, guts and skin
1 quart cold water
1 cup dry white wine
1 carrot, coarsely chopped
2 celery stalks, coarsely chopped
½ yellow onion, chopped
1 bay leaf
1½ teaspoons peppercorns
5 parsley stems
1 whole clove

PREPARATION

Combine all ingredients in a large pot, and simmer for 30 to 45 minutes; skim occasionally. Strain, cool, and refrigerate until ready to use.

Jean W. Hull

Jean Hull's culinary background began as a teen learning about food in her family's Michigan restaurant, which could explain her interest in guiding students in her role as food service coordinator at the University of Hawaii–West Hawaii. Through the curriculum she developed, students access 4 levels of completion within the Associate of Science 2-year degree. Her students get hands-on experience assisting noted local, regional, national and international chefs at community culinary events. Over the past 3 years, Chef Hull's food service students have taken a total of 10 gold, 4 silver and 2 bronze medals at the Hawaii Student Arts Culinary Competition. She was named Chef of the Year by the American Culinary Federation Kona-Kohala Chef's De Cuisine Association in 1992 and has been advisor to the Junior Chef's Chapter since 1990.

Hearty Mediterranean Seafood Stew

1½ pounds ono, swordfish or firm fish fillets
1 pound snapper or mahimahi fillets
½ pound medium shrimp, shelled and deveined
2 tablespoons olive oil
2 tablespoons minced garlic
1 large onion, coarsely chopped
1 leek, coarsely chopped
1 large fennel bulb, cut into ¼-inch pieces
1 tablespoon dried fennel seeds,
  broken or chopped
1 35-ounce can plum tomatoes, drained
2 8-ounce bottles clam juice
2 cups dry white wine
3 tablespoons tomato paste
2 large bay leaves
½ teaspoon dried marjoram
1 teaspoon dried oregano
1 teaspoon salt
2 tablespoons fresh lemon juice
½ teaspoon freshly ground pepper
½ cup minced parsley

PREPARATION

Heat oil in a large non-reactive pot over medium-low temperature. Add garlic, onion, leek, fennel bulb and seeds. Cover, and cook about 10 minutes Add tomatoes, clam juice, wine, tomato paste, bay leaves, marjoram, oregano and salt. Bring to a boil over high heat. Reduce heat to low, cover, and cook for 20 to 30 minutes.

Increase heat to medium. Add shrimp, and stir for 1 minute. Stir in the remaining seafood, and cook until the fish is opaque, about 4 minutes. Add the lemon juice, pepper and parsley, and simmer for a minute. Season with more salt (if necessary) and pepper.

SERVES 8

Kona Sportsman's Smoked Chowder

courtesy of Stafford DeCambra,
executive chef, American Hawaii Cruises

2 pounds smoked marlin or smoked firm fish
4 ears fresh corn
¼ cup butter
¼ cup diced onions
¼ cup diced celery
¼ cup diced leeks
¼ cup diced carrots
¼ cup diced red bell pepper
¼ cup diced green pepper
1 pound diced, unpeeled potatoes (3 medium)
2 cloves minced garlic
1 teaspoon dried thyme leaves
½ cup all-purpose flour
2½ quarts strong fish stock, hot
2 quarts heavy cream
1 cup Dijon mustard

PREPARATION

Place cleaned ears of corn in smoker, and smoke 20 minutes, or until dark brown. Remove kernels from ears; set aside.

In a heavy 8-quart pot, melt butter over medium heat. Sauté all vegetables, except corn, along with the garlic and thyme for 3 to 5 minutes. Add flour, stirring until well-blended and evenly cooked, 2 to 3 minutes. Remove from heat.

Stir in hot fish stock; simmer for 10 minutes. Add fish and heavy cream; simmer 5 minutes more. Stir in mustard and smoked corn.

SERVES 12

Pacific 'Ahi, Tomato and Basil Soup
courtesy of Chef Joel Schaefer, Angelica's Cafe

½ pound 'ahi fillet (sashimi grade),
  cut into ¼-inch cubes
1 tablespoon olive oil
2 tablespoons minced garlic
1 pound Maui onions, diced
  (approximately 3 medium)
3 pounds tomato concasse (blanched, peeled,
  seeded and chopped tomato)
5 cups chicken stock
1 cup slivered fresh basil
2½ teaspoons kosher salt
1 teaspoon freshly ground black pepper

PREPARATION

Heat olive oil in a 1-gallon soup pot until hot. Add garlic and onion pieces. Cook, stirring often, until onions are soft, approximately 5 minutes. Add tomato concasse, and cook over medium-high heat for 5 minutes to release juices. Stir often. Add stock. Bring to a boil, and cook for 10 minutes. Transfer solids to blender, or food processor, and purée to a smooth consistency. Reserve liquid. Return puréed mixture to liquid, and bring back to a boil. Turn off heat, add basil, salt and pepper. Place 6 ounces of soup into each serving bowl. Add 1 ounce 'ahi, and garnish with basil.

SERVES 8

Joel Schaefer

Chef Joel Schaefer sees food as an art form that responds to creativity. He uses the freshest ingredients, simplifies the combinations of flavors, and fashions dishes that appeal to the eye as well as the palate. As a member of the Chef de Cuisine, Honolulu Chapter, he is involved in cooking demonstrations, fund raising events and culinary competitions.

Three-Onion Seafood Soup

2 pounds white-meat fish fillets, cut into
  1-inch cubes
2 tablespoons olive oil
2 tablespoons butter
3 cloves garlic, minced
4 cups chopped round onions
4 cups chopped leeks
½ cup chopped green onions
¼ cup flour
1 cup dry white wine
8 cups fish stock
2 bay leaves
2 tablespoons black peppercorns
  Salt to taste

PREPARATION

Heat olive oil and butter in a large pot over medium-high heat. Add garlic, and stir briefly. Add the round onions and leeks; cook, stirring, until they are soft and golden brown. Add the green onions; stir briefly. Sprinkle in the flour, and blend well.

Add the wine, stir, and bring the mixture to a boil. Add the fish stock, bay leaves, peppercorns and salt. Bring to a boil, and let simmer, uncovered, for 15 minutes. Add the fish, and cook for 3 to 4 minutes, until fish is opaque. Remove pot from the heat. Remove bay leaves and peppercorns.

SERVES 8

FISHWIFE'S TIP
Securing the bay leaves and peppercorns in cheesecloth before adding them to the pot will make them easier to remove before serving. Otherwise, coarsely crack the peppercorns before adding to the pot.

'Ahi Tortino With Ogo Served With Calamari Salad in a Maui Onion Lilikoi Dressing

courtesy of Chef Roberto Aita,
Bistro Molokini, Wailea, Maui

3 ounces 'ahi fillet, sliced
1 tablespoon sliced Roma (Italian) tomato (seedless)
1 tablespoon peeled, sliced Japanese cucumber
1 tablespoon fresh tomato juice
½ teaspoon ogo, chopped

BROTH
½ celery stalk
½ round onion
½ carrot
1 tablespoon salt
2 pints water

MAUI ONION LILIKOI DRESSING
½ cup fresh lilikoi (passion fruit) pulp
1 Maui onion, steamed
½ tablespoon chopped cilantro
1 tablespoon rice vinegar
¼ cup fresh lime juice
½ teaspoon salt

CALAMARI SALAD
2 ounces squid, cleaned and cut into strips
½ cup finely diced mango
2 tablespoons finely diced roasted pepper
1 tablespoon diced green onions
1 tablespoon diced Roma tomato

Chef Aita's recipe was recognized by Project LEAN for its low fat content–only 1 gram of fat per serving!

Roberto Aita

Chef Roberto Aita has created a new cuisine, "Nuova Cucina Autentica," for Bistro Molokini at the Grand Hyatt Wailea. Chef Aita's "new" 1,000-year-old recipes, the food of his Italian forefathers, have been adapted to modern tastes and dietary needs by substituting stocks for cream and stressing the freshest produce and finest fish, meats and poultry. The result is rustic, farm-style cooking that becomes light and delicate in presentation, always with a touch of unexpected flavor. Chef Aita first learned about food by watching his grandmother create a delectable array of dishes. During his training, he worked in all 20 regions of Italy and discovered a variety of regional cooking styles and influences. By the time he was 25, Chef Aita had worked in 9 hotels and 15 restaurants. He has worked in many of the world's leading restaurants and hotels, including Sandro's in New York and the famed Villa d'Este in Lake Como, Italy.

PREPARATION

To prepare the 'Ahi Tortino, combine the sliced 'ahi, tomato, cucumber, fresh tomato juice and ogo. Place in a mold (use a small bowl, about 5-ounce size). Refrigerate for 1 hour.

To prepare the broth, put the celery, onion, carrot and salt in the water and bring to a boil. Cook the strips of squid in this broth for 2 minutes. Remove the strips, and set aside.

To prepare the dressing, blend the fruit pulp, onion and cilantro. Slowly add the rice vinegar. Slowly add the lime juice. Adjust with salt to taste. Set aside until ready to serve.

To prepare the salad, mix the mango, roasted pepper, green onion and tomato in a mixing bowl. Add the strips of cooked squid, and combine with ½ cup of the Maui Onion Lilikoi Dressing. Ladle the rest of the dressing on the plate, and arrange the 'ahi tortino on top. Garnish with fresh ogo and serve as an appetizer.

SERVES 4

Fish Stew With Eggplant

2 pounds firm fish fillets, cut into
  2-inch chunks
1 pound eggplant
  Salt and pepper
¼ cup olive oil
1 large onion, sliced
2 cloves garlic, minced
½ teaspoon oregano or thyme
1 bay leaf
4 cups tomatoes, seeded and chopped
2 tablespoons tomato paste
¼ cup chopped parsley
1 cup sliced mushrooms
1 cup bread crumbs
4 tablespoons butter

PREPARATION

Peel the eggplant, and cut it into 1-inch cubes. Sprinkle lightly with salt, and let stand for 30 minutes. Squeeze excess moisture out of the eggplant before using.

Heat 2 tablespoons of the oil in a skillet, and sauté the onion slices until they are soft. Add the eggplant and the remaining oil as needed, and sauté for 5 minutes. Add garlic, oregano, bay leaf, tomatoes and tomato paste. Cover skillet, and simmer mixture for 5 minutes. Uncover, and cook for 5 more minutes. Season with salt and pepper.

Gently blend the fish chunks, parsley and mushrooms into the mixture, and spoon everything into a baking dish. Sauté the bread crumbs in the butter, and sprinkle over the fish stew. Bake at 425° for 15 minutes, or until the fish is done and the stew is bubbly.

SERVES 6

Tropical Fish Soup With Shutome
courtesy of Rey Dasalla

4 ounces shutome fillet, diced
4 ounces opah fillet, diced
4 ounces uku fillet, skin on
1 cup diced onion
½ cup diced celery
½ cup diced leeks
6 tablespoons unsalted butter
1 teaspoon mashed garlic
6 tablespoons flour
¼ cup white wine
3 cups canned clam juice
2 cups milk
1 cup heavy cream
½ cup coconut milk
½ cup clams, chopped
½ cup crab meat
  Salt and pepper to taste
3 tablespoons parsley
2 tablespoons dry sherry
¼ cup green onions for garnish

PREPARATION

Combine onion, celery, leeks and butter in a large pot and "sweat" the vegetables over medium heat. Add garlic, and cook 1 minute. Add flour to make a roux. Add white wine and clam juice. Bring to a boil, and simmer for 15 minutes. Combine milk, heavy cream and coconut milk in a separate saucepan, and bring to a boil. Add milk mixture to the soup; simmer 15 minutes.

Remove soup from the heat, purée the mixture, and return it to the stove. Add chopped clams, crab meat and fresh fish. Season with salt and pepper. Finish soup by adding chopped parsley and dry sherry. Ladle soup into soup bowls, and garnish with green onions.

SERVES 4

Quick Fish Chili

2 pounds firm fish fillets or steaks
¼ cup chili powder
2 tablespoons olive oil
1 large onion, chopped
1 large green bell pepper, diced
1 large red bell pepper, diced
¼ teaspoon dried basil
¼ teaspoon dried thyme
¼ teaspoon dried oregano
¼ teaspoon ground cumin
¼ teaspoon cayenne pepper
¼ teaspoon dried red pepper flakes
1 teaspoon salt
3 bay leaves
½ cup tomato paste
2 cups fish stock (or chicken and clam juice)
½ cup red wine
1½ pounds ripe tomatoes, seeded and diced
1 large zucchini, sliced and quartered
2 cups cooked red kidney beans
  Salt and pepper to taste

PREPARATION

Cut fish into small cubes (¼ to ⅓ inch).

Heat the oil in a large, non-stick pot over medium heat. Cook the onion until limp. Add bell peppers, and cook for 3 minutes. Add herbs, cayenne pepper, red pepper flakes, salt, bay leaves and remaining chili powder, and mix well. Stir in the tomato paste. Cook for 2 minutes, then add stock, wine and tomatoes. Increase heat, and bring ingredients to a boil. Add the zucchini and beans, reduce heat, and simmer until beans are heated through. Add the fish, and stir constantly until it is opaque, about 3 minutes. Salt and pepper to taste.

SERVES 6

Alice's Seafood Kabobs With Parsley Pesto

1 pound ono, swordfish or other firm, white-fleshed fillets
1½ pounds medium shrimp (32 pieces)

PARSLEY PESTO
4 garlic cloves, peeled
4 medium Serrano or jalapeno chilies, seeded and quartered
1 cup Chinese parsley (cilantro) leaves, firmly packed
⅓ cup parsley leaves, firmly packed
2 tablespoons Worcestershire sauce
½ cup chicken broth
3 tablespoons butter, melted
3 tablespoons oil
  Zest of ½ lemon
  Juice of 2 limes (about ⅓ cup)
  Salt and black pepper to taste

PREPARATION

Cut fish into 48 ½-inch cubes. Peel and devein shrimp.

To prepare pesto, put garlic, chilies, parsleys, Worcestershire sauce and chicken stock in a food processor or blender. Process until mixture is coarsely puréed. Add butter, oil and lemon zest, and pulse to blend. Set aside.

To prepare kabobs, thread seafood (2 shrimp and 3 cubes of fish) on 6-inch bamboo skewers that have been soaked in water; cover and refrigerate kabobs until ready to grill.

Before grilling, brush kabobs with lime juice, season with salt and pepper, and brush on the pesto. Grill kabobs, turning once, until seafood is cooked, about 4 minutes.

MAKES 16

Camarónes Enchilados, Cuban-Style Shrimp Stew
courtesy of Lillie Garrido

2 pounds shrimp, shelled and deveined
½ cup cooking oil
1 onion, chopped
4 cloves garlic, minced
1 large green bell pepper, sliced
1 large red bell pepper, sliced
½ cup chopped cilantro
1 can (8 ounces) tomato sauce
1 can (6 ounces) tomato paste
½ cup dry white wine
¼ teaspoon cumin
¼ teaspoon crushed oregano
1½ teaspoons salt
1 teaspoon pepper
1 whole bay leaf
1 teaspoon Tabasco sauce

PREPARATION

Heat oil in a saucepan, and sauté onion, garlic, bell peppers and cilantro. Mix in tomato sauce, tomato paste and wine. Add spices and bay leaf, and top off with Tabasco sauce. Bring to a light boil, and add shrimp. Cover, and simmer 25 to 30 minutes over low heat. Serve over white rice.   SERVES 6

For Mariscos (seafood) Enchilados, use the same ingredients and add crab meat, squid, scallops and lobster.

Shrimp and Fish Creole

1 pound white-meat fish fillets
⅓ pound small shrimp, shelled
3 tablespoons butter
½ cup minced onion
¼ cup chopped bell pepper (red or green)
1½ cups sliced mushrooms
1 8-ounce can tomato sauce
   (or 2 fresh tomatoes, chopped)
½ teaspoon chili powder
½ teaspoon ground cumin
½ teaspoon ground coriander
   Salt and pepper
   Fresh Chinese parsley (cilantro) to garnish

PREPARATION

Melt 2 tablespoons of the butter in a large skillet, and sauté the onion, pepper and mushrooms briefly. Add the tomato sauce or tomatoes, chili powder, cumin and coriander. Simmer for 5 minutes. Add the shrimp and salt and pepper to taste, and cook until the shrimp is cooked, about 3 minutes.

Cut the fish into 4 serving-sized pieces, and place on a broiler pan. Season with salt and pepper to taste, and dot with the remaining tablespoon of butter. Broil until browned and just underdone (calculate 9 minutes per inch of thickness of fish). Remove fillets to a serving dish. (Drain into the creole sauce any juice that may have accumulated in the broiler pan.) Spoon the sauce over the fish, and serve. Garnish with fresh Chinese parsley.   SERVES 4

Three Hawai'i Fish With the Chef's Garnishes

courtesy of Roger Dikon, executive chef,
Makena Resort, Maui Prince Hotel

½ pound 'ahi fillet
½ pound mahimahi fillet
½ pound 'opakapaka fillet
½ spaghetti squash
1 avocado, sliced
Salt and freshly ground black pepper to taste

TOMATO VINAIGRETTE

2 medium tomatoes, peeled and finely chopped (about 1½ cups)
2 tablespoons finely chopped cilantro
1 tablespoon finely chopped scallions
1 tablespoon finely chopped fresh basil
2 tablespoons balsamic vinegar
1 tablespoon extra-virgin olive oil
¼ teaspoon finely chopped garlic
Salt and pepper to taste

AVOCADO BUTTER

1 ripe avocado, peeled and pitted (chef prefers Sharwil)
2 tablespoons extra-virgin olive oil
Juice of 1 lime
Salt to taste

CITRUS AIOLI

2 egg yolks
3 medium garlic cloves, very finely chopped
Salt
½ cup olive oil (approximately)
1 teaspoon each lemon, orange and lime juice
Ground white pepper

CUCUMBER-MIRIN SALSA

2 Japanese cucumbers, peeled
½ small red onion
½ red bell pepper
½ cup rice wine vinegar
¼ cup mirin
Freshly chopped mint leaves
Salt and freshly ground pepper to taste

(See Preparation on opposite page)

Roger Dikon

Hawai'i has been Roger Dikon's home for more than 14 years, by way of the eastern United States, France and the Virgin Islands. He opened the Kapalua Bay Hotel in 1978 with fellow chef Hans Peter Hager, joined the Hawaii Prince when it opened in 1986 and was promoted to executive chef in early 1989. His cooking reflects an intuitive grasp of indigenous ingredients, some of which he raises in his back yard and his garden on the hotel grounds. He takes much-loved island seafood, garden vegetables and spices in their freshest form and prepares them in the most sophisticated manner. Under his supervision, the Maui Prince is the only Hawai'i hotel to earn Gault-Millau "Best in Hawai'i" ratings for all 3 restaurants (Prince Court, Cafe Kiowai and Hakone) in 1991, 1992 and 1993. Chef Dikon shares his love of fine food and wine through cooking demonstration classes, guest chef duties locally and in the mainland United States, monthly vintner dinners pairing his food with some of the world's finest wines, and a monthly food and wine newsletter for his frequent restaurant visitors and guests.

Three Hawai'i Fish With the Chef's Garnishes

PREPARATION

To prepare Tomato Vinaigrette, combine all ingredients in a bowl, stir well, and chill for an hour.

To prepare Avocado Butter, purée avocado flesh in a food processor. Slowly add the olive oil, lime juice and salt to taste.

To prepare Citrus Aioli, beat the egg yolks one at a time with the garlic and a little salt until well-combined. Slowly drip in olive oil, beating constantly. As the sauce begins to thicken, stir in the lemon, orange and lime juices and continue to add oil. When the sauce becomes as thick as mayonnaise, stop adding oil. Season to taste with white pepper, and stir well.

To prepare Cucumber-Mirin Salsa, dice the cucumbers, onion and red bell pepper into ⅛-inch pieces and mix with remaining ingredients.

Steam the squash (cut piece in half) for about 12 minutes. Shred with a fork. Divide between 4 plates. On each plate, place 2 tablespoons each of the Cucumber-Mirin Salsa and the Tomato Vinaigrette as a bed for the seared 'ahi and grilled mahimahi. Lay down 2 slices of avocado as a bed for the 'opakapaka.

Portion the fish into 4 2-ounce pieces. Lightly season all the fish with salt and freshly ground pepper. Sear the 'ahi in a very hot pan (cast iron works best) for about 7 seconds on each side. Grill the mahimahi, and pan-sauté the 'opakapaka, taking care not to overcook.

Slice the 'ahi, and rest it on the Cucumber-Mirin Salsa; place mahimahi on the Tomato Vinaigrette, and top with 1 tablespoon Avocado Butter. Place the 'opakapaka on the sliced avocado, and top with Citrus Aioli. Garnish all with fresh steamed local vegetables, if you wish.   SERVES 4

Suzanne's Sweet and Spicy Seafood Sauté

1   pound fish fillets, cut into pieces
1   pound medium or large shrimp, shelled and deveined
2   tablespoons olive oil
¼   cup chopped green onions (use both green and white parts)
3   tablespoons minced ginger
3   garlic cloves, minced
3   tablespoons minced daikon or horseradish
1   cup chopped tomatoes
2   tablespoons sweet red wine
2   tablespoons shoyu
2   tablespoons brown sugar
½   teaspoon hot red pepper flakes
    Parsley for garnish

PREPARATION

Heat olive oil in a large skillet over medium heat, and add the green onions, ginger, garlic and daikon or horseradish. Sauté for 5 minutes. Add the tomatoes, wine, shoyu, sugar and red pepper flakes, and cook for 10 minutes. Add the shrimp and fish, and simmer in the sauce until done, about 8 minutes, depending on the thickness of your fish pieces. Put in a serving dish, and sprinkle with parsley.   SERVES 4

Sauces, Marinades & Relishes

Everything goes as an accent to seafood these days: a light drizzle of chili-soy sauce, a gentle dusting of Indian spices, a crunchy bed of cucumber-ginger relish, a zesty coat of minty mustard paste–boundaries no longer exist.

We have moved heavy, time-consuming sauces to the back burner and now produce big flavors with less effort. Ingredients are often raw, fresh fruits and vegetables that punctuate the meal with color and distinctive flavors. When we do cook up a sauce, it is quick, simple to prepare and light in consistency and calories.

Marinades can be a cook's best friend. The taste sensations you can create will elevate your seafood to a 5-star status. Marinades also double as basting sauces and protect your fish from drying out during broiling and barbecuing.

A subtle and simple dusting of herbs or spices will add extra "oomph" to an already flavorful fillet. Experiment, create your own–just wing it. You will be pleasantly surprised!

You'll find over 50 recipes in this chapter to accompany your seafood and inspire the creativity within you!

Vietnamese Lime-Mint Dipping Sauce

⅓ cup mint leaves
2 cloves garlic, pressed
¼ cup fresh lime juice
1 tablespoon lemon zest
¼ teaspoon minced lemongrass
⅛ teaspoon cayenne pepper
1 teaspoon tamari
2 tablespoons nuoc mam or Nam Pla
1 tablespoon rice vinegar
1 tablespoon water or sake
1 teaspoon sugar
  Pinch salt (or to taste)

PREPARATION

Combine all ingredients in a food processor or blender. Store in a glass or ceramic container, and refrigerate for up to 2 weeks. Bring to room temperature to use.
MAKES ⅔ cup

Garden Fresh Spinach and Yogurt Sauce

2 cups packed spinach leaves
1½ cups plain low-fat yogurt
1 green onion, coarsely chopped
1 tablespoon coarsely chopped fresh dill
1 tablespoon coarsely chopped fresh mint
1 clove garlic, chopped
1 anchovy fillet, finely chopped

PREPARATION

Process all ingredients together until smooth. Cover; refrigerate 1 hour (or up to 1 day in advance). Serve cold or at room temperature. MAKES 2½ cups

Suzanne's Mint-Garlic Yogurt Sauce

1 tablespoon minced garlic
2 tablespoons chopped fresh mint
1 tablespoon raspberry vinegar
½ teaspoon salt
½ teaspoon pepper
½ cup non-fat plain yogurt

PREPARATION

Mix all ingredients in a small bowl.
(Enough for 1½ pounds fish.)   MAKES ¾ cup

About the fish: Coat both sides of fish fillets or serving portions cut 1½ to 2 inches thick. Bake in a preheated 450° oven for 15 to 20 minutes, depending on thickness. Baste 2 or 3 times during baking.

Lime Cilantro Yogurt Sauce

¼ cup low-fat, plain yogurt
2 tablespoons fresh lime juice
1 tablespoon lime or lemon zest
1 to 2 teaspoons honey
1 tablespoon olive oil
1 tablespoon minced fresh Chinese parsley (cilantro)

PREPARATION

Combine all ingredients in a bowl. Adjust to suit your taste. MAKES ⅔ cup

---

FISHWIFE'S TIP
Strong-flavored sauces are best with red-meat fish. If you use them with white-meat fish, use them sparingly so they won't overpower the fish's delicate flavor.

Spicy Orange Dipping Sauce

¼ cup fresh orange juice
1 teaspoon balsamic vinegar
1½ teaspoons rice wine vinegar
1 teaspoon brown sugar
¼ teaspoon dry mustard
   Salt and pepper to taste

PREPARATION

Combine all ingredients. Excellent served with steamed spring rolls.

MAKES ⅓ cup

Lemon-Miso Spring Roll Sauce

2 tablespoons white miso
2 tablespoons fresh lemon juice
2 tablespoons shoyu
2 tablespoons rice vinegar
2 tablespoons mirin
2 teaspoons grated or minced ginger root
2 cloves garlic, minced
½ teaspoon sugar

PREPARATION

Combine all ingredients in a bowl, and blend well.

MAKES ⅔ cup

Garlic-Coriander-Miso Dipping Sauce

1 teaspoon minced Chinese parsley (cilantro, or coriander) stems
1 tablespoon minced green onion
¼ cup shrimp, fish or vegetable stock
⅛ teaspoon cayenne pepper
1 tablespoon tamari
1 tablespoon minced ginger root
1 tablespoon sake or white wine
1 tablespoon nuoc nam or Nam Pla
1 teaspoon white miso paste
   Pinch sugar

PREPARATION

Combine all ingredients in a glass or ceramic container. Refrigerate; bring to room temperature to use.

MAKES ½ cup

Ginger Sauce

1 tablespoon minced, fresh ginger root
3 tablespoons ground ginger
2 cloves garlic, minced
3 tablespoons shoyu
1 teaspoon sugar
¾ cup water
3 tablespoons olive oil
2 tablespoons minced Chinese parsley (cilantro) leaves
1 teaspoon freshly ground black pepper

PREPARATION

Combine the gingers, garlic, shoyu, sugar, water and oil in a medium saucepan, and bring to a boil over medium heat. Reduce heat, cover, and simmer for 10 to 12 minutes. Remove from heat. Add parsley and pepper just before serving. May be served hot or at room temperature.

MAKES ⅔ cup

Sharon's Moroccan Sauce

2 tablespoons sesame seeds, crushed
2 tablespoons honey
2 tablespoons orange juice
   Pinch cinnamon, no more than ⅛ teaspoon
   (optional)
½ teaspoon ground cumin
1 tablespoon shoyu
1 tablespoon olive oil
2 tablespoons lemon juice
½ teaspoon Szechwan chili paste
2 tablespoons minced green onions (garnish)

PREPARATION

Combine all ingredients except the green onions in a saucepan. Warm over medium-low heat. Serve over fish; sprinkle with green onion pieces.

MAKES ¾ cup

Ticia's Oriental Chili Sauce

2 tablespoons shoyu
½ teaspoon crushed hot red pepper flakes
1 tablespoon white vinegar
3 tablespoons water
½ teaspoon sugar
2 teaspoons sesame oil
1 clove garlic, minced
2 teaspoons minced ginger root
1 tablespoon sliced green onion

PREPARATION

Combine all ingredients in a small bowl; blend well. Let stand for ½ hour. Serve at room temperature.

MAKES ½ cup

Peanut Sauce for Fish

½ small onion, sliced
1 clove garlic, minced
¼ teaspoon powdered ginger
¼ cup water
4 tablespoons peanut butter
1 teaspoon shoyu
⅛ teaspoon Szechwan chili sauce
1 teaspoon red wine vinegar
1 teaspoon hoi sin sauce
2 tablespoons orange juice concentrate
1 teaspoon balsamic vinegar

PREPARATION

Briefly sauté onion, garlic and powdered ginger in a non-stick saucepan. Stir in all remaining ingredients; cook over medium-low heat until the sauce is well-blended and hot.

MAKES 1¼ cups

About the fish: Marinate fish in an orange juice-wine mixture; grill and serve with sauce. Or, serve sauce with fish that has been sautéed with black sesame seeds, minced ginger and minced garlic.

Chili-Peanut Sauce I

1 teaspoon peanut oil
½ teaspoon Szechwan chili sauce or paste
1 tablespoon tomato paste
1 clove garlic, minced
½ cup chicken broth
½ teaspoon sugar
1 tablespoon chunky peanut butter
2 tablespoons hoi sin sauce

PREPARATION

Combine oil, chili sauce, tomato paste and garlic in a saucepan over medium heat; cook 30 seconds, or until fragrant. Add broth, sugar, peanut butter and hoi sin; bring to a boil. Reduce heat, and simmer sauce until thickened, 2 to 3 minutes. If sauce is too thick, thin with additional broth, 1 tablespoon at a time.

MAKES ½ cup

Chili-Peanut Sauce II

¾ cup chunky peanut butter
1 cup chicken broth
2 tablespoons brown sugar
2 tablespoons shoyu
1 tablespoon minced ginger
2 teaspoons chili paste with garlic

PREPARATION

Combine all ingredients in a heavy saucepan over medium heat. Simmer, stirring frequently, until the sauce is smooth and slightly thickened, 3 to 4 minutes. Spoon over fish.

MAKES 2 cups

About the fish: Marinate the fish for 20 minutes in 2 parts shoyu, 1 part oil and a bit of ginger root before grilling or broiling.

Malaysian Barbecue Sauce

¼ cup firmly packed brown sugar
¾ cup rice vinegar
¼ cup shoyu
2 tablespoons water
1 tablespoon oil
2 tablespoons peanut butter
1 walnut-sized piece ginger root, peeled and julienned
½ teaspoon red pepper flakes
3 cloves garlic, minced
¼ cup chopped green onions

PREPARATION

Combine sauce ingredients; stir well, breaking up the peanut butter. Put in a saucepan, and bring to a boil over medium-high heat. Lower heat, and simmer for 5 minutes, until sauce thickens a bit. Remove from heat; let cool. Use as a marinade, or brush over fish before grilling; baste frequently.

MAKES 1⅔ cups

Beth's Special Tempura Sauce

1 cup orange marmalade
1 tablespoon freshly grated horseradish (or prepared, if you wish)
1 teaspoon minced ginger
1 shallot, minced
Pinch cayenne pepper

PREPARATION

Whisk all ingredients together in a bowl; blend well. Thin with orange juice if necessary, 1 teaspoon at a time.

MAKES 1 cup

About the shrimp: Prepare tempura style.

Nuoc Cham
Basic Vietnamese Dipping Sauce

2 to 3 cloves garlic, minced
1 small chili pepper with seeds, minced, or
 ½ to 1 teaspoon dried red pepper flakes
2 to 3 tablespoons sugar
¼ cup Nam Pla
2 to 3 tablespoons fresh lime or lemon juice
3 tablespoons water

PREPARATION

Combine garlic and chili pepper in a blender or food processor, and process until smooth. Add remaining ingredients, and blend well. Serve in individual dipping bowls, if you wish. If made in advance, sauce may be refrigerated for 3 days. Bring to room temperature before serving   MAKES ¾ cup

---

FISHWIFE'S TIP

Ingredients and amounts in this recipe may be altered to suit taste preferences. When experimenting, consider adding shoyu (low-sodium, for less salt), rice vinegar and mint leaves.

Sesame-Soy Dipping Sauce

1 to 2 tablespoons shoyu
½ to 1 teaspoon sesame oil
1 tablespoon sesame seeds, ground
1 teaspoon dry mustard
 Pinch sugar
¼ cup shrimp or chicken stock

PREPARATION

Combine the shoyu, sesame oil and seeds, dry mustard and sugar in a small bowl. Warm the stock, and whisk it into the shoyu mixture. Refrigerate; serve at room temperature.   MAKES ⅓ cup

Orange Sauce Oriental

3 tablespoons fresh orange juice
2 to 3 tablespoons hoi sin sauce
1 tablespoon oyster sauce
1 tablespoon ketchup
2 tablespoons minced green onions
2 teaspoons orange zest
¾ teaspoon sugar

PREPARATION

Combine all ingredients in a heavy saucepan over medium-high heat. Whisk together until the sauce comes to a boil. Reduce heat, and cook until sauce thickens, about 2 minutes.   MAKES ⅔ cup

About the fish: Marinate in 2 parts orange juice, 1 part oil, orange zest and black pepper before broiling or grilling.

Asian Sesame Sauce

½ cup sesame seeds, black and white
 (preferably toasted)
2 tablespoons shoyu
2 tablespoons tomato paste
2 tablespoons sherry
3 tablespoons sesame oil
1 tablespoon hoi sin sauce
1 tablespoon sugar
2 teaspoons rice vinegar
⅓ cup chopped shallots

PREPARATION

Reserve 2 tablespoons of the sesame seeds. Crush remaining seeds. Combine the reserved and crushed sesame seeds with all remaining ingredients. Blend well.   MAKES 1 cup

Fishwife's Peppercorn Sauce

1   teaspoon oil
1   tablespoon crushed dried green peppercorns
½   teaspoon dry mustard
1   tablespoon fresh lemon juice
¼   cup water or vegetable stock
¼   cup white wine
2   teaspoons fresh lemon juice
2   teaspoons shoyu

PREPARATION

Heat oil in a small non-stick skillet over medium-high heat. Stir in peppercorns and mustard; blend well. Add the lemon juice, water and wine, and cook mixture for 2 or 3 minutes. Reduce heat to low.

Put fish that has been grilled, sautéed or broiled in the skillet, coating both sides with the peppercorn sauce. Combine the 2 teaspoons fresh lemon juice with the 2 teaspoons shoyu. Spoon over the fish.
(Enough for 1⅓ pounds fish.)   MAKES ¾ cup

Cilantro-Miso Dipping Sauce
courtesy of Vernon Wong

2   cups fresh Chinese parsley (cilantro)
     Juice from 4 limes
¾   cup miso (shiro)
4   tablespoons olive oil
1   teaspoon ground black or white pepper
¼   cup mirin

PREPARATION

Chop Chinese parsley in a food processor. Add the rest of the ingredients, and blend until smooth.
MAKES 3 cups

Sashimi Dip

¼   cup shoyu
2   tablespoons rice vinegar
1   clove garlic, minced or pressed
1   tablespoon grated or minced ginger root
1   teaspoon sugar
2   tablespoons minced green onions
1   teaspoon roasted sesame seeds

PREPARATION

Combine all ingredients. Serve in small bowls.
MAKES ⅓ cup

Hot and Sweet Dipping Sauce

½   cup water
½   cup distilled white vinegar
1   cup sugar
1   to 2 cloves garlic, minced or pressed
1   teaspoon salt
½   to 1 teaspoon chili paste

PREPARATION

Combine the water, vinegar, sugar, garlic and salt in a heavy saucepan over medium-high heat. Bring to a boil; stir until the sugar dissolves. Reduce heat, and simmer until the sauce is syrupy, 15 to 20 minutes. Remove pan from heat; add chili paste, and cool before using. (Sauce will thicken further as it cools.)
MAKES 1⅓ cups

FISHWIFE'S TIP

Vary this recipe by using half rice vinegar and half white distilled vinegar; add ¼ teaspoon ginger juice; add minced green onions with the chili paste for an added bite.

Chili-Honey Sauce
courtesy of Vernon Wong

2 cups chili sauce
1 cup fresh orange juice
1 cup shoyu
1 cup honey
½ cup rice wine vinegar
½ cup salted black beans, rinsed and mashed
½ cup minced shallots
2 teaspoons grated fresh ginger root
2½ tablespoons Tabasco

PREPARATION

Combine all ingredients in a pan. Cook over medium heat; bring to a boil. Remove from heat, and cool. Brush on fish as it cooks.

MAKES 5 cups

Chunky Tomato-Ginger Sauce

2 tablespoons butter
6 green onions, chopped
4 cloves garlic, minced
2 teaspoons minced jalapeno
½ teaspoon turmeric
1 28-ounce can whole tomatoes, drained and chopped
2 tablespoons minced ginger

PREPARATION

Melt butter in a medium saucepan over medium heat. Sauté onions and garlic until the onions are limp. Stir in jalapeno and turmeric. Increase heat to medium-high; add remaining ingredients, and cook until thick, about 10 minutes. (Reheat if made in advance.)

MAKES 1¼ cups

Rahna's Favorite Thai Fish Sauce
(good served with shrimp or any kind of fish)

½ cup oil
1 small red pepper, seeded and chopped, or ¼ to ½ teaspoon dried red pepper flakes
2 cloves garlic, minced
2 teaspoons minced onion
2 teaspoons minced celery
2 teaspoons minced ginger
2 teaspoons minced Chinese parsley (cilantro)
½ cup chicken broth
½ teaspoon fish sauce or oyster sauce
1 teaspoon cornstarch

PREPARATION

Heat the oil in a skillet, and stir-fry the red pepper, garlic, onion and celery briefly. Add the ginger, parsley, chicken broth and fish sauce, and simmer for about 5 minutes. Stir in the cornstarch moistened with a little water. As soon as the sauce thickens, remove from heat. Serve on the side, or pour over cooked fish.

MAKES 1 cup

FISHWIFE'S TIPS
To Use a Marinade as a Sauce:
   1. Make extra marinade; set ½ cup aside to heat later and spoon over cooked fish.
   2. If your marinade calls for more oil than you want to put on the serving plate, mix together all ingredients except the oil, set aside ⅓ cup of the mixture to use as your sauce base. Add the proper amount of oil to the remaining ingredients and marinate your fish. To your ⅓ cup portion, add a stock, juice, wine, etc.; heat, and spoon over fish before serving.
   3. To kill any bacteria that might have seeped into the marinade from the raw fish, boil the marinade before using it to baste or as a sauce.

Marinades

Winners Circle 'Ahi Marinade

¼   cup shoyu or tamari
1   2-inch piece lemongrass, peeled and minced
1   dried red chili, crumbled
2   teaspoons grated ginger

PREPARATION

Combine all ingredients in a shallow dish. Marinate 'ahi for 1 hour before grilling.   MAKES ⅓ cup

'Ahi Marinade I

¼   cup oil
¼   cup shoyu
¼   cup fresh lemon juice
¼   cup chopped green onions or parsley

PREPARATION

Combine all ingredients in a non-reactive container. Marinate fish for 20 minutes, turning once.
(Enough for 2 to 3 pounds fish.)   MAKES 1 cup

'Ahi Marinade II

¼   cup oil
½   cup fresh lemon or lime juice
1   teaspoon dried oregano
¾   teaspoon garlic salt
½   teaspoon pepper

PREPARATION

Combine all ingredients in a non-reactive container. Marinate fish for 20 minutes, turning once.
MAKES ¾ cup

Hot and Sweet Marinade for Fish

2 cloves garlic, minced
½ jalapeno chili, minced (and seeded)
½ cup fresh orange juice
2 tablespoons orange zest
⅓ cup fresh lime or lemon juice
⅓ cup olive oil
2 teaspoons Dijon mustard
¾ teaspoon salt
¾ teaspoon ground cumin
1 teaspoon sugar

PREPARATION

Combine all ingredients, and blend well. Use to marinate fish or shrimp.   MAKES 1⅓ cups

Margo's Mediterranean Marinade

½ cup white wine vinegar
½ teaspoon Spanish paprika
½ teaspoon red pepper flakes
½ teaspoon dried oregano
½ teaspoon ground cumin
½ teaspoon dried thyme
3 medium garlic cloves, minced or pressed
1 bay leaf
2 tablespoons water
  Salt and freshly ground pepper to taste

PREPARATION

Mix all ingredients in a non-reactive pan. Marinate the fish (1½ pounds), cut into serving-sized pieces (or 1-inch cubes for kabobs), for 1 hour before grilling.   MAKES ⅔ cup

Margret's Southwestern Marinade

1 clove garlic, minced
½ jalapeno, minced
¼ cup fresh lime juice
¼ cup fresh orange juice
¼ cup olive oil
1 teaspoon Dijon mustard
½ teaspoon ground cumin
½ teaspoon sugar
½ teaspoon salt

PREPARATION

Blend together garlic, jalapeno, lime and orange juices, oil and mustard until mixture is smooth. (If you use a blender or processor, do not mince garlic and jalapeno first.) Add cumin, sugar and salt. Marinade may be made ahead and refrigerated, covered, for 12 hours. Marinate your fish (1¼ pounds) for 20 minutes before cooking.   MAKES ¾ cup

Chef's Note: Margret sometimes uses this recipe as a salad dressing.

Lemon-Ginger Marinade

⅓ cup fresh lemon juice
2 tablespoons lemon zest
¼ cup white wine
2 tablespoons oil
1 to 2 tablespoons shoyu
1 tablespoon minced fresh ginger
¼ cup minced green onions
2 cloves garlic, minced

PREPARATION

Combine all ingredients. Marinate your fish in mixture for an hour, turning fish once.   MAKES ¾ cup

Pickled Ginger Marinade

¼ cup minced sweet onion
¼ cup fresh lime juice
2 tablespoons shredded gari shoga
  (pickled ginger)
2 tablespoons shoyu
2 teaspoons sugar
½ teaspoon dried red pepper flakes (or to taste)

PREPARATION

Combine all ingredients in bowl large enough to hold ½ pound of cooked shrimp (small). Blend well, and coat shrimp. Refrigerate for 2 hours.

MAKES ⅔ cup

Indian Marinade

1 teaspoon coriander seeds
½ teaspoon white peppercorns
½ teaspoon ground cardamom
¼ teaspoon ground turmeric
8 ounces plain low-fat yogurt
1 teaspoon salt
1 teaspoon grated ginger

PREPARATION

Grind coriander and peppercorns to a powder; combine with cardamom and turmeric, and blend well. Stir 2 teaspoons of the spice mix into the yogurt; add salt and ginger. Cover and refrigerate overnight.
(Enough for 2 pounds fish.)   MAKES 1 cup

About the fish: Coat fish with marinade; let stand for 30 to 45 minutes in refrigerator before broiling, baking or grilling. Baste during cooking.

Kendra's Marinade for Shrimp

1 teaspoon dry mustard
1 teaspoon salt
½ cup olive oil
  Juice from 1 lemon
1 teaspoon dried basil leaves
½ cup chopped fresh parsley
3 cloves garlic

PREPARATION

Combine all ingredients.   MAKES ¾ cup

Citrus-Fennel Marinade

¼ cup oil
2 tablespoons fresh lemon juice
2 tablespoons Chinese parsley (cilantro)
½ teaspoon fennel seeds, crushed
1 clove garlic, minced or pressed
  Zest from the lemon

PREPARATION

Combine all ingredients; blend well. MAKES ½ cup

Ginger Marinade

2 tablespoons minced ginger root
2 teaspoons oyster sauce
1 tablespoon minced green onion
2 tablespoons sake or white wine
½ teaspoon sesame oil
1 teaspoon minced cilantro

PREPARATION

Combine all ingredients.   MAKES ¼ cup

Skewered Scampi Marinade

½ cup shoyu
½ cup oil
2 tablespoons lemon juice
½ teaspoon ground ginger
½ teaspoon garlic salt or powder
1 teaspoon Italian seasoning blend
Black pepper to taste

PREPARATION

Combine all ingredients, blending well. Marinate shrimp for up to 2 hours, refrigerated.
(Enough for 1½ pounds shrimp.) MAKES 1⅛ cups

Rahna's Delicious Cinnamon-Orange Marinade
courtesy of Rahna Rizzuto

½ cup Five Alive concentrate
¼ cup dry white wine
1 medium onion, finely chopped
3 cloves garlic, minced
1½ tablespoons finely chopped ginger root
1 teaspoon dried red pepper flakes
1½ tablespoons olive oil
1 teaspoon sugar
½ teaspoon salt
¼ teaspoon ground nutmeg
¼ teaspoon ground cinnamon

PREPARATION

Combine all ingredients. Blend well. Marinate fish for no more than 2 hours. Broil or grill.
(Enough for 2 to 2 ½ pounds fish.)
MAKES 1½ cups

Douglas Lum's Ginger Vinaigrette
This vinaigrette to be used with Douglas Lum's mahimahi recipe on page 50

1½ cups shoyu
½ cup rice wine vinegar
¾ cup sugar
5 ounces minced ginger root
¼ cup olive oil

PREPARATION

Mix well in a bowl or place all in a jar with a tight sealing lid. Shake until sugar is dissolved.
MAKES 2½ cups

Balsamic Vinaigrette

¼ cup balsamic vinegar
⅓ cup olive oil
1 to 2 sprigs fresh rosemary
½ teaspoon dried oregano
2 shallots, minced
Pinch hot red pepper flakes
Salt and freshly ground pepper to taste

PREPARATION

Whisk together all ingredients, and let stand for 2 hours. Before serving, heat sauce until warm, about 1 minute.

MAKES ¾ cup

About the fish: Marinate fish in half of the vinaigrette for 30 minutes before cooking. Discard marinade.

Simple Make-Ahead Miso Marinade

½ **cup white miso**
2 **tablespoons sugar**
3 **tablespoons sake or white wine**
1 **tablespoon mirin**

PREPARATION

Combine all ingredients. Spread half of mixture in a pan just large enough to hold fish (1 pound) in a single layer. Spread remaining marinade on top. Refrigerate overnight. Rinse marinade off fish; pat fish dry. Broil, turning once, until done.   MAKES 1¼ cups

---

FISHWIFE'S TIP

Lightly salt fish, and refrigerate for 2 hours before marinating.

Mustard-Dill Marinade

¼ **cup Dijon mustard**
1 **teaspoon dried mustard**
3 **to 4 tablespoons white wine vinegar**
2 **cloves garlic, minced**
½ **cup chopped fresh dill**
⅓ **cup olive oil**
1 **tablespoon sugar**
    Salt to taste

PREPARATION

Combine the mustards, vinegar, garlic, dill, oil, sugar and salt; blend well.   MAKES 1½ cups

---

FISHWIFE'S TIPS

1. Fish brushed lightly with olive oil will hold herbs and spices better. Press them into the flesh gently.
2. Salt and pepper the fish. Heat olive oil in a non-stick pan; add herbs or spices, and sauté briefly before adding fish.

Orange-Miso Marinade

2 **tablespoons orange juice concentrate**
3 **tablespoons water**
2 **tablespoons sake**
3 **to 4 teaspoons white miso paste**
1 **teaspoon black (or white) sesame seeds, crushed or minced for full flavor**
2 **tablespoons minced green onion**
    Salt and freshly ground pepper to taste.

PREPARATION

Combine all ingredients in a oven-proof baking pan. If you wish to dilute the marinade, use water or sake, a teaspoon at a time. Marinate your fish for 30 to 45 minutes. Turn fish once.

Preheat your broiler for 10 minutes. Place the pan as close to your coils as your oven allows. Broil fish for 2 to 3 minutes. Pour the marinade over fish, and continue broiling until the fish is done. The marinade will thicken into a nice sauce.   MAKES ¾ cup

FISHWIFE'S TIPS

1. Thin sauce with hot dashi, if necessary.
2. I use frozen juice concentrate because I can control the strength of the citrus flavor and substitute liquids other than water when I wish. Try this: defrost a can of juice, and freeze the concentrate in an ice cube tray. (I fill the compartments in my trays half-full, which gives me tablespoon measures of concentrate in each one.) When the juice is frozen, keep the cubes in a Ziploc bag and use as needed.

Relishes & Salsa

Cucumber-Ginger Relish

½ cup rice vinegar
¼ cup water
1 tablespoon shoyu
2 teaspoons sugar
1 teaspoon oil
1 tablespoon minced or grated ginger
2 medium cucumbers, peeled, seeded and thinly sliced
1 large carrot, peeled and grated
¼ cup minced green onions
2 tablespoons minced parsley (optional)

PREPARATION

Combine vinegar, water, shoyu, sugar and oil in a large bowl; blend well. Add remaining ingredients; mix well. Cover; refrigerate for up to 2 hours. Mix before serving.   MAKES 3½ cups

VARIATION

Add 1 tablespoon minced jalapeno or Thai chili pepper.

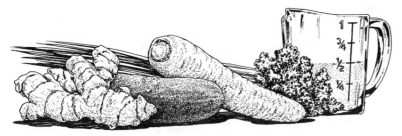

Chinese Black Bean and Mushroom Relish

3 tablespoons coarsely chopped fermented black beans
½ cup chopped fresh mushrooms
¾ cup chicken broth
3 tablespoons sake or white wine
   Zest from 1 lemon
2 tablespoons minced green onion
2 teaspoons sugar
1 tablespoon oyster sauce
1 tablespoon grated ginger

PREPARATION

Combine all ingredients in a saucepan. Bring to a boil; lower heat, and let simmer for 5 minutes. Thicken with cornstarch, if you wish. Serve over fish.
                    MAKES 1¾ cups

Basil-Tomato Salsa

10 ounces (about 5 medium) firm, ripe plum tomatoes, coarsely chopped
⅓ cup chopped fresh basil leaves
1½ tablespoons balsamic or red wine vinegar
   Salt and freshly ground pepper to taste

PREPARATION

Combine tomatoes and basil in a bowl. Add vinegar, salt and pepper.

                    MAKES 1½ cups

About the fish: Marinate your fish in oil and lemon juice, and sprinkle with additional chopped basil before cooking.

Tony's Super Onion Relish

1 cup diced onion
(use a variety–Bermuda, sweet, shallots, etc.)
¼ cup minced green onions
2 tablespoons chopped parsley
2 tablespoons olive oil
1 tablespoon fresh lemon juice
1 tablespoon fresh orange juice
2 tablespoons chopped orange segments
or pulp
1 teaspoon chopped fresh oregano, or
¼ teaspoon dried
1 teaspoon fresh thyme, or ¼ teaspoon dried
1 teaspoon orange zest
Salt and freshly ground pepper to taste

PREPARATION

Combine all ingredients in a bowl. May be served cold or at room temperature.

MAKES 1¾ cups

Peach 'n Onion Relish

2 medium peaches, unpeeled (ripe, firm fruit)
¼ cup thinly sliced green onion rings
¼ cup minced bell pepper (red and green)
1 tablespoon fresh lime juice
1 tablespoon chopped Chinese parsley
(cilantro)
1 tablespoon chopped parsley
1 tablespoon olive oil
½ teaspoon ground cumin
½ teaspoon salt
Freshly ground pepper to taste
Minced jalapeno chilies to taste

PREPARATION

Combine all ingredients *except* the jalapenos in a bowl. Mix in the chilies, 1 teaspoon at a time, and refrigerate, covered, for 30 minutes. Increase the amount of jalapenos, if you wish. (If prepared ahead, refrigerate for no more than 2 hours.) MAKES 1½ cups

Thai Flavored Cucumber Relish

1 small cucumber, peeled and seeded
2 small cloves garlic, minced
½ small Thai chili pepper, minced
(or ½ small jalapeno chili)
3 large green onions, cut into 1-inch lengths
5 tablespoons rice vinegar
1 tablespoon Nam Pla
1 tablespoon peanut oil
¼ teaspoon sugar
¼ teaspoon salt

PREPARATION

Chop cucumber; blend with garlic, chili pepper and green onions. Mix with remaining ingredients; let stand at room temperature for 1 hour. Relish may be made ahead and refrigerated for 6 hours. Return to room temperature before serving.

MAKES 2 cups

FISHWIFE'S TIPS

1. Experiment with ingredient amounts to suit your taste.
2. Before cooking, lightly season your fillets with herbs that will complement the flavors of the relish: cumin, turmeric, coriander, fresh minced Chinese parsley (cilantro), or mint.

Tropical Salsa

1   small cantaloupe
1   small papaya
1   medium cucumber
⅓   cup minced fresh mint
3   tablespoons lime juice
1   teaspoon lime zest
1   tablespoon honey
¼   teaspoon crushed red pepper flakes
     (optional)

PREPARATION

Seed, peel and dice the cantaloupe, papaya and cucumber. Combine all ingredients in a bowl. Serve slightly chilled or at room temperature.

MAKES 4 cups

Plum-Orange Salsa

2   firm, ripe plums, red or black
1   orange
1   tablespoon sliced green onion
2   teaspoons minced Chinese parsley (cilantro)
¼   teaspoon ground cumin
¼   teaspoon ground cardamom
¼   teaspoon dried red pepper flakes
¼   teaspoon ground coriander
¼   teaspoon powdered ginger
2   teaspoons lime juice

PREPARATION

Cut plums in half, remove the pits, and dice flesh. Peel orange, separate into segments, and cut segments into small pieces. (Remove the membrane from the segments first.) Put fruit in a non-reactive bowl. Add green onion and parsley.

Combine the spices, and sprinkle over the fruit, mixing well. Pour in the lime juice. Stir gently. Let salsa stand for 15 minutes before serving.

MAKES 1¾ cups

Summer Melon Salsa

3   cups diced melon, use a variety of types-
     honeydew, cantaloupe, et cetera
½   cup diced sweet onion
¼   cup chopped fresh basil
3   tablespoons fresh lime juice
1   tablespoon peanut oil
1   tablespoon finely slivered fresh mint
2   teaspoons lime zest
1   to 3 teaspoons minced jalapeno chilies
     Salt to taste

PREPARATION

Combine all ingredients *except* the chilies in a bowl. Add jalapenos, 1 teaspoon at a time. Add salt; let stand at least 15 minutes, but no more than an hour.

MAKES 4 cups

Kendra's Confetti Salsa

2 medium avocados
1 small, ripe papaya
⅓ cup lime juice
2 medium tomatoes, chopped
2 green onions, sliced
2 tablespoons sugar
2 tablespoons olive oil
1 tablespoon minced Chinese parsley (cilantro)
1 tablespoon minced fresh basil, or 1 teaspoon dried and crushed
   Zest of 2 small limes
¼ to ½ teaspoon dried, crushed red pepper (or to taste)

PREPARATION

Seed, peel and chop avocados and papaya into ½-inch cubes. Put in a glass bowl, and gently toss the cubes with lime juice. Add the tomatoes, green onions, sugar, olive oil, Chinese parsley, basil, lime zest and red pepper flakes. Cover, and chill.   MAKES 4 cups

Bob's Cilantro Salsa

¾ cup lime juice
⅔ cup thinly sliced green onions, green and white parts
1 to 2 pickled jalapeno chilies, stemmed and finely chopped
1½ cups loosely packed fresh Chinese parsley (cilantro) leaves, minced
⅓ cup olive oil
   Salt and pepper to taste

PREPARATION

Reserve 2 tablespoons of the lime juice to drizzle over your fish.

Combine the remaining lime juice, onions, jalapenos, cilantro and olive oil in a small bowl. Spread all but ½ cup of the cilantro salsa over 3 to 4 pounds of fish fillets. Bake, uncovered, at 350° until the fish is opaque in the thickest portion; baking time depends on thickness of the fish.

Serve with remaining salsa.   MAKES 4 cups

Mary's Papaya-Kiwi Salsa

2 ripe papayas, peeled and seeded
3 kiwi fruit
1 fresh jalapeno pepper
3 cloves garlic, pressed
½ cup minced red onion
¼ cup chopped fresh Chinese parsley (cilantro)
½ cup fresh lime juice
   Zest of 2 limes

PREPARATION

Cube papayas. Quarter and slice kiwis. Set aside.
Seed and chop the jalapeno. (Adjust the amount according to your heat tolerance.) Put jalapeno in a non-reactive bowl with the garlic, onion, parsley, lime juice and lime zest; mix. Add the papaya and kiwi.
          MAKES 4 cups
About the fish: Marinate the fish in Italian dressing before grilling.

Diced Vegetable Medley

2 to 3 tablespoons olive oil
1 small eggplant, diced
1 small red or yellow bell pepper,
  seeded and diced
1 small zucchini, diced
  Salt and freshly ground black pepper to taste
1 tablespoon chopped fresh parsley
1 tablespoon chopped fresh basil or oregano

PREPARATION

Heat 1 tablespoon of the oil in a non-stick skillet over medium-high heat. Sauté the eggplant first, until lightly browned, about 2 minutes. Remove from the skillet. Add more oil, if needed, and sauté the bell pepper briefly, about a minute. Add the zucchini (and oil only if necessary), and sauté for another minute. Return the eggplant to the skillet, season with salt and pepper, parsley and basil. Remove from heat.

MAKES 2½ cups

Fresh Tomato Salsa, Mediterranean-Style

3 large ripe tomatoes, chopped
2 tablespoons olive oil
2 tablespoons balsamic vinegar
2 tablespoons wine vinegar
¼ cup chopped onion or shallots
2 tablespoons capers, drained, or
  chopped Kalamata olives
2 tablespoons minced fresh parsley
2 cloves garlic, minced
1¼ teaspoons dried basil, crushed
  Salt and freshly ground black pepper to taste

PREPARATION

Combine all ingredients in a large, non-reactive container. Stir gently to mix well. If not serving immediately, cover and refrigerate for no more than 2 hours. Garnish with additional parsley, if you wish.

MAKES 3½ cups

Avocado-Tomato-Onion Salsa

¼ cup minced jalapeno peppers
  (degree of heat optional)
¼ cup diced, seeded tomato
¼ cup diced red onion
½ cup diced avocado (½-inch pieces)
3 tablespoons minced Chinese parsley
  (cilantro)
1 tablespoon lime juice
1 teaspoon olive oil
  Salt and pepper to taste

PREPARATION

Combine all ingredients in a non-reactive bowl. Serve immediately.

MAKES 1½ cups

FISHWIFE'S TIP

To make ahead, combine all ingredients except the avocado and lime juice. Add them just before serving, stirring in gently.

Seafood Herbs

Tarragon

Mint

Saffron

Savory

Coriander

Thyme

Fennel

Basil

Parsley

Sage

Rosemary

Bay leaves

Oregano

Chervil

Chives

Dill Leaf

Curry Powder

Lemon peel

Dill

Celery seed

Sesame Seed

Mustard Seed

Coriander Seed

Garlic

Red Pepper

Herbs

NOTES ON FRESH HERBS:

1. Delicate-flavored herbs (thin stems, tender leaves) are mild and can be used any time, alone or in combinations, with good results. Examples: Basil, chervil, chives, parsley.

2. Medium-flavored herbs hold up well in cooking and can be used with others herbs to add depth to the flavors of your food. Examples: Bay leaves, oregano, savory, thyme.

3. Distinctive-flavored herbs have to be chosen with care in their use. They can overpower the natural flavors of your food. Examples: Coriander, Chinese parsley (cilantro), dill, mint, rosemary, sage.

To store fresh herbs, be sure they are clean and thoroughly dry (or they'll rot!). Wrap them loosely in plastic wrap or in plastic bags, laying flat and uncrushed. Refrigerate. Fresh herbs are best used quickly, within 5 days if possible.

Remember that dried herbs are stronger flavored than fresh; powdered or ground herbs are stronger than dried or crumbled. Use this rule of thumb: ¼ teaspoon powdered = ¾ to 1 teaspoon crumbled = 2 teaspoons fresh.

Here are some final tips to remember:

1. The finer you chop your fresh herbs, the more flavor they'll produce.

2. Add fresh herbs to hot dishes (soups, stews, et cetera) no more than 45 minutes before serving; otherwise they'll begin to lose their flavor.

FISHWIFE'S TIPS

How To Use Herb Mixes and Blends

1. Sprinkle on both sides of fish, pressing herbs against the flesh to adhere. Let stand a few minutes, then cook.

2. Heat herb blend in hot oil (not much, maybe a teaspoon or 2) in a non-stick skillet. Sauté briefly before you add the fish.

3. To use in marinades, add herb blend to the liquid (usually oil-based) for flavoring.

4. Blends can be ground in a spice grinder, if you prefer working with a powder.

5. Make "herb cubes" by coarsely puréeing herbs in a blender or food processor with a bit of water. Freeze the purée in ice cube trays, and then transfer the cubes to plastic bags. This is a great way to season your dishes with no fuss!

Ancho Chili Mix

8 dried Ancho chilies, stemmed and seeded
1 tablespoon cumin seeds
1 teaspoon coriander seeds
2 tablespoons coarse salt
2 tablespoons brown sugar
1 teaspoon cinnamon

PREPARATION

Place chilies on a baking sheet, and bake in a preheated, 350° oven for 15 minutes, or until lightly roasted. Remove from heat; cool.

Heat cumin and coriander seeds in a heavy skillet over medium-low temperature until fragrant, about 2 minutes.

Halve chilies; put in a food processor with the cumin and coriander seeds. Add remaining ingredients. Process until the mix is the consistency of a coarse powder.

Rub your fish, preferably 'ahi, with seasoning on both sides before grilling, broiling or pan-frying. Use about ½ teaspoon per serving piece.

MAKES ¾ cup

Cheryl's Basic Herb Blend

1 bay leaf, finely crumbled or ground
1 teaspoon dried oregano
1 teaspoon dried basil
½ teaspoon salt
½ teaspoon pepper
¼ teaspoon dried thyme
¼ teaspoon dried marjoram
1 tablespoon minced fresh parsley

PREPARATION

Combine all dried ingredients; blend well. Mix with fresh parsley. Rub on seafood, and let stand 30 minutes before cooking.

MAKES ¼ cup

CHERYL'S NOTE
To use as an herb base for a marinade, mix with oil and a squeeze of lemon juice. Marinate seafood for 30 minutes. Turn fish once.

Cajun Seasoning

½ teaspoon salt
¾ teaspoon freshly ground pepper
   (mix black and white)
½ teaspoon onion powder
½ teaspoon cayenne pepper
½ teaspoon Hungarian sweet paprika
½ teaspoon dried thyme

PREPARATION

Combine all ingredients. Store in an airtight container.
MAKES 3¼ teaspoons

Citrus-Ginger Glaze

2 tablespoons orange marmalade
1 tablespoon minced ginger root (or to taste)
1 clove garlic, minced
3 tablespoons fresh lemon or lime juice
3 tablespoons white wine vinegar
¼ cup fresh orange juice
3 tablespoons olive oil

PREPARATION

Combine the marmalade, ginger, garlic, lemon or lime juice, vinegar and orange juice in a non-reactive saucepan. Bring mixture to a boil over medium heat, and boil until mixture is reduced to about ½ cup. Remove from heat, and cool; whisk in the olive oil.

Brush your fish with the glaze, and place on a heated barbecue grill that has been brushed with oil to prevent the fish from sticking. Turn fish once, and glaze frequently during cooking. Do not overcook. It is enough for 1½ pounds fish.   MAKES ¾ cup

Blackened Fish Seasoning

3 tablespoons paprika
2 teaspoons salt
2 teaspoons onion powder
1½ teaspoons garlic powder
1½ teaspoons cayenne pepper
1½ teaspoons black pepper
1½ teaspoons dried thyme, crushed
1½ teaspoons dried oregano, crushed

PREPARATION

Combine all ingredients in a shallow dish, and blend well. It is enough for 3 pounds fish.   MAKES 1 cup

Creole Seasoning I

2 teaspoons freshly ground black pepper
1 teaspoon cayenne or red pepper
2 teaspoons dried tarragon, crushed
2 teaspoons dried basil, crushed
1 tablespoon onion salt (see Fishwife's Tip)
2 teaspoons garlic powder
2 to 4 tablespoons paprika
2 teaspoons salt

PREPARATION

Combine all ingredients, and mix thoroughly.
MAKES about ⅓ cup

FISHWIFE'S TIP

Vary these ingredients according to taste preferences. If you are watching your salt intake, use onion powder in place of onion salt.

Creole Seasoning II

1 tablespoon salt
2 to 3 teaspoons freshly ground pepper
1 teaspoon cayenne pepper
2 teaspoons garlic powder
2 teaspoons thyme
2 teaspoons dried basil

PREPARATION

Grind together all ingredients until the mixture is fine. (May be stored in an airtight container up to a year.)
MAKES ⅓ cup

Lemon Marinade With Fennel

¼ cup oil
2 tablespoons fresh lemon juice
2 tablespoons cilantro
½ teaspoon fennel seeds, crushed
1 clove garlic, minced or pressed
Zest from the lemon

PREPARATION

Combine all ingredients; blend well.
MAKES ½ cup

Eloise's Crunchy Herb Rub

1 tablespoon curry powder
2 teaspoons freshly ground black pepper
¼ teaspoon anise seeds
¼ cup sesame seeds
Salt to taste
3 tablespoons oil

PREPARATION

Blend the curry powder, black pepper, anise and sesame seeds and salt in a bowl. Sprinkle mixture on both sides of fish; press on the herbs so that they stick to the fish. Brush oil on both sides of fish; cover, and let stand at room temperature for 15 minutes before grilling.
MAKES ½ cup

FISHWIFE'S TIP

This zesty rub is best used with 'ahi.

Lime Mustard

2 tablespoons coarse-grain mustard
2 tablespoons chopped lime zest
2 tablespoons fresh lime juice
½ teaspoon salt
¼ teaspoon freshly ground black pepper
  (or to taste)

PREPARATION

Mix together all ingredients. Brush fish with the mustard before grilling or broiling. It is enough for 1½ pounds fillets.   MAKES ¼ cup

FISHWIFE'S TIP
This mustard is best on oily fish.

Minty-Mustard Paste

½ cup Dijon mustard (smooth)
½ cup sugar
1 tablespoon lemon juice
1 tablespoon orange juice
1 tablespoon minced fresh mint leaves

PREPARATION

Combine all ingredients in a non-reactive, oven-proof dish that will hold your fish in one layer. Marinate your fish in the paste for at least an hour. Turn fish once.

Remove the fish, and place it on an oiled barbecue grill. Brush with the paste while the fish cooks. Turn the fish once. Serve immediately. It is enough for 1½ pounds fillets.   MAKES 1 cup

FISHWIFE'S TIP
Fresh thyme can be substituted for the mint.

Molasses Barbecue Basting Sauce

¼ cup shoyu
½ cup sake or white wine
2 tablespoons molasses
2 tablespoons minced ginger root
1 clove garlic, minced or pressed
½ cup minced sweet onion
1 teaspoon sesame oil (or mirin)
  Juice of one lemon
  Zest of 1 lemon

PREPARATION

Combine all ingredients in a non-reactive bowl; let stand for 1 hour. Brush sauce on fish frequently while barbecuing.

MAKES 1 cup

Spices of India Blend

3 tablespoons ground cumin
4½ teaspoons ground ginger
4½ teaspoons turmeric
3 teaspoons ground coriander
1 to 2 teaspoons cayenne, or to taste
3 teaspoons black pepper

PREPARATION

Combine all ingredients, and store in an airtight jar.
MAKES ½ cup

FISHWIFE'S TIP
To use as a marinade for shrimp, process 2 tablespoons of the blend with ½ cup tightly packed Chinese parsley (cilantro) leaves, ⅓ cup lemon juice, ¼ cup peanut oil, 4 cloves garlic and ¼ cup cashews to a smooth paste. Coat shrimp with paste, and marinate them for at least 2 hours.

Fishwife's Savory Herb Blend

2 tablespoons dried lemon thyme
2 tablespoons dried sage, rubbed
1 tablespoon dried rosemary
1 tablespoon dried parsley flakes
¾ tablespoon dried lemon peel
¾ tablespoon dried shallots
½ tablespoon dried green peppercorns

PREPARATION

Coarsely grind all herbs together. Store, tightly covered, for no more than 3 months.

MAKES ⅓ cup

Fishwife's Spicy Herb Blend

1½ tablespoons dried lemon thyme
1 tablespoon dried oregano
1 tablespoon dried shallots
1 tablespoon dried garlic
1 tablespoon coriander seed
1½ to 2½ tablespoons green peppercorns
2 teaspoons dried Szechwan peppercorns

PREPARATION

Coarsely grind all ingredients together. Store, covered, for no more than 3 months.

MAKES ⅓ cup

FISHWIFE'S TIP

When you create your own dried herb blends, purchase and use freeze-dried herbs for the best flavor and results.

Fresh Herb Seasoning for Shrimp

1 tablespoon minced parsley
1 teaspoon minced thyme
1 teaspoon minced marjoram
1 teaspoon minced chives
1 clove garlic, minced
¼ teaspoon minced, seeded jalapeno chili (or to taste)
½ cup chopped green onions (white and green parts)
1 tablespoon fresh lime juice
¼ teaspoon paprika
Pinch ground cloves
Dash hot pepper sauce

PREPARATION

Finely chop all ingredients together in a food processor. Refrigerate, covered, for up to 4 days. When ready to use, sauté seasoning and shrimp together in a tablespoon of olive oil. It is enough for 2 pounds of large shrimp.

MAKES ½ cup

Barbecue Herb Mix

1 tablespoon fennel seeds
2 tablespoons lemon zest
1 tablespoon dried tarragon
⅔ cup pickling spice

PREPARATION

Combine all ingredients in a food processor or blender until coarsely ground. Store in an airtight container for up to 3 weeks.

MAKES ¾ cup

Notes

A Guide to Microwave Fish Cookery

I confess. I've rarely used a microwave to cook fish, probably because I don't feel as much in control once I close that microwave door as I do when I cook fish on top of the stove. What if I "overzap" and ruin the fish? (It's easy to do, by the way, and the fish will be tough! The saving grace is it will be moist–for a while–and tough, rather than dry and tough, as it is when you overcook using conventional cooking methods.)

Anyway, I've succumbed, at least for the purpose of writing this section, but I was confused at first. Some books or recipes say to cook on "high," and others say "medium" is best. And what about covering the fish? Which method should we trust most–a tight seal of plastic wrap, or loose covering of wax paper or a paper towel? It's obvious the tight wrap will keep the liquid from evaporating, so you'd expect the fish would be very moist and tender when it is cooked tightly covered. And, you'll have an accumulation of mildly flavored natural juices to use as a sauce base.

So, I experimented, using kajiki. First, I cut the fish into 8 small pieces, each 1 inch thick. I cooked the pieces 1 at a time, using both the "high" and "medium" settings and changing the "cover" each time.

Here's what I learned: Whether the fish was cooked on "high" or "medium," there was little, if any, difference in the amount of liquid left in the dish. When covered tightly with plastic wrap, 1 tablespoon of liquid accumulated; with wax paper, only half that amount was left in the dish; with a paper towel laid on top, only one-fourth that amount was left; with no cover on the dish, the dish was almost dry and the edges of the fish seemed dry, too. (There wasn't a noticeable difference in the texture and moistness of the fish when cooked on these two temperatures, either. But once the fish cooled completely, the texture was best on the piece cooked on "high," tightly covered.)

I still don't really know how long you should cook the fish in the microwave; I just watched the fish turn from pink to white and then took it out. It seemed to work. But, to give you better guidelines, I looked up advice from Barbara Kafka, author of the "Microwave Gourmet," and included her timing method below.

To calculate cooking time on "high," work with these numbers: a ½-inch thick fillet (roughly 4 ounces): 1 minute. If the fillet's weight is 8 ounces: 2 minutes. If your fish is 1 inch thick and 8 ounces: 3 minutes. If you cook 2 pieces at once, double the cooking time.

FISHWIFE'S TIPS

1. Keep pieces under 4 inches thick for even cooking.

2. As it does with conventional cooking methods, the fish will continue to cook after you remove it from the microwave, so time your fish with "standing time" in mind.

3. Watch the fish as it cooks. You'll see it begin to turn white from the outer edges. Stop cooking as soon as the fish is opaque. It could be a bit underdone but will continue to cook as it stands. If the fish flakes and breaks up when you move it, it's overdone.

4. If you're using fillets, fold the thinnest edge under so that the entire piece is an even thickness.

5. When you're cooking the fish with other ingredients that create juices, like tomatoes or fresh mushrooms, you might want to use wax paper or vented plastic wrap (fold wrap back to form an opening along one edge of your dish) to keep from ending up with too much liquid in your dish.

6. Salt added directly to the surface of the fish can toughen the fish and distort the pattern of the microwaves.

7. Flavors intensify in the microwave, so don't use a heavy hand with herbs and spices.

8. Other options you can use (besides plastic wrap, wax paper and paper toweling) to wrap the fish include parchment paper and fresh, clean leaves of spinach, cabbage, lettuce or chard.

9. Arrange fish with thicker parts toward the outside of the cooking dish.

10. A general rule to converting a recipe for the microwave: reduce the amount of required liquid to three-fourths and cooking time to one-fourth of the original suggested time.

Snapper With Ginger

1 pound small snapper fillets
 (between ½ to ¾ inch thick)
2 tablespoons orange juice
4 teaspoons shoyu
2 teaspoons finely shredded or minced ginger
1 teaspoon orange zest
 Chopped green onion or Chinese parsley
 Orange wedges

PREPARATION

Set fillets on your cooking dish. Combine the orange juice and shoyu, and drizzle over the fish. Sprinkle ginger and orange zest over the fish. Cover with plastic wrap. Microwave at full power (100 percent) until fish is slightly translucent (it should still be moist and slightly underdone in the center), about 2 to 3 minutes. Let stand a couple of minutes. Garnish with green onion or Chinese parsley, and squeeze orange wedges over the fish before serving. SERVES 4

Mahimahi With Mushrooms and Herbs

1 pound mahimahi (or salmon, or any fish),
 cut into 4 serving-sized pieces
½ teaspoon dried Italian herbs or dill
6 medium mushrooms, cleaned and sliced
½ cup chopped chives
2 tablespoons water
2 tablespoons fresh lime juice
 Salt and freshly ground black pepper to taste

PREPARATION

Lay fish pieces in cooking dish. Add herbs, mushrooms and chives. Add water; cover with plastic wrap. Microwave for 4 to 6 minutes. Remove from oven and let stand 2 minutes. Pour lime juice over fish, and season with salt and pepper.

SERVES 4

Pat's Fish in Orange Sauce

1 pound fish fillets, or steaks
 (mahimahi, snapper, papio)
1 teaspoon finely shredded orange peel
1 cup orange juice
1 medium carrot, shredded
1 tablespoon cornstarch
¼ teaspoon salt (optional)
½ cup chopped cucumber

PREPARATION

Place fish in an 8-inch square baking dish. (If using fillets with thin edges, turn those edges under so the fillets will have an even thickness.) Cover with vented plastic wrap, and cook on "high" for 4 to 6 minutes. If your oven doesn't have a carousel, turn dish after 4 minutes. Keep fish warm while you make the sauce.

Stir together orange peel, orange juice, carrot, cornstarch and, if you wish, ¼ teaspoon salt, in a 2-cup glass measure or bowl. Cook, uncovered, on high for 3 to 5 minutes, or until sauce is thickened and bubbly, stirring every minute. Stir in the cucumbers. Pour over fish, and serve. SERVES 4

Tarragon Fish Fillets

1 pound fillets (snapper, papio)
2 tablespoons olive oil
  Juice of ½ lemon
¼ teaspoon salt
¼ teaspoon freshly ground black pepper
½ teaspoon dried tarragon

PREPARATION

Mix the olive oil, lemon juice, salt, pepper and tarragon in a plate. Add fish, and turn to get the oil/lemon juice mixture on both sides. Let fish marinate in the plate for 10 minutes.

Cover plate tightly, and microwave on high for 3 to 4 minutes, or until fish is opaque. Transfer the fish to a serving dish, and cover lightly (not with a paper towel because it will absorb any moisture that is on the fish) to keep warm.

Return the plate with the juices to the microwave, and cook, uncovered for 2 minutes, or until the juices are slightly reduced. Stir, and pour over the fish.

SERVES 4

Fish Fillets Olé

2 pounds fillets
1 small tomato, chopped
½ cup chopped onion
½ cup chopped green pepper
2 tablespoons butter
¼ cup green chili salsa
2 tablespoons lemon juice
3 tablespoons chopped black olives
1 tablespoon chopped parsley
1 clove garlic, minced
  Salt and hot pepper sauce (to taste)
¼ cup dry white wine

PREPARATION

Combine the tomato, onion, green pepper, butter, salsa, lemon juice, olives, parsley, garlic, salt and hot pepper sauce in a 13-inch by 9-inch baking dish. Cover with wax paper, and cook on high for 5 minutes. Stir, and add the white wine.

Place the fish fillets on top of the sauce, and spoon some of the sauce over the fish. Cover with wax paper, and cook on high for 6 to 8 minutes, depending on the thickness of the fish. Turn the dish once during cooking if you don't have a carousel in your oven.

SERVES 6

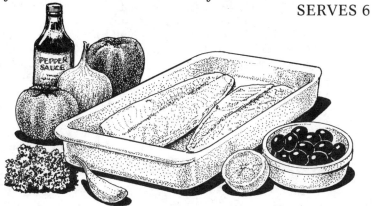

Notes

FISHWIFE'S TIPS FOR SMOKING FISH
with help from Luhr-Jensen and "Cooking Alaskan"

Fish Preparation:
1. Scale your fish, especially if you leave skin on, and clean them. Use the freshest fish possible.
2. If your fish are small, like 'opelu or akule, you can simply fillet them. For larger fish, cut your pieces into strips (as a guide, I always use the shape and size of my husband Jim's harmonica, sometimes making the strips a bit thinner). Remember, the thicker the pieces, the longer they will take to brine, dry and smoke.

Brining:
1. Salting is essential. It helps slow spoilage. The usual ratio of salt to water is ½ cup salt to 1 quart of water. Always use non-iodized salt.
2. Here's a general guideline from "Big Chief": brine chunks or strips 1 inch thick 8 to 12 hours, fillets to ½ inch thick 4 hours, and thin pieces from 2 to 4 hours. The length of time is up to you, but remember that it *is* possible to brine the fish too long, which could result in a finished product that is too salty (and too hot, depending on the ingredients). If the recipe says "brine 4 hours or longer," figure 4 hours is the ideal. If you have to leave it longer, make 6 hours the maximum.
3. *Never use wooden or aluminum containers.* Glass, crockery or plastic are fine. We use large, heavy-duty, Ziploc bags. They are convenient, you can *lomi* (rub) them to distribute the brine, and they stack well in your refrigerator. The plastic cooler tray that comes in your ice chest is perfect too.
4. Keep the brines as cool as possible. If you start with warm water, which helps dissolve the salt and sugar faster, cool down the brine before putting it on your fish.
5. You can reuse the brines, according to the "Big Chief" recipe book, but reuse should be limited to 2 or 3 times over a 1-week period. Remember that the brine draws out fish juices, which become part of the brine.

Desalting:
1. Rinse off the fish until all visible salt particles are gone. You might even have to soak the fish in several changes of water to remove saltiness.
2. Test for saltiness by cooking a small piece of fish and tasting it or by running your fingers over the flesh and then tasting them for saltiness.
3. Pat the fish dry and lay it on racks so the air can circulate on all sides. (We dry the fish directly on the Big Chief smoker racks, which saves us from having to move it later.)

Air-Drying:
1. Pellicle is the key word here. The pellicle is a gloss that forms on the fish's surface once it is dry. If the fish is not properly dried before smoking, it could "steam" in the smoker and white spots might develop on the flesh. It will taste good, though.
2. Depending on where you air-dry the fish, it could take several hours or a day.

Smoking:
1. The Big Chief takes it from here. It provides the proper temperature and air flow to raise the internal temperature of your fish to 165°, which pasteurizes it and inhibits natural deterioration. The only effort on your part is adding the wood chips every so often–every 3 hours or so. Length of smoking time depends on the fish's thickness: thick chunks, 8 to 12 hours, using 3 pans of wood chips; pieces to ½-inch thick, 5 to 8 hours, with 2 pans of chips; thin pieces, 2 to 4 hours, using 1 or 2 pans of chips.

Storing:
1. Cool fish first.
2. Wrap tightly, and store in the refrigerator if you plan to eat it right away. Otherwise, freeze and thaw as you need it.

Smoking Your Catch

Smoking fish is nothing new in Hawai'i, or in other parts of the world, for that matter. What began as a means of protection from spoilage has become a preferred way of preparing and eating fish. Smoked fish is available packaged in supermarkets throughout Hawai'i, but it's also easy and interesting to smoke your own. Whether you use an old, converted refrigerator, a wooden shed, a 50-gallon drum, an imu (underground oven) or an electric model, the results are wonderful.

We use a Big Chief, made by Luhr-Jensen, one of many electric brands on the market, and in it we've smoked 'ahi, mahimahi, swordfish, 'opelu, ono and even salmon with great results. (Catching salmon has become increasingly popular with island residents, and many bring home their salmon catch to smoke here.)

Because eating smoked fish is common in Hawai'i, 3 experts in the fish smoking arena share recipes and tips for beginners and "advanced" fish smokers alike: Juan Waroquiers, renown captain of the charterboat ILLUSIONS; Al Sullivan, owner-operator of Tanaku Lodge in Alaska and part-time resident of Hawai'i and Oregon; and Mike Dahlager, former Alaska commercial fisherman.

Although each has his preferred method of preparation and smoking techniques, all agree that the air-drying step is most crucial. Their message is this: "Don't rush it. Wait until you get a nice, hard glaze on the fish before you begin smoking it." Their second piece of advice is to experiment with the smoker and the length of time you smoke your fish to get the end product that suits you best.

First, here are 3 important facts to remember:

1. Salt is the preservative and is an essential part of the brine. The usual ratio of salt to water is ½ cup salt to 1 quart of water. Remember not to use wooden or aluminum containers!

2. Rinse the brine off fish before setting it out to dry.

3. Air-dry the fish until the water has dripped off and a glaze (pellicle) forms on the surface; this could take several hours or a day, depending on the thickness of your fish pieces. (Protect from flies with screening.)

Juan Waroquiers' Salmon Brine

Juan Waroquiers prefers fillets to chunks because he likes to slice off and serve thin pieces of salmon. If the fillets are too large for the smoker, he cuts them to fit, keeping those cut pieces as large as possible. He recommends you make your fillets as even as possible, gently pounding the thickest parts to flatten them, to ensure even smoking.

- 20 **pounds salmon fillets, skin on**
- 1 **gallon water**
- 1 **pound brown sugar**
- 1 **pound rock salt**
  Black pepper, jalapenos or additional spices optional, but not necessary

PREPARATION

Brine the salmon for 2 days to let the flavors really soak into the meat. Drain off the brine, but do not rinse the fillets because this brine isn't as salty as some can be. In cool weather, or in a cooler climate, air-dry the fillets outdoors in a screened enclosure (leave the skin on if you want to use this method, so you can hang the fillets by the skin) for 8 or 9 hours. If it is hot and sunny, as it often is in Hawai'i, the fish can spoil, so use the refrigerator, laying the fillets on racks with a tray at the bottom to catch the water that drips off. This drying method takes 1 or 2 days.

CHEF'S NOTE

Juan prefers to smoke salmon over hickory chips to a soft, pate-like texture, which he creates with the Big Chief by replenishing the hickory chips more frequently than is ordinarily necessary. "Once the chips in the tray turn totally black, I refill with fresh chips." He uses three trayfuls in 3 to 4 hours—the time it takes to complete the job. "But the hotter you smoke, the more perishable the product is, so you have to refrigerate it right away." Juan also freezes his smoked fish.

Al Sullivan's Tanaku Lodge Salmon Brine

Al Sullivan uses the Big Chief when he is at home in Oregon, but at Tanaku Lodge he smokes large quantities of salmon and halibut in a smokehouse he built (patterned after an old-fashioned outhouse). As is the case with many "creative" cooks, Al can't give us a specific quantity of fish for his recipe; he just "makes a gallon of brine in a 5-gallon, plastic bucket, fills the bucket with chunked fish," and calls it done. Nor does he give us amounts for the other ingredients–you'll see why when you read his recipe, which we give you with his step-by-step procedure.

PREPARATION

Cut salmon fillets into chunks, 2 by 4 inches. Leave skin on. Put 1 gallon of water in a large, non-metal container. Add enough salt to float a raw egg. (Al swears by this method, but be sure to measure the salt as you add it to the water because once the egg is floating, you will add ½ to ⅔ as much brown sugar to the amount of salt you just used!) The fish chunks should be submerged in the brine. Al uses another 5-gallon bucket, fills it with enough water to make it heavy, and uses it as a weight to hold the fish in the brine.

Al brines the salmon for 8 or 9 hours or overnight, drains the brine from the salmon, then swirls the fish around in cold water to remove the salt on the surface. (If your fish pieces are thin, rinse them more carefully because they'll absorb more brine than will thick pieces.)

Al drains and dries the fish on his smoker racks, laying them skin-side down, leaving ½ to 1 inch between pieces so the air circulates around them. While the pieces are still damp, he sprinkles them lightly with coarse ground pepper to taste. Depending on the weather, the fish could dry and glaze over in 2 to 3 hours.

Smoking time depends on taste and texture preferences and the size of your chunks: 8 to 12 hours. Al uses alder chips in Alaska and apple or cherry in Oregon.

'Big Chief' Basic Brine
suggested for all fish, meat and poultry

½ **cup non-iodized salt**
½ **cup white household vinegar**
1 **quart water**

PREPARATION

Mix salt and vinegar in a 1-quart jar, half-full of warm water. When thoroughly mixed, fill the jar to the brim with cold tap water. Refrigerate the solution if you are not going to use it immediately. The cooler the better.

VARIATIONS

Add the following ingredients to suit your preferences. You are limited only by your imagination.

Herbs: basil, bay leaf, dill, marjoram, oregano, parsley, rosemary, sage, tarragon, thyme.

Spices: allspice, caraway, cayenne, celery seed, cloves, cumin, curry, ginger, mace, nutmeg, pepper, turmeric.

Other: citrus juices, garlic, onion, prepared products (Tabasco, Worcestershire sauce, Kitchen Bouquet, Maggi, stir-fry sauce, et cetera), sesame seeds, shoyu, sugar and wines.

'Big Chief' Smokey Smelt
The Beer-Drinker's Friend–a Luhr-Jensen recipe

1 **cup non-iodized salt**
1 **cup brown sugar**
1 **cup shoyu**
½ **cup cider vinegar**
1 **tablespoon Worcestershire sauce**
1 **tablespoon paprika**
1 **tablespoon chili powder**
1 **tablespoon garlic salt (optional)**
1 **tablespoon onion salt**
½ **teaspoon black pepper**
3 **cups warm water**

PREPARATION

We used 'opelu, 20 fish, total weight about 10 pounds, scaled and filleted with skin on.

Mix all brine ingredients in warm water. Let brine cool before covering the fish. Brine for 4 or more hours; rinse and air-dry (See Fishwife's Tips on desalting and air-drying). Smoke 5 to 7 hours, or until the fish is smoked to your specification.

Mike Dahlager uses his smoker to hot-smoke and cool-smoke his fish. To get a cooler smoke, he sets the cover on top diagonally (or removes it completely) so the heat can escape and cool down the temperature. (Luhr-Jensen has directions for cool-smoking, using the cardboard box.)

Mike, who prefers alder wood over any other, shares two recipes for cooked smoked salmon from the University of Alaska's Cooperative Extension Service. To adapt the recipes for use in the Big Chief, he suggests you "crack the cover" to let the heat escape. The goal is to use a slow dehydration, because too hot a fire can result in a tough, rubbery product, Mike says. He leaves the skin on the salmon because "that's where the fat is and it seeps into the flesh and makes it even better." He rinses his fish to get all of the salt off the surface, and he pats the pieces dry with paper towels before setting them on racks to dry. "Look for a hard glaze to form before you start smoking," Mike says.

Cool-Smoked Salmon Brine

**Cleaned and filleted salmon
(no amount given)**
2 **cups salt**
1 **cup brown sugar**
2 **tablespoons white pepper**
1 **tablespoon** *each* **crushed bay leaves,
    allspice, crushed whole cloves and mace.**

PREPARATION

Dredge salmon fillets in salt mixture (you want it to cling to the flesh). Cover, and let sit for 6 hours in the refrigerator. Rinse under running water to remove all traces of salt. Soak salmon in running, or frequently changed water, for 4 to 6 hours. Air-dry for 6 hours.

Smoke in low temperature (below 100°) for 2 days.

Mike's Kippered Salmon
*Kippered salmon is dried in cool smoke,
then cooked in warm smoke for several hours.*

Salmon, cut into chunks
2 **quarts water**
2½ **cups salt**

PREPARATION

Soak the salmon chunks in the brine for ½ to 2 hours, making sure they're well-covered. Rinse pieces thoroughly in running water, and air-dry on racks for 1 or 2 hours, or until shiny and dry to the touch.

Smoke fish at low temperatures (80° to 90°, so remove smoker cover completely or set at a diagonal) until a glossy skin has formed (could be 8 to 15 hours, depending on temperature of the smoker). Increase temperature (put cover back on tightly), and smoke 1 or 2 more hours.

Cool Smoking
Juan Waroquiers sometimes slows the temperature and cooking by letting the first tray of chips smoke, then he unplugs the smoker to let it smoke slowly. (Sometimes he leaves it this way for 5 or 6 hours.) When the smoke has stopped, he plugs it in again, replaces the chips and repeats these steps. Although it takes 1 or 2 days, morning of day 1 to evening of day 2, he says the fish lasts longer.

Hot Smoking
The fish is smoked at a higher temperature (between 160° and 180°) and is fully cooked and flavored. It will not keep long unless it is refrigerated or frozen.

Cold Smoking
Used mostly to preserve fish for canning, this method does not cook the fish. However, the longer you smoke it at a low temperature, and the more salt you use to preserve it, the longer it will keep.

The following brine recipes were the first we experimented with when we first started smoking fish, and we still use them. They are simple and use ingredients that most of us always have on hand.

Savory Smoke Cure

1 cup Hawaiian or rock salt
1 cup firmly packed brown sugar
1 teaspoon black pepper
1 teaspoon ground ginger
1 teaspoon ground allspice
1 bay leaf, crumbled
2 cloves garlic, minced or pressed
⅓ cup maple syrup
1½ tablespoons shoyu

PREPARATION

We used ulua and ono loins, total about 15 pounds.

Mix the salt, sugar, pepper, ¾ teaspoon of the ginger, allspice, bay leaf and garlic. Sprinkle ⅓ of the salt mixture into a non-reactive container large enough to hold the fish pieces laid flat. Set fish on top of the salt mixture. (If the fish has skin, lay it skin-side down.) Pat remaining salt mixture onto fish; cover. (We had 2 layers of fish in 1 pan, so we put the salt mixture on bottom of container, added fish and more salt mixture, added second layer of fish, and topped it off with the remaining salt mixture.) Cover, and chill for up to 6 hours.

Rinse fish thoroughly under cool water, rubbing the flesh to get rid of the salt. Pat the fish dry with paper towels. Let fish stand at room temperature until the surface is dry and feels tacky, about an hour.

Mix the maple syrup, shoyu and the rest of the ginger (¼ teaspoon) in a small bowl. Baste the fish; let the glaze dry; turn fish over, and baste again. Be sure to let the fish dry before putting it in the smoker.
(See Fishwife's Tips.)

Smoked Fish á la Sid Weinrich
from "Modern Hawaiian Gamefishing"

½ cup Hawaiian salt
¾ cup brown sugar
4 cloves garlic, pressed or smashed
2 tablespoons ground red pepper
4 cups water

PREPARATION

We used ono and ulua loins and filleted 'opelu, about 6 pounds total.

Dissolve the first 4 ingredients in the water. Add fish, and marinate for 3 to 4 hours in the refrigerator. Wash the fish off carefully in cold water. Dry for 2 or 3 hours. Smoke until it is as hard and dry as you prefer.

CHEF'S NOTE

This recipe originally called for smoking in a 22-inch kettle-type barbecue grill. We followed the directions (igniting 16 briquets, placing them on each side of the fire grate once they turned gray, and sprinkling moistened wood chips over the hot coals) and found that our kettle didn't distribute the heat evenly. After 1 hour, some pieces were hot enough to cook while others felt cool to the touch. Although we tried to make it work (adding coals, adjusting vents), we quit and added it to the other fish in the Big Chief.

I also fried and oven-dried the fish, using this cure. Both were successful, and the fried version was especially tasty.

To oven-dry, set oven at lowest heat (but at least 165°) and place fish on a rack set over a cookie sheet or broiler pan. Baste with the maple glaze; after the glaze has set, turn fish over and baste the other side. Repeat occasionally. Remove fish from the oven when it has dried to the consistency you prefer.

To fry, baste the fish on both sides with the glaze, letting 1 side dry before turning the fish over. Heat a small amount of oil over medium heat in a skillet. Add sliced green onion and sesame seeds to the skillet. Sauté briefly. Add the fish, and sauté quickly on both sides. Remove from the heat.

Notes

Tips on Fish

How Shall I Cook This?

Fish vary in size, flavor intensity, texture and fat content or oiliness. Most of us just cook it and enjoy it! Fish is fish, right? Right, but we also know that certain factors can make the difference between a wonderfully succulent feast or a woefully dry fish.

Size and flavor intensity are easy to deal with; what's difficult is figuring out which fish are lean, which are fatty, and which are in-between. This isn't important from a nutritional standpoint, but it's crucial to the end result–your meal. By matching the cooking method with the fish's texture and fat content, and timing the fish properly, you'll be assured of perfectly cooked fish, every time.

'Ahi has a high fat content, which means it has rich tasting, firm flesh that can stand up to all the cooking methods in this book, including dry heat methods (grill, broil). Just be sure you marinate the fish in advance, or baste it as you barbecue.

The billfish, ono and opah are considered "dense and meaty," with distinctive flavors and medium-firm texture. The mahimahi has medium-firm flesh and moderately rich flavor. All can be prepared in the cooking method of your choice.

Snapper are mild-flavored and delicately textured, so they do best steamed, baked in a sauce, sautéed, or broiled with moist heat.

When substituting one type of fish for another, especially if you don't know how fatty or lean the fish are, you'll be pretty safe by sticking with the same color and denseness of the fish. You can count on baking, poaching, steaming and sautéing as safe methods for all fish. Otherwise, time fish carefully and baste when necessary.

Sashimi

Preparing sashimi, sliced raw fish, is an art. We may see it offered in haphazard chunks of all shapes and sizes, but in the true Japanese tradition it is finely sliced, thin and small enough to put into your mouth easily. How to do it?

1. Use only fresh, boneless, skinless fillets of fish. In Japan, it isn't uncommon to use only the back fillet of a fish.

2. Before you begin slicing the sashimi, prepare your serving dish with a lining of grated or thinly sliced vegetables, like carrot, turnip, red or green cabbage, leafy watercress tips or lettuce. To make a nice presentation, use a color that will enhance the sashimi. For white-meat fish, choose colorful vegetables, saving the lighter varieties for 'ahi or aku. Prepare the fillets by cutting them into segments or lengths that are the diameter you want your finished slices to be. If your fish fillets are large, cut them lengthwise into however many segments you need, being sure that the crosswise pieces you get will measure no more than 1 inch by 1½ inches.

3. Use cold fish, and for cutting ease keep your knife wet.

4. Aim for slices no more than ⅛ inch thick. This is easily done if you use an extremely sharp knife (I use the resident fisherman's filleting knife) and try to make the cut in one movement, rather than sawing the knife blade back and forth.

5. Let the slices fall as you slice. They will make a neat, domino-like row that you can transfer to your vegetable-lined serving plate row by row. (Slide your knife blade under the row to move it.) However, many folks prefer to place each slice, one at a time, on the vegetable bed so that guests can easily get the slice and vegetable to eat together.

6. It's best to slice the sashimi shortly before serving and return it to the refrigerator to stay cold until you want it.

Refrigeration Tips

1. Clean the fish. Refrigerate it whole, or cut into the serving size you're planning to use.

2. Be sure the fish is kept in the coldest part of your refrigerator. If your refrigerator is set at 32°F, you're in good shape and can count on the fish keeping for 2 or 3 days, depending on whether it's lean or fatty. The leaner the fish, the longer it will keep.

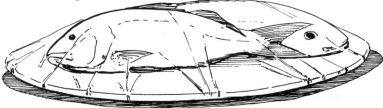

3. Store the fish on a plate, covered with foil or plastic wrap, or put the plate into a Ziploc bag. You want to keep the fish wrapped airtight.

4. For added insurance, add some ice cubes on the wrapped fish to keep it extra-cold.

FISHWIFE'S TIP
If you've purchased the fish from the market, don't rinse it off before following the storage rules above. The water could cause the flesh to break down faster. Do rinse it just before cooking, and then pat it dry.

How To Freeze

It can't be helped. Much as we'd like to do otherwise, we sometimes have to freeze our fish. The rule of thumb here is to protect the fish's flavor and texture by freezing it as soon as possible. After all, when you thaw the fish and eat it, you want it to taste as close to fresh as possible. The longer you wait to freeze the fish, the more likelihood there is that the quality of the fish will be poor. If you've left your fish in the refrigerator for a few days, chances are the natural fish oils have begun to turn rancid and bacteria have spread through the flesh.

Before we look at successful ways of freezing fish, remember never to freeze fish that you've purchased at the market unless you've asked the butcher whether the fish has already been frozen once. Markets often buy larger portions of fish than they can sell readily, freeze some, and then defrost them to sell at a later date. If a fish has been frozen once, eat it right away. Don't refreeze it.

Pre-Freezing Tips
1. Clean your fish first. Otherwise, body waste or even undigested food could spoil the fish.

2. Decide what sizes and shapes you want to freeze. Cut your fish into recipe-sized portions unless you wish to freeze it whole.

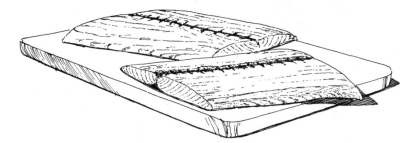

Freezing Tips

There are several ways to freeze your fish. Real fish connoisseurs say you should first determine whether you have a lean fish or a fatty fish. Freezing methods differ a bit depending on the fat content, but the general method used is the "dip and glaze." This method takes some time because it demands several steps, but the results are good.

FOR LEAN FISH

1. You'll want to freeze the fish in salted water.

2. Dissolve ⅓ cup of salt in each quart of water you use for freezing.

3. Get the water very cold or partially frozen if you can. Take the fish, immerse it in the salted water for 30 to 60 seconds, place the fish (wrapped if you wish) on a baking sheet in the freezer to turn the water into a glaze, then dip the fish again (for about 30 seconds) in the salted solution, remove, wrap it tightly in moisture-proof freezer paper while the fish is still wet, and freeze immediately. As you repeat the dipping and freezing, a thicker ice glaze results. If you can take the time to repeat this step 3 or 4 times, it will be to your advantage. Otherwise, twice is sufficient.

FOR FATTY FISH (usually a red-meat fish)

1. Use the same method, but substitute 2 tablespoons of ascorbic acid powder (vitamin C) for the salt.

2. Wrap the fish tightly in moisture-proof freezer paper while the fish is still wet. The wetter the fish, the better the protection. While wrapping, try to get all the air out of the package.

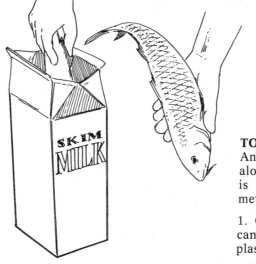

TOTAL IMMERSION

Another method that you can use alone or with the "dip and glaze" is the "immersion" container method.

1. Choose your container. You can use a clean milk carton or a plastic container.

2. Fill your container half full of water, put the fish into it, and fill with water to about 1 inch from the container top. (You can mix ice pieces with the water if you wish.) Don't worry if the finny part of the tail is above water. Close the top (staple or paper clip), and freeze. When you're ready to defrost, just peel the carton away. If you've used a plastic container, you'll have to thaw the block a bit before you can remove it.

Regardless of which freezing method you use, always label your wrapping. Be sure to put the type of fish it is, the date it was frozen and the amount frozen.

How Long To Freeze Fish

As short a time as possible. Prolonged storage will dry the fish out and deteriorate its flavor and quality. If your fish is fatty, use it within 3 months. If it is lean, store it no longer than 6 months.

How To Thaw Fish

You don't really need to thaw fish before cooking. If you cook it frozen, double the cooking time. If you want to thaw it, do so in its original container and in the refrigerator. Fish thawed at room temperature thaws unevenly, gets watery and mushy, and tastes worse than it looks. If you are desperate and must thaw it quickly, thaw the fish in its original wrapper under cold running water, about 30 minutes for each pound of fish. Use thawed fish immediately or, at most, within 2 days.

Thawed fish can have a strong fish smell or appear slimy. If this is the case, see next section.

Is the Fish Fresh?

Here are surefire ways to tell whether the fish you're purchasing (or receiving) is fresh.

In a whole fish, check for the following:

1. Bright eyes, not dull, cloudy or sunken.

2. Reddish gills and taut skin.

3. Scales firmly attached, not loose or dropping off.

4. Firm flesh that bounces back when poked, kind of like a cake does when you test it for doneness. If an indentation remains in the fish where your finger poked it, don't buy it.

5. Fresh smell, like ocean water, not fishy.

6. Rigidity. If the fish is not wrapped or packaged, pick it up and see if it flops down around your hand. If the fish is fresh and has been properly iced, it should be rigid.

In chunks, fillets and steaks, check for the following:

1. Firm flesh as above.

2. A solid piece of meat. If the piece looks like it is separating or the layers are coming apart, don't buy it. If there is a backbone attached to the piece, as there sometimes is in a fish steak, the flesh should not be pulling away from the bone.

3. Moist meat, not dry or dull. The color should be consistent and not discolored around the edges or in the center, as sometimes happens with beef.

4. Proper packaging, tight wrapping around the fish and little liquid in the plastic tray. If the fish has been poorly packaged, it will not stay as fresh.

5. No fishy smell. If you detect a strong fishy smell, don't buy the piece.

> In a warm climate, fishing is a favorite pastime. Whether standing patiently on shore or skimming the ocean waves, fishing enthusiasts never tire of trying to catch their favorite fish for dinner. But fish can spoil rapidly, especially if it isn't properly cared for upon catching. Under the best circumstances, we've given several steps to take to insure that your catch remains fresh until you get it home.

Keep It Fresh on Land or Sea

1. Kill the fish quickly. Letting it bang around on the rocks or aboard the boat can cause the easily damaged flesh to bruise, and this spoils the meat. Also, during a prolonged dying process a chemical change takes place in the flesh that could change the texture and quality of the meat.

2. Bleed the fish immediately after catching because the blood spoils the fastest. Many fishermen don't take the time to do this unless the fish is a tuna or ulua. (These fish spoil quickly, so every precaution should be taken to keep them fresh.) You bleed a fish by cutting through to the bone on one side of the tail, or by making a diagonal cut into the flesh behind the side fin, or by cutting into the gill area, or by reaching in and tearing the gill loose. Basically, you want to break an artery.

3. Put the fish on ice immediately. Small chunks of ice are better than one large block because the fish can be packed down into and surrounded by smaller pieces.

Getting Rid of Fish Odors

Fish can smell, especially if kept refrigerated too long or after thawing. Assuming that the fish is not spoiled, but has been improperly wrapped or stored, there are ways to get rid of this fishy odor.

1. Rub both sides of the fish with a paste of baking soda and water. Let the rubbed fish sit for 30 minutes. This paste will help absorb the fish odor.

2. Soak the fish in tomato juice, or cook it in a tomato-based recipe. The tomato magically rids the fish of any strong taste or odor.

3. Wipe the pieces with fresh lemon juice to help reduce bacteria. This tip is from Peter Merriman of Merriman's Restaurant.

Tips on Cooking Fish

How To Time Fish

There is only one way to cook fish: quickly! Nothing is worse than overcooked fish; it is tough, dry and unappetizing. Even the tastiest sauce won't save fish from being terrible if it's overcooked. And don't fall for recipe directions that suggest the "flake test." Digging up the surface of a piece of fish while you wait for it to flake creates a messy-looking fish. Canadians claim a foolproof method that you can use with confidence: cook your fish no more than 10 minutes for each inch of thickness. It's easy!

BUT: Remember that all rules have exceptions!

1. Fish continues to cook after it is removed from the heat, so it's better to remove the fish before the clock says it's done. After 8 minutes of cooking per inch, consider removing the fish from the heat. An extra minute could mean the difference between moist and dry fish.

2. Take the cooking method and heat into consideration when figuring the amount of time you'll need to cook the fish. If you're poaching, you need to begin timing when the poaching liquid begins to simmer. If you're baking a casserole-type dish, or covering your fish with sauces and cheese, plan on additional time. Lemon or lime juice marinades partially "cook" the fish, so cut your cooking time down, accordingly.

3. If you're cooking frozen fish, double the cooking time per inch of thickness.

4. If your fillets are thinner at the ends than in the middle, as is the case in large fish, cut down a bit on the cooking time so the ends won't be too dry. Other options are to turn the thin end of the fillet under to create an even thickness for even cooking, or cut off the thin ends and cook them separately. Keep covered until the thicker pieces on the grill are cooked.

Now that you've been cautioned and can see all the exceptions to the rule, back to the Canadian method. Measure the thickest part of the fish, and plan on a cooking time of 8 to 10 minutes per inch of thickness. Whether the fish is whole, stuffed, filleted, steaked, butterflied or whatever, measure it at its thickest part and calculate 8 to 10 minutes per inch. For example, if the fish or piece of fish measures 3 inches thick, you'll need to cook it between 24 and 30 minutes.

If you feel uncomfortable just timing, or are one of those cooks who likes to touch or test, try these tips:

1. Watch the color change. Raw fish is translucent; cooked fish is opaque. As you fry, the bottom of the fish will begin to turn white. Turn the fish over when the bottom half of the fish is white. Then, watch it carefully and remove it from the heat before it is completely white.

2. My fork test is neater than the old flake test. When the fish is cooked, a fork will slide into the flesh smoothly, with no resistance. If the fish is still raw inside, the fork will meet resistance, as though the flesh is rubbery. The nice thing about this testing method is that the fork holes don't show at all.

As a general rule, you can use the following temperatures for each method of cooking, but don't feel locked into any one of them. Each recipe will vary.

BAKE ....325° to 450°.

BROIL .... 550°, 8 to 10 minutes per inch of thickness when placed 3 to 4 inches below (or above if on an outdoor grill) the heat source.

SAUTÉ ....Medium-high.

POACH or STEAM .... 8 to 10 minutes per inch of thickness.

Baking

Baking is a versatile method of cooking fish, but it can be tricky. Some consider it the method in which you have the most control because there is no intense, direct heat on the fish as there is in broiling and grilling. However, the fish must be protected from the dry oven heat. Fish can be baked whole, stuffed, in steaks or fillets, but always *in a sauce or liquid that will keep it moist (see braising). Baked fish recipes include a sauce or a basting liquid to protect the fish; otherwise, that oven will dry out the fish in a flash. Temperatures for baking can range from 350° to 450°; some prefer to bake fish uncovered at 325° to 350° while others swear by 450°.*

To make a parchment paper pouch:
1. Begin with a 12- by 18-inch piece of parchment paper. Fold in half (to measure 12 by 9 inches).
2. Beginning at the folded edge, draw half a heart shape, as large as the paper will allow.
3. Cut out the heart with scissors.
4. Open the heart and brush lightly with oil. Leave a 2-inch border along the edge unoiled.
5. Place your fish (and "veggies") in the oiled center of one side of the heart. It can touch the fold, but not the unoiled part.
6. Fold over, and seal the pouch: make folds, beginning at the bottom point, incorporating old folds into new ones. Tuck the end under the pouch to secure it.

7. Place on a baking sheet. Bake at 400°. If sealed and folded correctly, steam will puff up the pouch, signifying that the dinner is done. If your pouch does not puff, remove it when you think the fish is done.

How to Make a Foil Package for Baking Fish
1. Place your fish lengthwise in the center of a sheet of foil 2½ or 3 times as long as the fish. (If you have a sauce that you are baking or steaming with the fish, put the foil on a plate that is large enough to hold the fish. The slight bowl shape of the plate will hold the sauce at the bottom of the foil.)
2. Bring the sides of the foil together above the fish. Fold the edges down together, 2 or 3 times, leaving some air space between the fish and foil.
3. On each end, fold the edges together 2 or 3 times toward the fish.

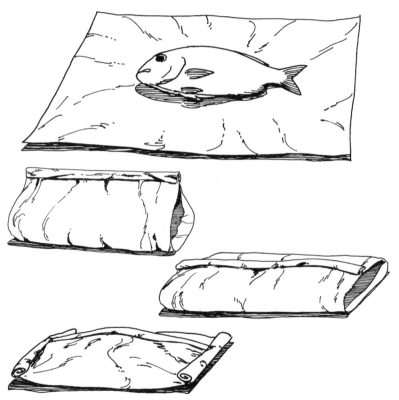

Note: Foil pouches can be refrigerated up to 24 hours. Paper pouches should be used within 4 hours.

FISHWIFE'S TIP
Cooking time should be increased by 3 to 5 minutes per inch of thickness if the fish is heavily sauced or covered with vegetables or cheese, or if the dish was prepared in advance and is going into the oven ice-cold.

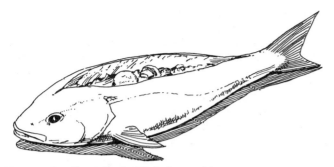

How to Stuff a Whole Fish for Baking

1. To stuff the conventional way, wash and dry a cleaned (gutted and scaled) whole fish. Slice the fish from the base of the head, on the stomach side, to the beginning of the tail.

   If you prefer to stuff the fish from the backside, remove the backbone of a whole fish by slicing along the length of the spine. Cut along the side of the fish that seems fatter to you. This is where the darkest meat will be. Carefully cut the flesh away from the spine by following the rib bones. Pull out the spine and attached rib bones. Clean the fish from the top. (If the head has been removed prior to removing the spine, most of the innards will have come out with the head. But finish the cleaning job, anyway. Rinse cavity.)

2. Sprinkle inside the cavity with some lemon juice, and rub it around. If you prefer, you can rub the cavity with onion or garlic powder, depending on the stuffing you plan to use.

3. Stuff.

4. Close the fish with small, oiled skewers, like those you would use on a turkey or a chicken. For a sure closing, use a heavy cord to lace the fish shut, crisscrossing the cord over the skewers.

5. If you prefer, you can bake the fish without closing it. Just lay the stuffing on the exposed flesh of the fish and mound it up everywhere.

6. If you've used the standard method of stuffing the stomach cavity, brush the skin surfaces of the fish with vegetable oil or melted butter (if you're not among the cholesterol conscious), so the fish won't stick to the baking pan or rack.

7. Measure stuffed fish at its thickest part (including stuffing), and calculate 8 to 10 minutes of cooking time per inch of thickness.

Braising

Braising is cooking with moist heat, on the stove or in the oven—a method that insures tender and juicy results with little effort. If you were braising beef, chicken or pork, your recipe would tell you to brown the meat before adding the liquids. In the case of fish, browning the fish first isn't necessary, but you can briefly brown the fish before you braise. Here are basics for this cooking technique:

1. Chop or dice some vegetables (a carrot, an onion, and 2 or 3 celery stalks). Sauté in a bit of liquid until softened; remove to a baking dish just large enough to hold fish.

2. Place fish on top. Season.

3. Add liquid (wine, fish stock, et cetera, about ½ cup per pound or pound and a half of fish).

4. Bake at 350°, basting often, until done. To cook on the stove, place vegetables, fish and liquid in a stove-top pan; bring the liquid to a boil; lower heat and cook slowly until done. Remove fish to a plate. If it sits in the hot broth, it will overcook.

5. Make a sauce of the broth: strain liquid into a saucepan; add chopped shallots or green onion, herbs, fresh tomatoes, et cetera

6. Oven temperature will vary (between 350° and 425°) according to the recipe.

FISHWIFE'S TIPS

General Cooking Techniques
1. Use non-stick cookware.
2. The faster fish is cooked, the juicier it will be.
3. With stove-top cooking, your skillet should be large enough to hold fish in one layer without crowding. Ideally, you'll have space between pieces. Otherwise, cook in 2 batches. (If pieces are too close together, they'll steam.) In the oven, space between pieces will allow the sauce to fill in between pieces.
4. Denseness of fish matters when cooking. "Meaty" fish, like ono or swordfish, will take longer than soft-textured ones. Pick your cooking method accordingly.

Barbecuing

One taste of grilled tuna, or any fish for that matter, can convert even the most confirmed meat-lover to fish. Although all fish tastes wonderful when cooked over the coals, the tuna family is special and ends up tasting like a filet mignon! *The major drawback to barbecuing is that it can dry out your fish quickly, but certain precautions can help you avoid that problem: add moisture to your fish; make sure the coals aren't too hot; and cook the fish quickly.*

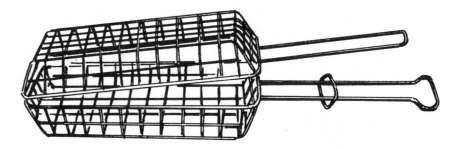

Tips for the Fire

1. Coals should be grayish-white before you put the fish on. If they're still an angry, flaming red, your fish will overcook and maybe even burn. Depending on the type of hibachi you use, the proper cooking stage should come between 30 and 45 minutes from the time you start the fire. If you can hold your palm a couple of inches over the fire for 4 or 5 seconds, it is about the right temperature (between 300° and 375°). You'll know that the fire is at the right temperature when your fish picks up the imprint of the rack as soon as it is put down.

2. If your hibachi or grill rack can be adjusted, set the cooking height 4 inches above the coals for best results.

3. Clean your grill after every use.

4. When your fire is ready, remove your grill and oil it so your fish won't stick to it (fish can stick even if they've been marinated).

5. Invest in a hinged grill basket. You can put all your fish pieces in the basket, cook them, turn them over and remove them from the heat together, so no pieces will be overcooked. If you can't find the basket type, a flat hinged grill will do, but it will leave indentations in the fish. This won't hurt the fish in any way. Be sure to put some shortening on whatever type of hinged grill you use.

6. During cooking, tap the coals occasionally to remove any ash build-up. This will help maintain an even heat while the fish cooks.

About the Fish

1. Have your fish at or near room temperature before cooking.

2. Oily fish are best to grill. They don't dry out as quickly, and somehow the combination of their own oils and the marinades result in the appetizing blend of flavors. You may barbecue oily fish without marinating them in advance, but not without brushing them with oil before and during cooking.

3. White meat (or lean) fish *must* be marinated to protect them from drying out on the grill. In addition, you want to sear in the juices quickly. Cut the steaks ½ to ¾ inch thick, and cook quickly over very hot (but not flaming) coals.

4. Firm-textured fish hold up best especially on skewers–all the fish in this book qualify!

5. If you use bamboo skewers, soak them first in water (about an hour) so they won't burn over the coals.

6. Concerned that your thin fillets (papio, small snapper, et cetera) will overcook and burn? Wrap them in (or cook them on) ti, banana or cabbage leaves, or on bunches of herbs tied together, or place the fillets on sliced vegetables (like zucchini) or citrus fruits. This is where your basket grill will come in very handy!

7. Because fish is delicate and can break apart easily, figure out in advance the length of time needed to cook the fish so that you need to turn it only once. Let the fish sear at least a minute before turning it, or the flesh will tear. Thin fillets will cook through without being turned.

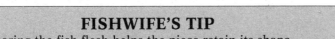

FISHWIFE'S TIP

Searing the fish flesh helps the piece retain its shape.

FISHWIFE'S TIP

Want your fish rare in the center? Time cooking at 3 minutes total for a ¾-inch thickness of fish.

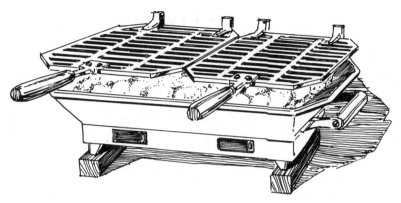

Stir-Frying

Stir-frying is similar to sautéing (high heat, minimum fat), but it requires constant motion and advance preparation (fish and ingredients to cube), and a flavoring liquid is usually added at the end.

1. Cut fish into cubes no more than 1 inch thick. Fish in the medium- to dense-texture categories hold their shape best so are less apt to break apart during cooking.

2. Slice accompanying raw (or partially steamed) vegetables into small pieces; set aside.

3. Combine ingredients for your stock or liquid; set aside.

4. Heat a non-stick wok or skillet over medium-high or high heat.

5. Add a small amount of oil, and heat it.

6. Keep ingredients in constant motion during cooking.

7. Stir-fry ingredients that take longest to cook first; remove them before you stir-fry the next ingredients.

8. Lean fish will dry out during cooking, so marinate it for at least 30 minutes before grilling. Baste it often during cooking. Fish with a higher fat content can also be marinated (although it isn't necessary) and should be basted during cooking.

9. Cooking fish with skin still on helps seal in the juices during cooking. Brushing the skin with a lemon-butter sauce or a sauce of some kind gives a delicious flavor and crispness. Make shallow (¼-inch maximum) slashes in the skin, or the fillet will curl up (the heat shrinks the skin). When grilling a fillet, do so flesh-side down first; otherwise you'll lose the juices. Cook the skin side last. For timing purposes, cook it longer on the skin side than on the flesh side.

10. If you're cooking in foil, a wonderful way to seal in those juices is to put a splash of wine or a few pats of butter in the foil package to provide some moisture. Opening the packet halfway through the cooking process will allow the fish to pick up some smoky flavor.

11. To ensure even cooking, try not to use whole fillets with ends that are thinner than the mid-section. If you must use these fillets, don't gauge your doneness by the thickest part. Remove the fish before that mid-section is done or the thinner ends will be dry, dry, dry. Other options are to turn the thin end of the fillet under to create an even thickness for even cooking, or cut off the thin ends, place on grill and remove them when they're done. Keep covered until the thicker pieces on the grill are cooked.

FISHWIFE'S TIP

To add an herb essence to the finished product, throw fresh herb sprigs directly on the coals just before you grill your fish. Remember to soak those herbs first–the water in them will create some steam and protect them from immediately burning to a crisp.

FISHWIFE'S TIPS

1. Olive, canola and peanut oils top the list of "good" oils. They contain monounsaturated fat, now found to be beneficial to our health. Consider your method of cooking when selecting your oil. Olive and peanut oil have high smoking points, so they are best for deep-frying and sautéing at high temperatures.

2. Butter, which brings out the flavor of fish like nothing else can, is high in saturated fats and burns more easily than oil unless is it clarified first.

3. To fry more healthily and still get the flavor of butter, mix 1 part melted butter with 3 parts of oil. Besides the buttery flavor benefit, it won't burn as quickly as pure butter would.

4. If the price of olive oil sends you into orbit, try the trick my sister, Kendra, uses: plop 5 or 6 black olives into a pint of oil, and let them marinate at least a few hours before using.

5. Don't use such a high heat that your oil (or butter, if you're a diehard) smokes or burns. It will ruin the flavor of your fish and any sauce that you planned to make in the same pan.

Sautéing (or Pan-Frying)

Sautéing is a simple way to prepare a quick fish dinner. It's especially successful with pieces under an inch thick because they only take a minute or two of sautéing on each side to brown nicely and remain moist inside. Here's how:

1. Coat your fish lightly before sautéing, with flour, bread crumbs, or other seasonings, to give it a crisper look and taste, if you wish.

2. Use a non-stick pan in which you've heated 1 tablespoon of olive oil (or 1 teaspoon per serving piece) over medium-high temperature.

3. Place the most attractive side of the fish down first. The side in first contact with the hot pan and whatever amount of oil is in it, browns best.

4. For best results, keep thickness of fish an inch or less.

5. When fish is done, remove; make a quick sauce by adding wine or a stock to the pan and scraping loose bits of fish (deglazing). Add onions, herbs and diced tomatoes if you wish. Spoon over fish.

SPECIAL TIPS

Peter Merriman of Merriman's Restaurant specializes in creating tantalizing fish dishes. He offers these general tips for fish cookery:

1. To avoid overcooking, turn sautéed fish only once and broiled fish twice.
2. Feel fish with your fingers as it's cooking. Its resistance should be similar to pushing lightly on the tip of your nose.
3. Fish will continue to cook after removal from the heat, so don't be afraid to cook it to only 90 percent done before removing it from the heat. Also learn to judge doneness by the color of the fish.
4. First cook the side that will show on the plate. The skin side should be last.
5. Parsley lends an excellent flavor to the fish; use it often.
6. For sautéed fish, press each side of the fish piece into flour and then pat away excess flour.
7. If your sautéed fish must be cooked ahead of time, dredge it in whipped whole eggs before sautéing. The eggs will seal the natural juices inside.

Deep-Frying

Although this is the most caloric method of cooking, deep-frying tastes wonderful. If you take the time to get the oil to its proper temperature before adding the fish, the fish will start cooking and sealing itself off before it has a chance to absorb much oil. Keep the following in mind:

1. Use fresh oil. Peanut oil and olive oils are best for deep-frying. (Use pure olive oil; it's not necessary to use the more expensive extra-virgin grade.) Previously used oil has particles of food, egg, fish or whatever you've been cooking, which spoil and turn the oil rancid. In addition, your fish will take on the flavor of whatever was cooked in the oil before.

2. Deep-frying temperature is between 360° and 375°.

3. Keep checking the temperature of the oil. Don't let it get too hot or smoke. You can tell when the oil is hot enough by using a thermometer or by dropping a small bread cube into the oil. If it rises to the surface immediately and sizzles, the oil is ready to use.

4. The amount of oil you use varies. If using a deep-fat fryer with a basket, you must be sure to add enough oil to cover the fish. If you're using a regular deep-sided pan, you'll have to turn fish as it browns anyway to get both sides cooked, so you can get away with using less oil. With a regular pan, be sure to keep the oil no higher than the halfway level.

5. Check the temperature and oil level as you're cooking. Cold fish can cause the temperature to drop, and cooking will cause the oil level to drop. If you need to add oil or raise the temperature, do so slowly.

6. When you've finished cooking, let the oil cool completely and then discard.

FISHWIFE'S TIP

Did you know that the strong "fishy" smell of fish cooking is really not the fish at all, but the fat or oil in which you are cooking? Always use clean oil, not oil you've previously cooked in and saved, and don't let it reach the smoking stage. Your cooking odors will disappear.

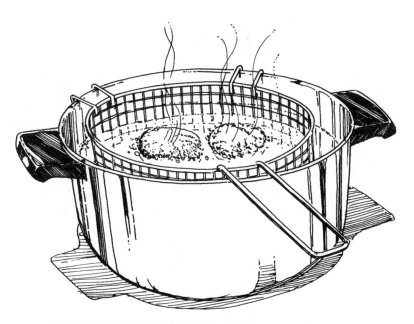

ABOUT FISH FOR DEEP-FRYING

1. The size of your pieces will determine the cooking time. Keep the thickness under 1 inch, particularly if you are coating them with batter before frying. You won't want the batter to burn while you wait for the fish to cook through.

2. Cut fish into pieces that can be easily handled when turning over in the oil.

3. Pat fish pieces dry before seasoning, flouring, coating or battering. Otherwise the coating won't adhere well, and the moisture will cause the oil to spit and spatter.

4. The fish will cook faster than you think. It's safe to judge doneness by the color of the batter, but you should also keep the Canadian method of time in mind. If you're unsure, do one piece first, break it open to see if it's done, and then do the rest.

5. Cook only a few pieces at a time. Never crowd.

FISHWIFE'S TIP
For even-width pieces, either steak the fish (cutting in cross-sectional slices) or fillet it, cut each fillet down its length to make 2 pieces, and cut crosswise into pieces to the thickness you desire.

Steaming

Unlike poaching, steaming means cooking fish above, not in, the liquid. Steaming is an extremely healthful way to cook fish, and it is especially suited to whole, small fish or fillets. Steaming is also a good way to cook fish like ono, marlin and any other species that tends to dry out fast. To steam, follow these steps:

1. Choose a fish steamer, fish poacher or a covered pot large enough to hold a plate or rack with the fish on it. You will put water or some liquid in the bottom of the pot and set the fish on the rack or plate above the water during cooking.

2. Use a heat-proof plate or pan to hold your fish. If your rack ordinarily sits on the bottom of the pan, as most poacher racks do, put some cookie cutters (the kind with no top or bottom) in the bottom of the pan to raise the rack above the level of the water. If you use a plate, prop the plate above the level of the water. Otherwise, when the water boils it will splash onto your plate and wet the fish.

3. Bring the liquid to a boil before placing the fish on the rack or plate, and the rack or plate into the pan. Cover the steamer. Always use oven mitts to protect yourself from the steam when you are placing the fish in the steamer or taking it out. Your steamer or pot must accommodate the plate or steaming dish with clearance of an inch all around so steam can escape. If you're steaming whole fish that will take longer than 10 minutes to steam, check the water level occasionally so you can add water if necessary.

4. Cook your fish for 8 to 10 minutes per inch of thickness, measured at the thickest part of the fish.

5. Removing the fish after it has been steamed can be tricky, especially if the fish is large. To aid you with this task, slide 1 or 2 large spatulas under the midsection of the fish so it won't break or cave in. Or, prior to steaming the fish, line the rack or plate with ti leaves, which can be used later to lift the fish out. Or, instead, before steaming the fish, wrap it in cheesecloth. Moisten the cheesecloth first by wetting it or dipping it into your liquid or marinade. Wrap it loosely around the fish, allowing about 10 to 12 inches of extra cheesecloth on each end of the fish. This extra cloth can be used as handles when the time comes to remove the fish to a serving plate.

Broiling

In these days of staying fit, being vigorous, and eating right, broiling gets an A+ for health-consciousness. Not only is broiling healthier for us, it's fast, too. Its major drawback is that the high heat can dry fish out very quickly. If you're cautious in your timing, you'll end up with a fast, delicious way to prepare your catch. Remember these tips to make broiling easy:

1. Lightly oil your broiling pan for easy cleanup and to keep the fish from sticking. Or, if the fish has been marinated beforehand or brushed with oil, just cover the pan with foil and do away with greasing the pan.

2. Preheat the broiler for at least 10 minutes, and put your broiler pan in the oven to heat up, too. Brush the broiler pan or rack with oil after it's been heated. The hot pan will help cook the underside of the fish, sort of like a pizza crust.

3. When calculating the cooking time, remember the temperature will be extremely hot, so figure 8 to 9 minutes per inch of fish, measured at its thickest part. (If your fish is frozen, double the cooking time.) Do test the fish for doneness before the allotted time is up.

4. Let the thickness of your fish determine the cooking time and the distance from the heat.
a) Thin steaks or fillets or lean fish: broil close (3 to 4 inches from coils), about 3 minutes. No need to turn over. To keep the fish moist, place fish in a pan that holds it comfortably; add a little stock or wine.
b) Medium steaks or fillets (up to 1 inch in thickness): broil 4 to 6 inches from coils; baste during broiling; turn once.
c) Thick steaks, fillets or whole fish (up to 2 inches thick): brown under the broiler; remove to a baking dish; and cook until done. This is a good method to use when you cook ahead. Broil to brown, set aside to finish in the oven just before you serve. Refrigerate until you need it.
d) Whole fish must be turned and should be placed no closer than 4 inches from the heat source.

5. Regardless of whether or not you turn your fish during cooking, baste the fish with oil or your marinade during cooking to keep it moist. Try to keep your basting liquid or oil only on the fish. If it drips all over the cooking rack or pan, it will smoke and may even catch fire.

6. To further assure that your fish will be moist, put ½ inch of water in the broiling pan that holds the rack to create steam. With this method, fish shouldn't need turning, unless it is very thick.

Poaching

In poaching, fish is immersed in a gently simmering liquid. It is an excellent and healthful way to cook and is versatile, too, because you can serve all kinds of sauces to enhance your dish. It's also an excellent way to prepare flaked fish that you want to use in salads, soufflés, mousses and sandwiches.

You can poach whole fish, chunks, steaks or fillets, but be sure the liquid remains at a very low simmer. If it begins to boil hard, your fish will break apart.

What if you don't have a poacher?

Although commercial fish poachers–oval-shaped pans with a rack and cover–are available, you don't need one to poach. You can use any pan with a cover, preferably a frying pan with high sides, or you can even make a foil packet and oven-poach your fish.

To oven-poach, place a piece of heavy-duty foil, large enough to wrap around the fish, on a baking sheet or pan. Place the fish in the center of the foil, add your seasonings and poaching liquid, and then close the foil packet so no liquid can seep out. Put in a 375° oven, and bake 10 minutes per inch of thickness of the fish, measured at its thickest part.

Poaching Liquids

You can poach in any liquid, even water, but it's fun to use different liquids and herbs for new and exciting flavors. Your poaching liquid can often be used as the base for your serving sauce; strain the liquid before making the sauce. So, depending on how you plan to serve the fish, you can experiment with milk, wine, beer, chicken or shrimp broth, various juices and canned, clear soups. The most common liquid is a Court Bouillon–a combination of water and white wine (about 3 cups), chopped onion, celery and carrot (2 of each), seasoned with parsley and herbs. You can add other ingredients as well.

If you are among the cooks who prefer to use a fish stock or base, see the "Soups, Stews and Seafood Combos" chapter. (Many chefs consider fish stock as too intense to use as a poaching liquid. Diluting the fish stock with water, wine or chicken broth helps the problem.)

To Poach a Whole Fish

1. Clean the fish.

2. Measure your fish at its thickest part, and plan to poach it 7 to 8 minutes per inch of thickness. Watch it carefully, though, because it can overcook easily.

3. A large, whole fish can be difficult to remove intact from the liquid, so it should be placed on the rack of a fish poacher or on an oiled dish to be submerged in a pot.

4. It's also a good idea to wrap the fish in cheesecloth before putting it on the rack or dish. Wet the cheesecloth first, by putting it in your cooking liquid or water. Then place your fish in the center of the cheesecloth. Leave extra cheesecloth on each end of the fish, enough to tie knots at both ends to use as handles when you remove your fish after cooking.

5. How much liquid should you use? Some say the poaching liquid should cover the fish; others say the liquid should be at least 1 to 2 inches deep. Once you decide which of these you prefer, here's how you make sure the proper amount of liquid is in your pot before you start cooking: put the fish in the pan, pour in cold liquid until you have the right amount and then remove the fish before you begin heating the poaching liquid.

6. Bring your broth to a gentle boil. Look for the "shiver" or "shimmer" of the liquid to know you have the perfect temperature. At this point, the liquid begins to simmer (you'll see small bubbles); add the fish. Continue to simmer, covered, until the fish is done.
Remove the fish by lifting the rack or dish from the liquid the instant the fish is done. Let the fish sit with the cheesecloth still around it for a few minutes. This will give the flesh a chance to cool and firm up a bit.

7. When you remove the fish from the liquid, it might have some "residue" clinging to it. Simply blot it on toweling.

8. If you used cheesecloth, unwrap the fish carefully so you don't remove its skin.

To Poach Fish Pieces

1. Keep your pieces in one layer in the pan so they will cook evenly.
2. Some cooks prefer to bring liquid to a simmer before adding the fish. In this case, start timing when you add the fish.
3. During cooking, the liquid will bubble gently around the edges of the fish. If it's more vigorous than that, your heat is too high.
4. Remove carefully from the pan. Pieces may break apart.

Another poaching method that made the rounds in the early '90s is credited to a mainland chef named Steve Mellina. It works well when you want your fish cold or at room temperature.

For up to 2 pounds of fish:

1. Coat the bottom of your pan lightly with olive oil; add 2 tablespoons or so of chopped onion or shallots and herbs, if you wish.

2. Lay the fish in the pan; season with salt and pepper.

3. Add ½ cup white wine and enough water to cover your fish.

4. Cover the fish with a wet towel (not a fuzzy one–use a dish towel) or parchment paper.

5. Bring the liquid to a boil slowly.

6. As soon as the liquid boils (gently, not rolling) remove the pan from the heat. After 2 minutes, remove the dish towel.

7. Let stand until the liquid has cooled. The fish will be done to perfection.

Here's still another way:

Place fish in a frying pan; cover with stock (fish, chicken, vegetable). Lay a piece of oiled parchment paper over the fish. Don't worry about the fit–you want the heat to evaporate. Slowly bring the stock to a gentle boil. Turn off heat, and let fish sit in the stock until the fish is cooked. To use the stock as a sauce base, remove the fish and bring the stock to a boil until it is reduce by half or more. Add chopped plum tomatoes, fresh herbs, a teaspoon or 2 of butter, salt and pepper; and serve over the poached fish.

Low-Fat Cooking

We're addicted to fat because it enhances the flavor of food, so the key to low-fat cooking is to fill that flavor void. Experiment with ways to boost flavors in your cooking as you cut down on fats you add *to your food. Follow these suggestions, and you won't miss the fat:*

- Drizzle fish with a mixture of herbs and citrus juice before and after cooking.

- Use fresh herbs for more flavor.

- Intensify flavors by adding ingredients with zing; the list is endless: mustard, horseradish, balsamic vinegar, onions, garlic, ginger root, fresh herbs, zest of citrus fruits, sun-dried tomatoes (rehydrated, NOT packed in oil), rice vinegar, shoyu, salsas, Worcestershire sauce, ground peppercorns, 1 tablespoon of Parmesan, Romano or feta cheese.
Try this simple, high-flavor, low-fat recipe: Blend together 1 teaspoon olive oil, 2 teaspoons Dijon mustard, 1 clove minced garlic, a pinch of dill and 4 teaspoons lemon juice. Coat fish; broil.

Here are some other tips to get you on the road to healthier cooking:

1. All the cooking techniques in this volume are suited for low-fat cooking, including cooking in foil or parchment paper.

2. Purchase non-stick cookware, a most important element in low-fat cooking. When using a non-stick pan or skillet, you need no oil or butter. (To cook onions or "veggies" that are part of the recipe, put them in the heated skillet, add a small amount of any liquid that is compatible with your recipe–white wine, *sake*, water, chicken broth, V-8 juice, et cetera–to "sweat" or braise your veggies to desired softness before adding the fish.)

3. If you MUST use oil, to sauté fish for example, use 1 teaspoon of olive oil *per serving* in your non-stick pan (but no more than a tablespoon). Heat it, spread it around the pan; add fish. Heating the oil first is important: hot oil will begin cooking the fish immediately, so less oil will be absorbed into the fish.

4. Use non-stick cooking sprays.

FISHWIFE'S TIPS

Alter your favorite sauce recipes to suit your low-fat life style: in a recipe that calls for 6 tablespoons of butter, begin with only 1. Follow the recipe; at the end, add 1 more tablespoon of butter for good measure if you want. The sauce will be excellent; you won't miss the butter you left behind.

Fattening ingredients like butter, cream or mayonnaise aren't necessary to thicken soups or sauces.

- In a soup: sauté your veggies first. Remove some from the pan and purée them in your processor. Return the purée to the stock as a thickener.

- In a sauce: purée papaya or mango, season with lemon or lime juice, add minced sweet (or green) onion and mint or basil, and top your fish before serving.

- For a sandwich: purée papaya, and blend in some whole grain mustard and lime juice. Use in place of mayonnaise for a great fish sandwich.

FISHWIFE'S TIPS

1. You almost never need the amount of fat called for in a recipe. If you use a non-stick skillet, you can cut the amount of butter or oil in the recipe by half without sacrificing the end result. If the amount of fat is crucial to the success of the recipe, substitute oil (canola, safflower, olive) for at least half of the indicated amount of butter.
2. Some vegetables, especially mushrooms, eggplant, zucchini and onions, soak up oil or melted butter in your pan, so you use far more than is really necessary. Try this: use just a bit of butter, if you must, and a flavored liquid of your choice (wine, beef, chicken or fish stock) to cook those vegetables. The liquid will boil off, and your vegetables will be nicely flavored without too much fat.
3. Experiment with low-fat ingredients: part-skimmed mozzarella for Cheddar, or plain, non-fat yogurt instead of sour cream; cooked vegetable purées instead of flour-butter roux to thicken sauces or soups.
4. Alternate your methods of cooking: even if your family prefers fried or deep-fried fish, introduce them to steamed, poached and baked dishes.
5. Think flavor! The addition of small amounts of shoyu, salsas, flavored broths (especially fish stock you make yourself and freeze!), wine, anchovy paste, tomato paste, balsamic and wine vinegars, and herbs can add big flavor to your recipes. Herbs that are good with fish include basil, chives, coriander, curry powder, dill, sage and thyme.

How Much To Serve?

Many nutritionists and home economists say that we should serve each person 3½ ounces of fish. But the amount of fish you serve depends on several things:

1. How you're cooking it. If vegetables are part of the recipe or if a rich sauce is to be served with it, you'll need less.

2. The type of meal you're having. If you're planning a big dinner with appetizers, soup and dessert along with the entrée, you'll need less fish than you would if you were serving just the fish, a starch and a vegetable or salad.

3. The fish itself. If it's whole, you have to allow for the weight of the head, tail and bones when figuring out serving amounts.

4. And, most important, how many fish lovers you're feeding.

Here are some guidelines:
Whole fish with head and tail .... 1 pound per person
Whole fish, dressed .... ½ pound per person
Fillets or steaks (no bones) .... ⅓ pound per person
Cubed .... ¼ pound per person
(as in stir-fry or soups cooked with vegetables)

How Fresh Is Your Catch?

Fish is known to be one of the most tasty, healthy and nutritious forms of food available. However, there are certain precautions you should take and knowledge you should have as a consumer to avoid certain health hazards.

Consuming Raw Fish

Many of you are from island and coastal areas and are from fishing families or are fortunate enough to have friends, neighbors or family members who share their catch with you. If this is the case, you can be reasonably sure of both the freshness and care of the fish (which should be iced immediately after capture for maximum freshness). Such is not always the case for store-bought "fresh" fish.

Included in the chapters of this book are numerous recipes that call for the use of raw fish for sashimi, poke, ceviche *and seared preparations (which leave the center of the meat very rare). We've included these recipes because they offer exciting, flavorful dining experiences, which explains their extreme popularity in Central Pacific island fine restaurants and at family gatherings.*

If you are fortunate enough to know the source of the catch and can be certain that the fish is fresh and has been properly handled, these recipes can be prepared and served with the confidence that there will be no ill effects. However, we offer the following warnings and cautions you should be aware of and heed before choosing a raw fish recipe for consumption.

According to the "University of California at Berkeley Wellness Letter" (vol. 11, issue 9), "Fish and shellfish marinated in lime juice–known as ceviche, a Latin American specialty–are still raw fish. Like sashimi, ceviche could make you sick.

"Marinating infected seafood might kill cholera bacteria on the surface, but the interior is another matter. And E. coli, which can cause severe food poisoning, is hardly fazed by lime juice. Parasites could be a problem, too." Blanching before marinating is not sufficient, either.

"The FDA says that if the raw fish used in ceviche is commercially frozen first and then thawed, it might be safe. . . . But even frozen shrimp should be cooked for three to four minutes in boiling water to kill any microbes and other stowaways. This doesn't mean that ceviche is certain to make you sick. But, as with [sashimi] and poke, you're taking a risk.

"You could try cooking shrimp or other fish first and then adding the lime juice marinade for a cold dish. It's really not that different, except that it's reliably safe to eat."

In conclusion, if you do not have certain knowledge of who caught the fish, when the fish was captured and how it was cared for, it should be properly cooked and never eaten raw.

Notes

Adding The Final Touch

Contrast is the key to adding the final touch to your seafood creation. Through contrasts in color, texture and flavor, you can easily elevate your recipe from family favorite to the great-for-company category.

Think "color contrast" from start to finish through your choice of ingredients, tableware, and the culinary accompaniments that share the menu with your fish. With the varieties of fruits, vegetables, grains, greens and even edible flowers that are available today, you have interesting options to the "sprinkle of parsley" that was once your primary garnish.

It's simple, especially if you decide that an ingredient that is already part of the recipe would make a perfect finishing touch. For example, julienned nori, a dusting of black and white sesame seeds or thin slivers of pickled ginger are easy ways to dress up recipes that include these Oriental flavors. Or, put your creative juices to work—that touch of color could be a bed of shredded zucchini and carrots for seared swordfish, a ruffle of green and purple lettuce leaves tucked under a pink snapper, or citrus zests in yellow, orange, and green to set off a tasty fish chowder. Fresh herbs sprigs are naturals with fish; dill, fennel and cilantro offer the visual grace of seaweed along with complementary flavors, and mint, basil and oregano remain old, always-in-vogue standards.

Simple touches include cracked peppercorns of red, black and green for a flavorful zing and confetti-like look; minced Greek olives for Mediterranean appeal; rings of tiny, colorful chili peppers enhance Mexican or Thai flavors; and a bundle of enoki mushrooms, tied with a ribbon of chive, completes an elegant presentation.

Your side dishes can provide flavorful and colorful contrasts for the entrée as well. For example, a trio of diced fruits like mango, kiwi and strawberries dressed with mint and a squeeze of lime juice complement a flavorful seared tuna, crispy fish tempura or curried shrimp. Wild rice, as opposed to white, provides color and texture as do pastas in various shapes, sizes and hues, and charred sweet bell pepper rings of red, green, yellow and purple top a barbecued fillet in an inviting manner.

Textures create visual and appetizing contrasts. Varying textures, like flavors, put your senses on alert. Consider a velvety mahimahi paired with a salsa of diced, raw vegetables or a crunchy fish-filled taco served with creamy avocado and papaya wedges—no textural boredom with these simple combinations!

As you work with contrasts, don't overlook the importance of tableware as part of the final presentation. A dramatic plate may be the perfect frame for your fish dinner, providing texture and color contrast at the same time. A bold placement or colorful tablecloth will liven up white dinnerware, and flowers, strategically placed, become a bright and fragrant focus your diners will appreciate.

Make "contrast" a focus in your recipes and surprise yourself with the variations and combinations you'll discover. The extra bonus is that cooking will be more interesting, appealing and rewarding than ever before!

Glossary

ARUGULA. Greens with a peppery flavor.

BALSAMIC VINEGAR. Sweet-tart, intensely flavored vinegar made from unfermented grapes; aged in wooden barrels for 6 or more years.

CHILI PASTE WITH GARLIC. Spicy, coarse grained; made of red chilies, bean sauce and garlic.

CHILI PEPPER OIL. Fiery seasoning made from chili extract and soybean oil.

CHINESE BLACK BEANS. Fermented, preserved in salt.

CHINESE BLACK VINEGAR. Made of vinegar and rice.

CHINESE CABBAGE. Pale green, celery-shaped cabbage, similar in appearance to romaine.

CHINESE PARSLEY. Flat-leafed, pungently flavored herb (also called cilantro, coriander).

CHINESE RICE WINE. Wine made from rice.

CURRY PASTE. See red curry paste.

DAIKON. White, carrot-shaped Japanese radish.

DASHI. Soup stock made of kelp and dried fish shavings.

DIJON MUSTARD. Medium-hot French mustard.

FARMER'S CHEESE. Semi-soft cheese made of part-skim milk.

FRIED ONION FLAKES. Fried or toasted dried onion.

FRISSEE. The sweetest member of the curly endive family; slightly bitter.

GALANGAL POWDER. Made from the galanga root; sometimes called young ginger or laos.

GRUYERE CHEESE. Full-flavored, semi-firm cheese from France.

HOI SIN SAUCE. Thick sauce made of soybeans; sweet and slightly pungent.

IRA GOMA. Roasted sesame seed.

JALAPENO PEPPERS. Hot green chilies sold fresh and canned.

KAFFIR LIME LEAVES. Bitter; dried from kaffir tree.

KALAMATA OLIVES. Greek origin, packed fresh in brine or oil.

KOREAN BARBECUE SAUCE. Bottled sauce made with soybeans, shoyu, sesame oil, Korean seasonings and other ingredients.

LAOS (also called galanga root). Similar in appearance to ginger, but mild-flavored.

LAULAU. Steamed meal of taro, pork and fish wrapped in ti leaves.

LEMON ZEST. Thin, outer rind of fruit; yellow part only.

LIQUID SMOKE. Flavoring made with hickory smoke concentrate.

LOLA ROSA. Greens.

LOMI. To knead.

MAI FUN NOODLES. Dried, thin rice noodles.

MIRIN. Syrupy Japanese flavoring made of sweet rice wine.

NAM PLA. Dark bottled Thai fish "sauce" made with anchovy or mackerel extract and water; used as seasoning. (Vietnamese fish sauce is nuoc mam.)

NIÇOISE OLIVES. Grown in Provence; a large-pitted olive.

NORI. Thin sheets of dried seaweed (green or dark purple in color); also sold in strips or shredded.

ORANGE ZEST. Thin, outer rind of fruit; orange part only.

ORIENTAL SESAME OIL. Made of pressed sesame seeds.

OYSTER SAUCE. Thick flavoring; made with oyster juices.

PICKLED GINGER. Thinly sliced ginger root, pickled in vinegar.

POHOLE FERNS. A green curly fernlike vegetable sometimes used in poke dishes and often in Japanese salads.

POKE. Cubed raw fish, seasoned with spices, seaweed, etc.

RED CURRY PASTE (also called krueng gaeng pet). Made of Thai ingredients including chilies, shrimp paste and lemongrass.

RICE FLOUR. Made of finely ground glutenous rice; used as coating for sautéing.

RICE PAPER WRAPPERS. Round, brittle, translucent wrappers; need rehydration before using.

SAKE. Japanese rice wine.

SAMBAL OELEK. Brand name; ground fresh chili paste.

SHIITAKE MUSHROOMS. Large, brown, meaty mushrooms; smoky flavor; sold dried and fresh.

SHOYU. Seasoning made of soybeans and grain, fermented 2 years; milder than Chinese soy sauce.

SPRING ONION. Scallions that appear in early spring.

SZECHWAN PEPPERCORNS. Small, red-brown and podlike.

TERIYAKI SAUCE. Basic Japanese sauce made with shoyu, ginger and garlic; used mostly as a marinade or flavoring.

THAI BASIL. A member of the basil family.

THAI FISH SAUCE. See Nam Pla.

TI LEAVES. Smooth leaves of the ti plant; used as wrappers.

TOBIKO. Flying fish roe (eggs).

TOFU. Soybean curd; sold fresh (packed in water) and in a box (sealed and pasteurized), and deep-fried; bland tasting, it absorbs flavors in which it is cooked or served.

WASABI. Japanese horseradish; sold as powder and paste.

WON TON WRAPPERS. Wheat flour-based dough squares.

YAKINORI. Toasted seaweed.